Wielding the Hoe

SCHO

SCHOOL O   RIE

Unive

LWK.   THREE

Cross-Cultural Perspectives on Women

General Editors: Shirley Ardener and Jackie Waldren,
for The Centre for Cross-Cultural Research on Women, University of Oxford

ISSN: 1068-8536

Women Wielding the Hoe

Lessons from Rural Africa for Feminist Theory and Development Practice

Edited by
Deborah Fahy Bryceson

BERG PUBLISHERS
Oxford/Washington, D.C.

First published in 1995 by
Berg Publishers
Editorial offices:
150 Cowley Road, Oxford, OX4 1JJ, UK
13590 Park Center Road, Herndon, VA 22071, USA

Library of Congress Cataloging-in-Publication Data

A catalogue record for this book is available from the Library of Congress.

British Library Cataloguing-in-Publication Data

A catalogue record for this book is available from the British Library.

ISBN   1 85973 068 X (hardback)
       1 85973 073 6 (paperback)

Printed in the United Kingdom by **WRP** Book Manufacturers, Bridgend,
Mid-Glamorgan.

Contents

Preface

The condition of the rural African woman continues to hold the attention of western governments, aid institutions and development practitioners. This is as a result of the abiding general perception that she is a marginalized, downtrodden and docile chattel of an exploitative social system which has taken advantage of her attributes, both biological and physical, for the survival of the society. This notion has triggered sympathetic, external interventions intended to lighten her burden and improve her lot. Well-meaning though these intentions have been, the results have not always been satisfactory in terms of the impact and sustainability of the programmes subsequently launched. This can be attributed, at least in part, to theoretical premises and on occasion dogmatic approaches which have not necessarily demonstrated a genuine understanding of the historical, cultural and social milieu of the African situation.

This volume, which presents contributions from twelve social scientists with extensive field experience in Africa, critically examines key concepts grouped around themes of great relevance such as agricultural production, reproduction, women's workload in their multiple roles, and women and AIDS. Some chapters call into question the appropriateness of indiscriminate application to African women of models and concepts more suited to western society. They touch on biases in the assumptions of external development and donor agencies which influence the packaging of their interventions in support of rural women. The volume has the added strength of presenting the point of view of the rural women themselves. The various themes have been treated without compromising the central focus of the volume, that is, the woman as the backbone of agricultural production in Africa with the hoe continuing to be the main tool at her disposal for cultivation.

Among the many lessons that the book offers is the importance which needs to be attached to empirical data assembled through participatory and field-based research as the only way to guarantee faith with the African reality in the packaging of external assistance in support of the rural woman. It is clear that this is the surest way of validating the theoretical framework for action, and ensuring the best return on resources. Another clear message is that fresh perspectives, concepts, approaches and strategies are needed to forge viable responses to the challenges faced by the African woman.

This book should be an invaluable reference for policy-makers in Africa as well as for the international community, and also for researchers and scholars involved in the search to find a scenario which would give the African woman the pride of place she has so well earned. The book's publication in 1995 is opportune in view of the Fourth World Conference on Women in Beijing. As an African woman and as someone who has spent many years working within the United Nations system, it is my hope that *Women Wielding the Hoe* will stimulate further reflection and action aimed at improving the condition of the rural woman in Africa whose situation, despite decades of debate, has registered change at a pace too slow.

Mary Chinery-Hesse
Deputy Director General,
International Labour Office, Geneva.

Acknowledgements

A number of people have in one or another capacity been instrumental in getting this book to press. We are grateful to all of them. Special mention should be made of: Shirley Ardener's supportive encouragement, Afshaan Shaafi's copy-editing, Anne Reeves' indexing and Lynne Hancock's willingness to prepare the manuscript for final publication at short notice. Han Bantje kindly supplied the book cover photo of Zambian women hoeing. Thanks goes to the Afrika Studiecentrum, Leiden for its assistance throughout this endeavour.

Deborah Fahy Bryceson
Cross-Cultural Centre for Research on Women, Oxford
and Afrika Studiecentrum, Leiden

I

INTRODUCTION

1

African Women Hoe Cultivators: Speculative Origins and Current Enigmas*

Deborah Fahy Bryceson

Over time, western attitudes towards African women have ranged from admiration for their autonomy and strength as agricultural producers and family provisioners, to sympathy, as victims of history and the inequities of their own societies, to disdain for their 'lack of mastery' of technology and their frequent childbearing. For many accustomed to the comforts of industrial societies, the lives of African women cultivators epitomize the dilemma of the non-industrial, developing world – hard physical labour in response to heavy family responsibilities, with low material output and high material uncertainty. There is, in other words, a great deal of normative opinion and emotionalism which colours western attitudes and indeed western research about African rural women.

Written primarily by scholars and development practitioners of western origin or by non-westerners with extensive work experience in western aid agencies, the papers in this collection self-consciously explore former and prevailing western theories about African women hoe cultivators. In some cases revised or opposed theories are advanced. The book's contributors, all social scientists with long-standing field experience of different parts of Africa, identify biases in the existing literature which often have as much to do with features of western social organization as they have with African rural societies.

A book about African women hoe cultivators is necessarily wide in scope. This book reflects the long-term research experience, varied disciplines and widespread geographical coverage of its twelve contributors. The disciplinary and geographical spread is wide but by no means comprehensive. The focus is primarily on African women hoe cultivators' patterns of production and reproduction and associated social

3

relations and resource control. In many cases, the authors have been deliberately personal in describing their field perceptions over time. While hints of their methodological approaches are occasionally revealed, the book is not intended as a review of field methodology. Rather it is the authors' findings and changing perceptions which are of most interest, providing a way of becoming aware of some of the subtle and not so subtle aspects of western bias in 'knowing' and 'aiding' African women hoe cultivators.

This introduction seeks to draw attention to some of the key themes as well as obvious gaps in the existing literature. The first section discusses the mystique that African rural women represent to western feminists and development practitioners. The second section delves into the origins of women hoe cultivators in Africa's prehistoric past and outlines where and in what contexts women currently engage in hoe production in Sub-Saharan Africa.

Following this introduction, the book is divided into five main sections which deal with African women hoe agriculturalists' productive role, their reproductive role, the way that they have been approached and portrayed by western development agencies, and efforts to record African women's own views. The concluding section of this book summarizes some of the areas of disagreement and accord between the various contributors of this volume. As the book's sub-title suggests, emphasis is on the lessons that can be drawn from the sustained fieldwork of the contributors for western feminist theory and development practice.

The Mystique Surrounding African Women Hoe Cultivators

Ester Boserup (1970), in her book *Woman's Role in Economic Development*, drew the developmentalist community's attention to the centrality of female labour in African farming systems. Both in terms of labour force participation and time input, she argued that women make a greater contribution to African agriculture than men, hence the use of the term 'female farming'. The evidence that she collected showed that the gap between male and female labour contributions in farming was widening and women's working day was lengthening. These findings held deep significance for western development aid agencies which, in an era of relatively tranquil world politics, were embarked on a drive to 'modernize' rural Africa. Boserup gave the western development camp an economic rationale for putting women on their agenda.

While Sub-Saharan Africa is not alone in having such female farming systems, the continent has by far the world's greatest concentration of women directly engaged in field cultivation. Boserup associated the incidence of female farming with low population density and 'shifting cultivation', i.e. agriculture characterized by low crop yields per land unit, but comparatively high output per labour unit resulting from the long fallow periods under which soils have time to rejuvenate fertility. Boserup identified these features with tribal societies where land is abundant and collectively possessed by the community.

Boserup observed that, not infrequently, such communities are organized on the basis of matrilineal descent. She argued that there is a marked tendency for more patrilineal inheritance practices to be incorporated as population pressure leads to reduced land accessibility and capital goods of one form or another assume importance in the society's production and consumption pattern. The presence of polygyny is not uncommon. Wives and cattle can become objects of wealth accumulation for men. Additional wives are vital for increased agricultural production in the absence of hired labour or investment in capital goods such as ploughs, fertilizer, etc. According to Boserup (1965): 'Many wives in polygamic tribes are domestic and agriculture slaves in disguise.' However, she tempered her views in her later work with the observation that African women in shifting cultivation systems 'are hard working and have only limited right of support from their husbands, but they often enjoy considerable freedom of movement and some economic independence from the sale of their own crops' (Boserup 1970).

Boserup emphasized that in shifting cultivation systems there is a tendency for women to have spheres of operation separate from men: separate crops, usually food crops, which only women grow; separate tasks in the agricultural production process, especially weeding and cultivating tasks, while men are more involved in clearing work; and even separate agricultural plots for crop cultivation. This economic separateness, however, is believed to erode with the intrusion of commodity, labour and land markets. Boserup (1970) argues that as population densities increase and land replaces labour as the scarce factor of production in the long-term transition from shifting hoe cultivation to permanent plough agriculture, women's participation in agricultural production declines.

Boserup's views have been criticized for taking a fixed, evolutionary perspective based on a western 'modernization' model. Beneria and Sen (1981) believe that Boserup 'tends to ignore the process of capital accumulation ...[and]... the different effects of capital accumulation on women of different classes'. Afonja (1981) identifies Boserup with the international development policy approach which encourages women to enter the workforce without giving adequate consideration to the relationship between production and reproduction. Citing the case of Yoruba women traders, she charges that Boserup and other western researchers cannot 'reconcile women's low status in the domestic domain with their high participation rates in the public domain' (Afonja 1981).

Many have challenged Boserup's generalizations that Sub-Saharan Africa is a 'female farming' zone. Guyer (1984), for example, rejects the association made between female farming and 'primitive' agriculture in an evolutionary sense. Countering this model of 'naturalism', she argues that the cultivation of Africa's oldest staples, namely yams, millet and sorghum did not rely on female labour alone. Rather, ritualized divisions of labour with a sequential mix of male and female tasks were the norm. Thus, 'female farming' did not precede male farming nor are gender patterns of agricultural production determined by the inherent characteristics of the crops in question or by women's childbearing and child rearing responsibilities which are believed to restrain their labour input. In this way, Guyer roundly dismisses all aspects of the essentialism of the naturalist model.

Whitehead (1991), commenting on the links made between the 'feminization' of African food production and the depiction of the continent's food supply problems in current literature, also stresses that so-called female farming systems are actually based on a complex inter-relationship of male and female labour. Men have been hoeing for centuries and continue to do so. Only some of the male farming population have adopted ploughs, together with much smaller numbers of women. Whitehead mocks the exaggerated notion that:

> The archetypal female farmer scratches the impoverished earth around her homestead with a hoe to produce 'subsistence' crops. Her husband, meanwhile, manages the complex technology of hybrid seeds, small-scale irrigation schemes, tractors, etc. to produce export agricultural crops. So powerful is this image in contemporary thought that this structural dualism is often conceptualized as lying at the heart of the link between the food crisis and the sexual division of labour. (Whitehead 1991)

Similarly, Wright (1983) questions Boserup's stark opposition between female hoe and male plough agricultural systems. She argues that the introduction of plough agriculture into what is now Zambia did not result in a diminution of women's farming effort. Men monopolized the ploughs whereas women continued in close proximity with hoe cultivation (Wright 1983), a pattern noted in Bundy's (1988) historical review of agricultural change in South Africa as well. Although women were largely excluded from ploughing, their labour as unwaged family labour increased. A transition from matrilineal to patrilineal inheritance and from male bride-service to single lump sum bridewealth payments by men for women cemented women's function as productive assets for their husbands. Polygyny was thus a form of male wealth accumulation. Women were 'farmhands', not 'partners' to their husbands (Wright 1983). Furthermore, men had the right to make only discretionary payments to family support.

Recent detailed studies of changing male and female work patterns following the introduction of ox ploughs are inconclusive (Mettrick 1978; Tobisson 1980; Venema 1980). Kjaerby (1983) and Bradley (1990) question any general tendency for women's workload to be reduced, given the likelihood of women's continued or increased involvement in weeding. Women are responsible for weeding in many African farming systems and ox ploughing, which facilitates the farming of larger acreages per household unit, can result in more weeding, contrary to Boserup's view that weeding is reduced. Both Kjaerby and Bradley predict that women's workload can only be eased following the introduction of *comprehensive* animal-powered mechanization including ox-drawn weeders and carts and/or irrigation, which tends to be associated with men's increased involvement in weeding.

These and other critiques of Boserup's portrayal of African female farming systems and evolutionary tendencies offer important challenges to the theory, but they have not dislodged the fundamental premise that female labour is central to African agriculture. Many of the criticisms of Boserup relate to the observation that the transition from hoe to plough agriculture has not alleviated women's agricultural workload. However, the transition from hoe to plough in Sub-Saharan Africa is far from complete and in most areas it has barely surfaced or has been skipped altogether as mechanized agriculture has been introduced.

On the other hand, the differentiated pattern of women's participation in agriculture throughout the world is readily apparent and seems to support Boserup's thesis. In Asia and Latin America, not only does agricultural production tend to be more capital-intensive and less reliant on female labour but the rural 'household' is more consolidated as a residential unit in which production, consumption, distribution and investment of its members intersect. To understand why African agriculture and social structures are distinctive, the relationship between women, hoe agriculture and associated social structures must be examined.

Most countries of Sub-Saharan Africa are predominantly rural in character: roughly 70 per cent of the population live in the rural areas. Agricultural production is relatively uncapitalized and in most countries hoe production prevails. Approximately 68 per cent of the labour force in Sub-Saharan Africa are estimated to be working in agriculture (UNDP 1992). Dixon[1] (1983), using revised International Labour Office (ILO) statistics, estimates that women's labour comprises at least 46 per cent of total agricultural employment. What is the status of female labour in agriculture? Does the principle of strength in numbers apply?

In searching for answers to these questions, one quickly confronts the curious blend of autonomy and vulnerability of women hoe cultivators. Gender and age, rather than class, predominate in the delineation of social standing and work allocation in hoe societies. While both women and men are generally considered capable of hoeing, women tend to be more strongly identified with this work activity in their role as food provisioners. The motor force of hoe agriculture is human labour. Where there is relative land abundance and virtual non-existence of capital, as is the case in so much of Sub-Saharan Africa, labour has tended to be the limiting factor of production. Control over the labour of others is the key to male power and authority in the society. But hoes have an individualizing effect on work organization since they are designed to be handled by only one person. Thus there is a tension between the technical possibility of women acting as direct producers and their social designation as men's means of production.

While the issue of labour control is central to understanding the position of women in hoe agriculture, it would be misleading to infer that women's labour is slavishly exerted in the service of men. On the contrary, existing evidence suggests that women tend to think of their labour effort in terms of being part of a natural order to ensure adequate food production and basic survival of their dependents and themselves, as illustrated by Obbo in Chapter 9. Force of habit, rather than male coercion, is seen as the basis for the prevailing gender division of labour. But what is the past history of women's role in African agriculture? When and why did women get so heavily involved in farming?

Adoption and Adaptation: Malleability of the Division of Labour under Hoe Agriculture

Agricultural Origins

Fragmentary evidence of African food plants, such as the West African forest yam *Dioscorea* and Sahelian pearl millet *Pennisetum americanum* and sorghum *Sorghum bicolor,* dates back to the second and third millennium BC (Shaw 1976; Phillipson 1982), but domestication of crops is a long evolutionary process. Selective gathering precedes conscious cultivation and, as Harlan (1982) stresses, hunting and gathering activities are far more nutritionally reliable and are more economical in terms of labour expenditure at low levels of population density.

According to archaeological and linguistic evidence, hunting and gathering, as well as pastoralism, were the primary means by which people obtained food, until agricultural production gradually started to increase in importance over the last two to four thousand years depending on the region one is examining (West Africa: Anquandah 1993; Stahl 1993; East Africa: Schoenbrun 1993a). While the nature and shape of the movement to an agricultural way of life is still subject to more conjecture than proven fact, archaeologists now believe that the impulse for such movement was an acceleration of desertification in the Sahara (Clark 1976; Blench 1993). Bold theories of the spread of a more agricultural diet and lifestyle southwards through the continent has been associated with Bantu-speaking people (Oliver and Fagan 1978). These agricultural pioneers had knowledge of both iron-working and farming with crops, notably sorghum. Some early version of hoe digging tools was considered to be part of their technology kit. It is useful to review the main components of the Bantu agricultural expansion theory since it has been highly influential, and is now under attack by current schools of archaeological and linguistic thought (Andah 1983; Shaw, Sinclair, Andah and Okpoko 1993).

Greenberg (1966) identified the heartland of Bantu languages to be south of the Sahara in what is now northern Cameroon. Traces of early stone age agricultural endeavours exist in West Africa (Andah 1993). It is believed by the Bantu expansionist school that knowledge of iron-working acquired en route from Sahelian sources was instrumental in the expansion of agriculture. From a starting point in the northwestern part of Sub-Saharan Africa, the influence of Bantu agriculture spread in a two-pronged fashion, a western prong descending along the western coast of the African continent and an eastern one through eastern and southern Africa. In this way the Congo forest was largely circumvented. Available evidence suggests that many agricultural innovations were made on the forest fringe but the spread of agriculture, notably cereals like sorghum, was away from the forest into the savanna.[2] What is considered most striking about this historical movement is its speed (Oliver and Fagan 1978). Between roughly 500 BC and 1000 AD, Bantu-speaking agriculturalists established semi-permanent settlements in the higher rainfall areas of savanna Africa between the Sahara and the Kalahari deserts. These settlements represented localized concentrations of higher population densities compared with the settlement pattern of surrounding groups more specialized in hunting and gathering or pastoralism.

While there would have had to have been a substantial degree of human migration involved in the Bantu expansion, given its short time span, it is important to stress that the expansionist school of thought does not view the Bantu agriculturalists as a distinct racial stock. Rather, it is argued that absorption in various ways, ultimately by intermarriage, gave rise to a people whose commonly held characteristics were language, technology and an agrarian culture rather than genes.

The question of the actual mechanisms by which such human migration and technological innovation took place has been the sticking point in the theory. Since Africa was not densely populated at the time of the Bantu expansion, it is believed that only a limited amount of geographical displacement of indigenous peoples would have been likely. Rather, the newcomers occupied restricted environmental niches that offered complementarity between different groups of people and the possibility of trade. Historians Oliver and Fagan (1978) explain the impetus for the physical movement of Bantu people in terms of their combined means of livelihood. They speculate that Bantu agriculturalists retained a heavy hunting component to their way of life which would have compelled them to persistently search for more plentiful supplies of wildlife in new terrain. Because of the sparseness of population, they would have been able to move to higher rainfall areas which afforded both good hunting and favourable agricultural prospects. Through a process of fission, younger generations with knowledge of farming and iron-making spread to new areas. It is fairly safe to assume that the hunters Oliver and Fagan refer to are men. Vansina (1990), tracing the more forest-biased western Bantu expansion, has a similar perspective: '... villages moved to fresh sites once or twice a decade ... Given what is known about the ancestral social tradition and its emphasis on leadership by achievement, one expects some young and ambitious men to have struck out in search of a land of plenty, sometimes going much farther than usual.'

The productive role of women in early Bantu societies is largely overlooked. On the other hand, women's reproductive role is seen as pivotal: '[I]t must have been the comparatively rapid rate of population growth among the food-producers which was mainly responsible for the absorption of the earlier hunting and gathering populations, and for the emergence of the many and varied Bantu peoples which have occupied the scene during the past thousand years' (Oliver and Fagan 1978).

Since it is generally assumed that the influence of Bantu agrarian forms of livelihood spread through peaceful means, it is strange that there has been little discussion of the role of social relations and marital alliance. Ahmed (1991) addresses this gap, arguing that the matrilineal and matrilocal social structure of Bantu groups would have been critical to the agricultural synthesis and assimilation of neighbouring Cushitic and Sudanic peoples in East Africa. In this scenario, women's agricultural expertise would hold centre stage since either non-Bantu men would marry into Bantu societies and thereby come in contact with the productive skills of Bantu women with the children of such unions speaking a Bantu language as their first language, or Bantu-speaking women could have married into Sudanic and Cushitic societies but maintained very strong ties with their natal homesteads, while raising bilingual children. Certainly, this perspective is more in tune with current archaeological thought which emphasizes small-scale movements of individual communities, related to the life cycle of component homesteads, as highly effective means of cultural transmission over time and space (Kopytoff 1987).

Between the eighth and the thirteenth century AD, a Late Iron Age periodization has been applied to much of Sub-Saharan Africa. According to Schoenbrun (1993a), in the Great Lakes region of East Africa, this period coincided with increasing population pressure arising from population growth of Bantu agrarian communities as well as with the environmentally degrading effects of iron mining and smelting on soils, and with the migration of central Sudanic, Nilotic and Para-nilotic pastoralists in a southerly direction to eastern Africa. It is believed that Bantu agricultural innovations at this time served to enhance soil fertility, increased the carrying capacity of existing settlements and, most significantly, allowed Bantu agriculturalists to infiltrate the vast, but drier, less agriculturally hospitable savanna areas. Complex mixed farming practices, combining plant and animal husbandry, the planting of nitrogen-fixing legumes, and inter-cropping made this possible.

Broadly, the Late Iron Age influence brought about a differentiation of agricultural communities into four main types in East and southern Africa. First, there were areas where Nilotic peoples displaced the earlier Bantu settlers and/or indigenous people and established a semi-pastoralist mode of existence, for example, amongst the Luo of Kenya. Second, there were areas where incoming Nilotic people encountered relatively densely populated Bantu cultivators and established a ruling stratum based on patron/client relations and complementary exchange of horticultural and dairy products, e.g. the Tutsi pastoralist/Hutu cultivating societies of present-day Rwanda and Burundi. Third, and far more numerous, there were the welter of Bantu and Khoisan societies from central Tanzania southwards down to the Kalahari desert which incorporated cattle-keeping and milking practices with their cultivation. Finally, there were Bantu farming communities living in zones marginal for cattle-keeping which continued to farm without cattle.

In comparing and contrasting these various agro-economic types of agricultural communities one is struck with the social implications of the more pronounced cattle-keeping component of Late Iron Age communities. Cattle-keeping was strongly associated with polygamy, patrilineal inheritance patterns, chiefly rule, age-grade stratification and often militaristic tendencies directed at cattle-raiding. However, it is important to note that to this day many cattle-keeping societies display lateral forms of inheritance between siblings similar to what is found in most matrilineal societies. In cattle-keeping societies, cattle-linked siblings are pivotal, yet women play an important role in agricultural production through the 'house-property complex' (Gluckman 1950). This is a form of transmitting property which utilizes the division between wives in a polygamous household, assigning land utilized by an individual wife to be property inherited by her sons (Ardener 1954). Goody and Buckley (1973) see this system as social recognition of women's major role in agricultural production, conforming to the view that women are central to family food provisioning. In any case, it is clear that many systems of patrilineal inheritance in Sub-Saharan Africa are not steadfast, being influenced by forms of matrilineal practices. Monica Wilson (1977), describing bridewealth practices in the richly endowed agro-pastoralist Nyakyusa community of southern Tanzania, notes: 'One can hardly escape the conclusion that two separate traditions, that of marriage by [male labour] service [to in-laws] with matrilineal descent, and that of marriage with cattle [as bridewealth payment] and patrilineal descent has not been fully reconciled, and that some of those who married with cattle felt that they were due greater command over a wife than poor men who married by service.'

Vansina (1990) suggests a similar process of consolidation of male power amongst certain forest groups after 1000 AD. He points to the growth of settlements of unequal size, military innovation and the gradual appearance of patrilineality associated with status and power gained in giving rather than receiving a wife into a settlement. However, the internal development of social classification systems of these forest communities as well as the effect of successive layers of political centralization of local communities created a diverse array of 'matrilineal' and 'patrilineal' societies. On closer examination, such diversity revealed complex combinations of matrilineal and patrilineal features, strongly hinting at the inadequacy of bipolar labels.

Having presented this sketchy review of literature dealing with the origins of agriculture in Sub-Saharan Africa, we can now turn to the central question posed by Boserup's predecessor, Hermann Baumann (1928), who asked: 'Can we draw any conclusions from African evidence as to the invention of hoe culture by women?' It has been commonly assumed that women as traditional plant-gatherers are the 'inventors' of agriculture. In the case of Sub-Saharan Africa, we see that the issue in the current literature is not 'invention' as much as 'technology transfer', i.e. the spread of a technical package, be it cultivation techniques or tools associated with vegetable/cereal production. Women's role in this process is open to conjecture. Inferences are based largely on the observation of current patterns. Thus Boserup's and Baumann's general observations tend to hold sway, i.e. in African hoe agriculture, men generally do the heavy but sporadic clearing, while women do the year-round work of cultivating the soil. Baumann (1928) argued further: 'Where women undertake the hoe culture, it is often very superficial; where the man takes part, it is intensified, and the intensity of cultivation increased in proportion to the man's share in the hoe culture.'

Feminists have reacted against Baumann's male bias, but the bulk of current scientific literature on the origins of agriculture provides little evidence to dispel preconceived notions of women agriculturalists as primaeval provisioners and men as agricultural pioneers. Given the emphasis on African agriculture as an innovation rather than an invention, the issue revolves around the mechanisms for technology dissemination. Historians such as Oliver and Fagan (1978), preoccupied with the identification of stratified patrilineal societies and state systems and dismissive of subsistence-based matrilineal societies, seem to suggest that the iron spear, be it for hunting or cattle-raiding purposes, was the compass determining the direction of agricultural dynamism.

There is very little about the design and usage of the hoe in the existing Anglophone literature. Francophone scholars (e.g. Jean 1975; Marzouk-Schmitz 1984; Raulin 1984; Seignobos 1984 and Dupré 1993) have devoted more attention to the role of agricultural tools in African farming systems through time. But there is an eery silence about women's use of hoes over the centuries. Archaeologists and historians caution that the use of iron hoes was probably not universal or even commonplace (Schoenbrun 1993b). Early metal working was no doubt primitive and iron hoes would have required constant renewing. Many agricultural areas would have been far removed from sources of iron ore or any trade channels from which iron could have been obtained. Wooden hoes and wooden digging sticks were undoubtedly widespread. Women's hoes would have most likely been wooden. Iron could have been saved for axes and spears. Since bush clearance and hunting were primarily male tasks, iron tools could have been the possessions of men rather than women. In the nineteenth and twentieth centuries, the wide availability of iron hoes, in part due to foreign importation, made their ownership and usage ubiquitous. It is in this period of relatively recent recorded observation that the hoe has become so strongly identified with women agriculturalists.

Influences on the Agricultural Division of Labour

It is somewhat easier to piece together a general understanding of the division of labour in rural Africa when the time-frame is restricted to a few hundred years rather than millennia. Whilst the specific divide between male/female agricultural tasks and work time devoted to agriculture varies tremendously throughout Sub-Saharan Africa, it is possible to identify historical factors that have shaped the degree of female farming in hoe agriculture regionally. These factors have been direct influences on rural labour availability, conditioning the range of mechanisms for both the internal and external control of labour in rural areas. They include: slavery, colonialism, the influence of Islam and Christianity, post-colonial urbanization and development initiatives and most recently, the re-ordering of state and market relations under structural adjustment.

The European-instigated slave trade in Africa dates back to the sixteenth century in West Africa, whereas East Africa became a source of slave labour for export by European agents more recently in the eighteenth century (Sheriff 1987). In both areas, the slave trade fostered domestic forms of enslavement. A substantial percentage of slaves in Africa were women who performed farming as well as housekeeping tasks (Law 1991; Wright 1993). Robertson and Klein (1983) have suggested that African 'free' women were the main beneficiaries of domestic slavery. Free women acquired slaves as gifts from their menfolk and in some instances they were in a position to purchase them. The legacy of slavery in West Africa has been cited as a contributing cause for comparatively less involvement of women in agricultural hoe production in several West African ethnic groups such as the Yoruba of Nigeria, the Fon of Benin (Afonja 1991; Wartena 1993). Women's access to slave labour enabled them to direct their energies into commerce and trade. Furthermore, the high incidence of slave raiding was considered, by some ethnic groups, to make it unsafe for women to cultivate in the fields. To the present, the stigma of agricultural labour as the work of slaves has provided women with the rationale for not engaging in agricultural production in some ethnic groups (Wartena 1993). In other areas, women's non-involvement in agricultural production has been re-inforced, or replicated by the spread of Islamic purdah practices.

But this apparent ascendance of the hierarchical principles of class over gender have never been very robust. Roberts (1988) demonstrates that female ownership of slaves was contingent on domestic circumstances. A husband was entitled to marry his wife's slave and thereby appropriate the slave's labour from his wife. Going further, Hay (1988) notes that the words 'slave' and 'wife' can be interchangeable. Amongst the Luo of Kenya, the term 'my slave' is an affectionate way for a man to refer to his wife.

The range of women's productive roles under the influence of slavery illustrates how the wider historical context sets the boundaries for women's room to manoeuvre. Women attempted to seize the opportunities and mitigate the constraints that existed in their communities. In so doing, they actively moulded the gender division of labour which was then subject to sanctions by the community. Old and new factors enter into the equation. Similarly, Roberts (1988) stresses the continually negotiable status of women's 'freedom' to pursue non-agricultural activities at present in West Africa vis-à-vis the domestic and farming duties that they have to their husbands and other male kin.

Throughout the centuries of the slave trade, women, especially in the chiefless societies that tended to be raided for slaves, were vulnerable to enslavement. Their labour, as farmers and domestic help, was valued. Life histories of women from the nineteenth century indicate how they could be shunted from place to place as tradable assets depending on the vicissitudes of war and economic fluctuations (Wright 1984). Polyethnic communities and weak, ad-hoc judicial systems often resulted. With the coming of colonial rule, European administrators endeavoured to stabilize their territories. Outlawing of the slave trade went hand in hand with efforts to revitalize lineage authority. Wright (1993) argues that the early years of colonialism were characterized by a 'hardening of "tradition" and a strong disposition to enforce patriarchy'. Nowhere could this be seen more clearly than in relation to the way women's role in subsistence production in their native rural communities was designated, if not encoded. Despite the appearance of new trading opportunities and non-agricultural livelihoods, women were actively discouraged from responding to these economic impulses and migrating to the towns and settlements that opened up in connection with colonial enterprise. Through local by-laws, women who left their home areas faced heavy sanctions and were labelled prostitutes (e.g. Ghana: Roberts 1983; Tanzania: Mbilinyi 1989; Schmidt 1991; Malawi: Wright 1993).

Colonial government economic policies were aimed at increasing agricultural commodity production and raw material extraction. Almost invariably the labour they sought to involve in these economic activities was male. In many of the moderately to densely populated areas of West and East Africa, colonial agricultural officers encouraged African men to grow export cash crops like coffee, tea, cocoa and cotton. In the sparsely populated areas, where the physical distances between scattered settlements was a major obstacle to the development of peasant cash cropping, men were recruited for colonial mining and plantation work. Male circular migration from these rural areas and the associated 'bachelor wage system' were premised on women remaining in their villages and producing the basic foodstuffs required for their own and their children's well-being.

During the colonial period, rural African women hoe cultivators' food provisioning activities were elevated to a living legend. Sir Roger Swynnerton, whose career in the British colonial agricultural service in East Africa spanned three decades, relates the views of his colleagues:

In Kenya twice a year we called our provincial agricultural officers together for a conference to discuss programmes ... About the middle of the 1950s, one of our subjects of discussion was whether we should push for crop specialization in different areas of the country ... leaving food crop areas to produce the subsistence requirements of the cash crop areas. One very experienced provincial agricultural officer said this just would not work. The

African was so inured to securing his food supplies that when the first rain started pattering on the roof of his hut, the wife in her sleep would reach over on one side and pick up a hoe, the other side to pick up a bag of seed and in the middle of the night she would go out and start planting food. In no way would she stop doing that whatever the cash crop being grown. (Swynnerton 1985)

Following roughly seventy years of colonialism, in the 1960s, the newly independent African economies' dash for 'development' gave room for some women to circumvent the stereotyped view of women's occupation as subsistence food farmers. More girls' education, the launching of the 'family wage' to support African family life in the towns, and rapid urban class formation served to disengage a growing segment of the female population from rural farming throughout Sub-Saharan Africa (Bryceson 1985). Young girls in the countryside had new role models. Academic success or life circumstances such as marriage or divorce could propel them to seek residence and non-agrarian occupations in the city. Even in the countryside the direction of change was increasingly towards emphasis on non-agricultural, income-generating projects for rural women.

During the last decade, under the influence of IMF-enforced structural adjustment programmes, new complex patterns have emerged. The economic exigencies of these years led rural women to diversify their income-earning, more as a way of reducing the risk of livelihood failure than as a strategy for income maximization. In this way, women farmers in many rural areas of East Africa have been increasingly involved in trading activities, often encouraged by market liberalization policies of the state (Bryceson 1993). Conversely, in certain West African communities, women traders are turning increasingly to farming, as demonstrated by Guyer in the next chapter. These new activity patterns are superimposed and do not alter the fact that during the past decade of economic duress and, in some areas, war-torn conditions, 'women wielding the hoe' are in evidence as the mainstay of rural existence much as before. Even in urban areas women's hoeing skills have often been crucial to urban families who resort to farming either for direct household consumption or to earn income for household maintenance in the face of economic crisis (Rakodi 1988).

Many aspects of the twists and turns of women hoe cultivators' lives over recent decades are documented in Sections II through V of this book. Suffice to conclude this section by observing that what we know of African history and prehistory suggests that the gender division of labour in hoe agriculture is malleable, responding to forces which act on the internal dynamics of African agrarian societies. Equally, it must be noted that the cataclysmic political events and severe economic circumstances of the past two decades, have not shaken the bedrock role women play in African hoe agriculture. Complex combinations of continuity and change abound. Disentangling various strands, the authors of the following chapters provide graphic portrayals of women's position in the production, reproduction and consumption patterns of rural Sub-Saharan Africa.

Notes

* I am grateful to Shirley Ardener, Sally Chilver, Ian Fowler, Peter Geschiere, Jack Mapanje and the authors of the other chapters in this volume for their advice and comments on this introduction and the conclusion, but I bear full responsibility for the views expressed.

1. Dixon (1983) provides estimates of the proportion of total subsistence and remunerative agricultural labour performed by women using the 1980 Food and Agricultural Organization agricultural census as a basis for adjusting 1970 ILO female agricultural labour estimates. The adjustments are always upwards, compensating for the degree of under-counting in the national statistics. Anker (1993) discusses the widespread problem of under-reporting of female participation in the labour force.

2. A quite separate phenomenon, the spread of Southeast Asian root crops, like yam and cocoyam, and banana cultivation is believed to have taken place in the opposite direction from about the third century AD onwards (Shaw 1976). Introduced by Indonesian traders and migrants visiting the East African coast, the new food crops would have probably traversed the wetter highland areas around Lake Malawi, spreading up the valley of the Western Rift, passing both to the north and south of the Congo forest as well as along the riverine routes through the forest. This innovation had the effect of gradually displacing the indigenous pygmy occupants of the forest, with almost complete displacement in the southeastern zone and the area around the great bend of the river, leaving intact communities in the more northerly areas in what is now southern Cameroon, northern Gabon and the Congo Republic.

References

Afonja, S., 'Changing Modes of Production and the Sexual Division of Labor among the Yoruba', *Signs*, Winter 1981

Ahmed, C., 'Not from a Rib: The Use of Gender and Gender Dynamics to Unlock Early African History', Paper presented at the African Studies Association Meeting, St. Louis, USA, 1991

Andah, B., 'The Bantu Phenomenon: Some Unanswered Questions of Ethnolinguistics and Ethnoarchaeology', *West African Journal of Archaeology*, vol. 13, 1983

—, 'Identifying Early Farming Traditions of West Africa', in T. Shaw et al. (eds), *The Archaeology of Africa*, 1993

Anker, R., 'Measuring Women's Participation in the African Labour Force', in A. Adepoju and C. Oppong (eds), *Gender, Work and Population in Sub-Saharan Africa*, London, James Currey, 1994

Anquandah, J., 'The Kintampo Complex: A Case Study of Early Sedentism and Food Production in Sub-Sahelian West Africa', in T. Shaw et al. (eds), *The Archaeology of Africa*, 1993

Ardener, E., 'The Kinship Terminology of a Group of Southern Igbo', *Africa*, vol. 24, no. 2, 1954

Baumann, H., 'The Division of Work according to Sex in African Hoe Culture', *Africa*, vol. 1, 1928

Benería, L. and G. Sen, 'Accumulation, Reproduction, and Women's Role in Economic Development: Boserup Revisited', *Signs*, Winter 1981

Blench, R., 'Recent Developments in African Language Classification and Their Implications for Prehistory', in T.Shaw et al. (eds), *The Archaeology of Africa*, 1993

Boserup, E., *The Conditions of Agricultural Growth*, New York, Aldine Publishing Company, 1965

—, *Woman's Role in Economic Development*, London, Earthscan Publications Ltd., 1970 (1989)

Bradley, C., 'Women Weeding and the Plow: A Comparative Test of Boserup's Hypothesis', *African Urban Quarterly*, vol. 5, nos. 3/4, 1990

Bryceson, D.F., 'Women's Proletarianization and the Family Wage in Tanzania', in H. Afshar (ed.), *Women, Work, and Ideology in the Third World*, London, Tavistock Publications, 1985

—, *Liberalizing Tanzania's Food Trade*, London, James Currey, 1993

Bundy, C., *The Rise and Fall of the South African Peasantry*, London, James Currey, 1988, 2nd edition

Clark, J.D., 'Prehistoric Populations and Pressures Favoring Plant Domestication in Africa', in J.R. Harlan, J.M. de Wet and A.B. Stemler (eds), *Origins of African Plant Domestication*, The Hague, Mouton Publishers, 1976, pp. 67–105

Dixon, R., 'Land, Labour, and the Sex Composition of the Agricultural Labour Force: An International Comparison', *Development and Change*, vol. 14, 1983, pp. 347–72

Dupré, M-C., 'From Field to Kitchen: Women's Tools in the Forest of Central Africa', Paper presented at the 'Transformation, Technology and Gender in African Metallurgy' Workshop, Centre for Cross-Cultural Research on Women, University of Oxford, May 1993

Gluckman, M., 'Kinship and Marriage among the Lozi of Northern Rhodesia and the Zulu of Natal', in A.R. Radcliffe-Brown and D. Forde (eds), *African Systems of Kinship and Marriage*, Oxford, Oxford University Press, 1950

Goody, J. and J. Buckley, 'Inheritance and Women's Labour in Africa', *Africa*, vol. 43, 1973

Greenberg, J.J., *The Languages of Africa*, The Hague, Mouton, 1966

Guyer, J., 'Naturalism in Models of African Production', *Man*, vol. 19, no. 4, 1984

Harlan, J.R., 'The Origins of Indigenous African Agriculture', in J.D. Clark (ed.), *The Cambridge History of Africa: From Earliest Times to c. 500 BC*, vol. I., Cambridge, Cambridge University Press, 1982

Hay, M.J., 'Queens, Prostitutes and Peasants: Historical Perspectives on African Women, 1971–1986', Boston University, African Studies Center Working Paper No. 130, 1988

Jean, S., *Les Jacheres en Afrique Tropicale: Interprétation Technique et Fonciere*, Mém. Inst. Ethn., Musée de l'Homme, Paris XIV, 1975

Kjaerby, F., *Problems and Contradictions in the Development of Ox-Cultivation in Tanzania*, Copenhagen, Centre for Development Research, Research Report No. 66, 1983

Kopytoff, I. (ed.), *The African Frontier*, Bloomington, Indiana University Press, 1987

Law, R., *The Slave Coast of West Africa 1550–1750: The Impact of the Atlantic Slave Trade on an African Society*, Oxford, Clarendon Press, 1991

Marzouk-Schmitz, Y., 'Instruments Aratoires, Systemes de Cultures et Différenciation Intra-Ethnique', *Cahiers ORSTOM*, série Sciences Humaines, vol. 20, 1984, pp. 399–425

Mbilinyi, M., 'Women's Resistance in "Customary" Marriage: Tanzania's Runaway Wives', in Abebe Zegeye and S. Ishemo (eds), *Forced Labour and Migration: Patterns of Movement within Africa*, London, Hans Zell Publications, 1989, pp. 211–54

Mettrick, H., *Oxenization in the Gambia: An Evaluation*, London, Ministry of Overseas Development, 1978

Oliver, R., 'The East African Interior', in R. Oliver (ed.), *Cambridge History of Africa from AD 1051 to c. 1600*, vol. III, Cambridge, Cambridge University Press, 1977

Oliver, R. and B.M. Fagan, 'The Emergence of Bantu Africa', in J.D. Fage (ed.), *Cambridge History of Africa from c. 500 BC to AD 1050*, vol. II, Cambridge, Cambridge University Press, 1978

Phillipson, D.W., 'Early Food Production in Sub-Saharan Africa', in J.D. Clark (ed.), *The Cambridge History of Africa from Earliest Times to c. 500 BC*, vol. I, Cambridge, Cambridge University Press, 1982, pp. 770–829

Rakodi, C., 'Self Reliance or Survival? Food Production in African Cities with particular reference to Zambia', Paper presented at the School of Oriental and African Studies Workshop 'The New Urban Poor in Africa', London, May 1988

Raulin, H., 'Techniques Agraires et Instruments Aratoires au Sud du Sahara', *Cahiers ORSTOM, série Sciences Humaines*, vol. 20, 1984, pp. 339–58

Roberts, P., 'Rural Women's Access to Labor in West Africa', in S.B. Stichter and J.L. Parpart (eds), *Patriarchy and Class: African Women in the Home and the Workforce*, Boulder, Westview Press, 1988, pp. 97–114

Robertson, C. and M.A. Klein (eds), *Women and Slavery in Africa*, Madison, University of Wisconsin Press, 1983

Schmidt, E., 'Patriarchy, Capitalism and the Colonial State', *Signs*, 1991, pp. 732–56

Schoenbrun, D.L., 'We are What We Eat: Ancient Agriculture between the Great Lakes', *Journal of African History*, vol. 34, 1993a, pp. 1–31

—, 'Cattle Herds and Banana Gardens: The Historical Geography of the Western Great Lakes Region c. AD 800–1500', *African Archaeological Review*, vol. 11, 1993b

Seignobos, C., 'Les Instruments Aratoires en Afrique Tropicale: La Fonction et le Signe, *Cahiers ORSTOM, série Sciences Humaines*, vol. 20, 1984, pp. 3–4

Shaw, T., 'Early Crops in Africa: A Review of the Evidence', in J.R. Harlan, J.M. de Wet and A.B. Stemler (eds), *Origins of African Plant Domestication*, The Hague: Mouton Publishers, 1976, pp. 107–53

Shaw, T., P. Sinclair, B. Andah and A. Okpoko, 'Introduction', in T. Shaw, P. Sinclair, B. Andah and A. Okpoko (eds), *The Archaeology of Africa: Food, Metals and Towns*, London, Routledge, 1993

Sheriff, A., *Slaves, Spices and Ivory in Zanzibar: Integration of an East African Commercial Empire into the World Economy 1770–1873*, London, James Currey, 1987

Stahl, A.B., 'Intensification in the West African Late Stone Age: A View from Central Ghana', in T. Shaw et al. (eds), *The Archaeology of Africa*, 1993

Swynnerton, R., 'Interview with Sir Roger Swynnerton concerning his work in the Tanganyikan Colonial Agricultural Service', interviewed by D.F. Bryceson, April 1985, Rhodes House Library Archive, Oxford

Tobisson, E., 'Women, Work, Food and Nutrition in Nyamwigura Village, Mara Region, Tanzania', Dar es Salaam, Tanzania Food and Nutrition Report No. 548, 1980

United Nations Development Programme, *Human Development Report 1992*, New York, Oxford University Press, 1992

Vansina, J., *Paths in the Rainforests*, Madison, University of Wisconsin Press, 1990

Venema, L.B., 'Male and Female Farming Systems and Agricultural Intensification in West Africa: The Case of the Wolof, Senegal', in U. Presvelon, and S. Spijkers-Zwart (eds), *The Household, Women and Agricultural Development,* Miscellaneous Papers No. 17, Wageningen University, The Netherlands, 1980

Wartena, D., 'Ethnicity and Differential Development of Female Farming: The Case of the Fon and the Adja in South Benin', Paper presented at the 'Globalization and the Construction of Ethnic Identity' Seminar, June 1993, Leiden

Whitehead, A., 'Rural Women and Food Production in Sub-Saharan Africa', in J. Dreze and A. Sen (eds), *Political Economics of Hunger*, Oxford, Clarendon Press, 1991, pp. 425–73

Wilson, M., *For Men and Elders: Change in the Relations of Generations and of Men and Women among the Nyakyusa-Ngonde People 1875-1971*, London, International African Institute, 1977

Wright, M., 'Technology, Marriage and Women's Work in the History of Maize-Growers in Mazabuka, Zambia: A Reconnaissance', *Journal of Southern African Studies*, vol. 10, no. 1, October 1983

— (ed.), *Women in Peril: Life Stories of Four Captives*, Lusaka, Neczam, 1984

—, *Strategies of Slaves and Women*, London, James Currey, 1993

II

'SISTERS OF THE SOIL': AGRICULTURAL PRODUCTION AND SOCIAL ORGANIZATION IN AFRICAN HOE-BASED SOCIETIES

2

Women's Farming and Present Ethnography: Perspectives on a Nigerian Restudy*

Jane I. Guyer

Introduction

From the changed vantage point of the 1990s, the work we carried out on African women's farming in the 1970s could seem dated: Africa has changed, theory has changed, we have changed, and perhaps most important, our colleagues and constituencies have changed. It requires concentration to relive the sense of revelation, of entire new terrains opening up, that Ester Boserup's famous book (1970) inspired. We have to remind ourselves of the powerful combination of analytical leverage and political concern that was embodied in that work. A generation of researchers launched themselves with enormous energy into the application of their own favoured theoretical tools to a landscape that was virtually unexplored (for a review see di Leonardo 1991; Guyer 1991).

More than we realized at the time, those theoretical tools turned out to have hidden assumptions that we were forced to unpack. As we struggled to apply what was in those days the only 'theory' available, more and more of the propositions became questionable when matched against the findings from that other strand of the anthropological tradition: the empirical acuity and openness of ethnographic method. Above all, there was an underlying evolutionism built into them, such that in one way or another African women's hoe agriculture was seen as an earlier stage of development: of population density and intensive land use, of technique, of specialization and commercialization, of social differentiation. Gradually, over the past twenty years, the whole evolutionary model has needed to be broken down into separate concepts, hypotheses and interpretations. This has been an awkward,

25

not always graceful process. The short, self-contained, *self*-reflexive loop advocated in the anthropological theory of the 1980s was not often achievable. The actuality was long, ragged chains of *inter*-personal abrasion and mutual support, cross-cutting influences of unanticipated kinds, and the sheer surprise seeing demonstrated – in oneself or in others – dispositions that simply did not fit a cherished theory or an imagined self-image. And the world itself moved rapidly on, often before new reflections could be coherently assimilated. 'Rapid intellectual appraisal' has been the order of the day: an intuitive – rather than deeply and logically considered – weaving together of personal experience, shifted intellectual logics and exposure to change. The present results are provisional. Evolution has been replaced by history, but not completely and not yet entirely coherently. Boserup's original generalized account of women's predominance in hoe farming and of colonial history remains more or less in place, but we are no longer sure about the dynamics that produced the patterns.

The form that this set of questions took in my own mind was the apparently dry and abstract question: what is the relevant *time-frame* for interpretation of the division of labour? And what kind of time-frames do we have in the conceptual repertoire? The present paper is a brief history of the various components and stages in my own thinking from my first fieldwork on the topic in the mid-1970s to the present. Although the paper is short, I try to include at least some of the varied inputs into 'rapid intellectual appraisal' that were the crucible and catalysts of change. I cannot, with apologies, do justice to all of them; it remains a personal exposition rather than a review (see, however, Guyer 1988; 1991).

Encounters with Evolutionism

In her publication in 1970, Ester Boserup put African women's enormous contributions to the agricultural economy back on the intellectual map. Her basic starting point came from the work of the founding father of all subsequent research on African divisions of labour, Hermann Baumann, who suggested that women's farming was associated with sparse population, the dominance of root crops over cereals and minimal cultivation of the soil 'in the African primeval forest ... from time immemorial' (1928). To this model Boserup added the colonial articulation, in which the particular kind of commercialization that the colonial encounter fostered, mainly for the export market and mainly by men, set up a differentiation process into elites and the rest, into male and female. We had, then, three main time-frames of empirical enquiry: the very close view of the ethnographic present and the very distant view of great spans of evolutionary time, and a structural account of a particular historical interlude during which the tendencies of evolution were forced out of shape. And the three could be fitted together quite neatly.

Only as we used the frameworks in research did we begin to see changes in crops, techniques and the social organization of production that spilled beyond them. In my own first research on women's farming, I followed closely Boserup's structural and historical benchmarks. Working in two very different systems early in my career was not entirely planned, but it has provided extraordinary, insistent and humbling challenges. Having worked first in a Yoruba community in western Nigeria in 1968-9, I immediately had the parallels and contrasts in mind when I started to work on women's farming in the Beti area of southern Cameroon in the mid-1970s. While the two peoples share certain attributes of agro-ecology and economic history – a savanna/forest border environment, proximity to rapidly growing cities, cocoa as the major export crop – they seem to exemplify quite different gender divisions of labour. For a very long time, Beti women have carried out most of the tasks of food cultivation. Yoruba women's farming on their own account, by contrast, was very much a minority enterprise when I worked in southwestern Nigeria in 1968-9. The vast majority of women fit the famous Yoruba pattern of female enterprise in processing and trade, while men were responsible for farming and the staples of the diet. To use Boserup's phraseology, the Yoruba system was a male farming system in a relatively high population density area and the Beti a female farming system in a relatively low population density area. Classic social anthropology would also have placed the two systems in different categories: the Beti a segmentary society, the Yoruba with centralized administration of large urban settlements.

My first historical work on the division of labour was a comparison of the two systems under the common influence of the cocoa economy of the colonial period (1980). That analysis was based on the typological distinction between the two, and the conclusion tended to reaffirm it. In both cases, the gender division of tasks with respect to food cultivation had been very largely preserved over the expansion of cocoa production during the colonial period. Yoruba men continued to farm and to provide dietary staples in kind or through cash income, while women stepped up their activities in distribution. Beti men added cocoa farming to their older forest activities, leaving women with food cultivation.

Figure 1: The Gender Division of Labour in Agriculture

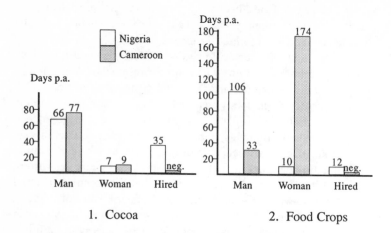

1. Cocoa   2. Food Crops

In both cases, the broad framework of the old task-specific division of labour of male and female farming was recognizable in the colonial and post-colonial economies. Theoretically-inclined comparativists, such as I was at that time, could argue that both mainstream socio-cultural and Marxist interpretations of social change could be supported by this finding: locally specific values and relationships – whether thought of as the *cultural* definition of male and female tasks or as the male-female differential in *economic* returns to labour – seemed to persist tenaciously over the 100 years of dramatic political and economic transformation. The colonial and commodity economies took the local systems as they found them; the local systems assimilated novelty to their own norms of thought and activity. At the same time, these conclusions could be assimilated to Boserup's evolutionism because the two societies continued to work under very different conditions of population density.

While this was a neat and persuasive conclusion I was never entirely happy with it, and for two reasons. First, it seemed uncanny and dissatisfying that the results could be made to fit any one of the then competitive theories. And second, the key analytical parameters had been left rather vague in that persistence was inferred but its dynamics were not sufficiently explored. The conclusion remained impressionistic, a quality one can often mask by quantification. But in the end, one looked at those bargrams and responded intuitively to their difference, with no criteria for judging how different 'different' had to be, nor how long 'difference' might take to develop, in order to be really significant.

I was bothered, not that the logic of inference was necessarily wrong, but that it remained unexamined. If persistence in the face of both the passage of time and articulation with the colonial world is a key characteristic, then its qualities need to be specified, including its dynamics: that is, ways of differentiating between stagnation and tradition, between reasonable caution in the face of economic and political volatility and the outright rejection of innovation, between inability to articulate a collective vision for change and powerlessness to implement one. We were ourselves living out – in the late 1970s and early 1980s after a pioneering period in feminist anthropology and feminist consciousness – the ongoing implications of what we had thought were unambiguous innovations in our own divisions of labour. By that time we had seen enough 'change' to know that diagnoses of complex situations did not yield easily, even to concentrated effort. Was it the 'fear of success', the 'glass ceiling', the 'double work-day', 'the mommy-track', 'the biological clock', sexism in the unions, the cultural 'backlash', poverty, or all of the above that made our own changes less dramatic and our situations more persistent than we had anticipated? For existential as well as ethnographic reasons, trust in knowing how to 'place' the present in its most powerful interpretive framework has been increasingly brought into question.

In scanning the horizon for landmarks and beacons for exploring this territory, the situation in Africa itself has loomed large. When one is there, the changes and persistences seem far more diverse, surprising and intellectually stimulating than the models can cope with, a fact that lies behind – I believe – at least some of the difficulties of African scholars with work coming out of western social science traditions. An interchange witnessed at a session of the African Studies Association meetings several years ago has been a graphic reminder to me; to a perfectly reasoned comparative and typological discussion of Yoruba's women's economic freedom, a female Yoruba participant responded with profound exasperation: 'We are *not liberated*!'

Different vantage points, different views. And undoubtedly our African colleagues have the acute sensitivity of the water diviner to hidden evolutionary assumptions that we have to actively train ourselves to locate, given the comfortable accommodation that our discipline once made between the uniqueness of cultures and their classification into evolutionary series from 'primitive' to 'civilized', from 'acephalous' to 'centralized', or in this case, from egalitarian to hierarchical. But there are also formal analytical differences between the two vantage points, stemming from assumptions about the nature of time. The first scholar is reflecting in a comparative and static mode on the nature of cultural assumptions and social structures; the second is thinking in an experiential mode whose temporal reach is back into her immediate past and forward into her potential future. The first is a framed definition of time, and the second is a centred definition. The first takes a boundary – a persistent Yoruba culture – and then explores the canvas within it; the second starts with a focal point and works outwards with no initial concern about the positioning of the frame which may, in the end, be quite arbitrary.

This contrast between framed and centred assumptions about relevant time makes them seem opposed and perhaps mutually exclusive. What I was hoping, however, was to see them as part of a repertoire of time concepts that might be built up, and then combined in ways that highlighted key processes. C. Wright Mills (1959) wrote that the intellectual journey of social science was incomplete until biography and history had been illuminatingly intersected. Biography and history are only two temporal concepts. Clearly, coming from anthropology with its long tradition of work on indigenous and analytical temporalities, including developmental cycles (Goody 1958) and structural duration (Gluckman 1968), there were more.

The first and most obvious experiment to do with my own empirical problem of the dynamics of the division of labour was to move the time-frame around, to shift the classic pre-colonial, colonial, post-colonial three-act play out of the centre and try to incorporate pre-colonial change (Guyer 1984). Prevailing approaches to pre-colonial change in agricultural production and the division of labour came from evolutionary theory, understandably since the data are thin. Boserup incorporated Baumann's assumptions. The female farming he saw at the end of the nineteenth century in the forest regions of central Africa preceded – as he saw it – the male farming of the savanna, as extensive agricultural techniques precede intensive techniques, and as segmentary societies precede centralization. Female farming was individuated and technically simple; male farming was collective and complex. Female farming was primitive; male farming more advanced.

Moving these assumptions of a given temporal order out of the way for the moment was a liberation; it allowed me to see another, different regularity that I had not noticed before. When I looked again at the ethnographic data on African farming around the turn of the century, when it was first described in some detail, it seemed that the syndrome defined as 'female farming' was particularly characteristic of maize and cassava production and hardly at all of yam, sorghum, millet and rice. All of the latter crops were grown in complex group and individual, male and female, interdigitated task sequences, and sacralized in a manner that made production seem like a ritual, a choreographed movement, at some stages literally set to music. In fact, the anthropology of performance was an inspiration to understanding the economies of these staple crops. Audrey Richards (1939) captured both the social and aesthetic nature of the contrast with maize and cassava, whose cultivation – she wrote – was not only individual, but 'considered hard and unromantic work, quite unlike millet cultivation'.

The contrast, then, is obviously not between roots and cereals because there are both root and cereal crops in both categories. The two different categories of crop correspond, rather, to the New World staples introduced from the last years of the fifteenth century on the one hand and the indigenous African staples on the other. One had an empirical basis from which to argue then, that African farming had not started out female and individual, as evolutionary theory suggested; it had shifted in that direction with the adoption of maize and cassava. To see this, one had to remove the temporal frame defined by evolutionary and social structural theory, and reposition it around a central focus, in this case the introduction of the New World staples into production repertoires.

Positioning the time-frame in an exploratory and experimental way to throw a focal historical process into relief gives some purchase on the problem of persistence by highlighting the shifts that have taken place, however slowly and however little trace they have left in written sources. Perceptions, questions and methods are reoriented away from the evolutionary issue of why men come into the basically female work of farming, to the social historical question of how crop innovations in African history have been the catalyst for reshaping the gender division of labour: for both sexes, and in ways that affected the entire pace and social context of work. To address this latter question, it is clear that a simple task-based description – men do this and women do that – must be inadequate because it fails to capture the dimensions of farm work that we know have changed: the crops and the performative sequencing of activities.

In a more recent paper (1988), I suggested that analysing the rhythmic structures enacted in production – rather than the more classic description of tasks – might be a micro-level method of seeing the 'practice', the turbulence of the customary division of labour revealed in the macro, multi-century, continent-wide vision. With a set of temporal frames provided by the nested calendrics of a particular system, one could centre and re-centre on what I thought of as 'the beat', the moments of maximum social and cultural emphasis and possibly of contention as the rhythm of work picked up or syncopated in new ways over time with the addition of new crops, new techniques and new processes.

While I have felt somewhat satisfied – so far – that the distant vision of history and the close vision of practice have the same logical properties with respect to framing and centring, a further problem nags: their magnifications are dizzyingly far apart. One is too close, for the analyst and perhaps the actor as well, to discriminate the historically significant – the transformative – from just movement. The other is too far away to see the forays, experiments and struggles through which a particular path – recognizable to the analyst and plausible to the actor – gets taken. Other magnifications of vision were needed, intermediate temporal frames, to discriminate significant shifts of configuration from, on the one hand, structural or revolutionary change and, on the other, just 'practice'. This is a critical analytical issue: the problem of being able to scale up and down within a single theoretical framework, rather than having to shift assumptions at different levels of analysis. But differentiating *degrees* and *kinds* of significance is also a cultural and experiential issue. Understanding the step-by-step cumulative and configurational nature of change is not just an ivory tower challenge; people face it themselves by applying discrimination and establishing interpretations to draw on the past and take hold of the future.

Having thought about the scale and significance issue for some time, I returned to Nigeria to plan a new field research project in the community where I worked in 1968-9, explicitly experimenting with an intermediate time-frame, namely the past twenty years. Twenty years falls neatly into no common anthropological time-frame, not even a generation, except perhaps a female generation. It is not long enough to support an argument about major structural change, much too long for the ethnographic present, and it lends itself temptingly to the application of a kind of interpretation to which most anthropologists are – I think – allergic, namely the tracing of linear trends. This era had, nevertheless, been undeniably significant in Nigerian political, economic and cultural history. It begins during civil war, the Biafran War, goes through the oil boom of the 1970s, the return to civilian rule in 1979, another military period from 1984 projected to last until 1992, and the jolting economic conditions of devaluation and structural adjustment beginning in 1985. My own two pieces of 'ethnographic present' field research had been done in moments of crisis, not stasis: the civil war and the structural adjustment period.

I have mentioned my good fortune. While men's farming in this community had undergone a certain expansion and technical modification over those twenty years (Guyer 1992), I found that the female processors and traders had effected more striking change by going into farming on their own account in unprecedented numbers (Guyer with Idowu 1991). The male farming/female trade picture no longer held. Both men and women were crossing with some alacrity the categories of occupation I had implied – and mistrusted – as stable in my earlier paper, and the whole development seemed to be going in the opposite direction to the 'evolutionary' path from female to male farming. The arguments briefly summarized above certainly left space for this kind of turn of events, but witnessing a real example offered new possibilities for trying out framing and centring concepts, and locating persistence and transformation, over a period of rapid change.

The paper's title – 'present ethnography' – is used to express the difference between this and description in an ethnographic present that fits into an implicitly evolutionary frame of interpretation. It refers to an ethnography of the moment in all its particularity and incoherence, set in as many types of time-frame as seem necessary to gain a sense of the direction of social and cultural dynamics, as seen from within as well as without. One is asking – in this case of the gender division of labour – where did it come from and where does it seem to be going? Having set out the intellectual run-up, the remainder of this chapter is a quite prosaic first approach to the situation.

A Present Ethnography of Yoruba Women's Farming

In 1968, I worked in a small town of about 6,000 inhabitants. While small by Yoruba standards, it is fully constituted, with a beaded-crown *oba* ('king'), a full hierarchy of chiefs, residential quarters, cults and occupational organizations. It was settled in the mid-nineteenth century by refugees fleeing from the fall of Old Oyo, and throughout a quite turbulent political history had fallen under the regional domination of Ibadan. Land is owned by compounds, residential and administrative units that are ideologically defined as patrilineal, but historically quite mixed in ways that are punctiliously preserved for customary legal purposes. As John Peel (1983) has put it, the past is in the Yoruba present in clearly and fully articulated ways. History and precedent are passionately explored and invoked.

This community lies outside the famous cocoa belt, in derived guinea savanna land. For at least 100 years, the area has supplied savanna products to Ibadan, including food crops such as egusi-melon, yams and dried cassava that are produced less easily in the forest zone. It is an area of fairly low population density (about 50 per sq. km for the district as a whole, but as low as 14 in some farm areas), one in which the land frontier has not yet been reached, at least, not in the technical sense of carrying capacity, although land can be a cause of dispute.

So to women's farming. First, obviously, one frames: 1968 and 1988, women's farm activities then and now, similarities and differences. While in 1968 decision-making and control of farm income was predominantly in the hands of men, all women did carry out agricultural work. Teams of women hired themselves out for harvest work for which they were paid, even by their husbands or close kin (Idowu and Guyer 1991). Wives helped to dry soaked cassava. Some women worked as day labourers picking tobacco. All women head-loaded crops from farm to village and from village to wholesale market; husbands expected this service and generally did not pay for it. In fact, the entire commercial side of agriculture was deeply dependent on women's porterage because of the limited road network. In brief, a large proportion of women had regular duties related to agriculture. It was a version of the classic interdigitated task structure, but with an unusually heavy emphasis towards women's specialization in ancillary processing and trading tasks in a farming economy that became partially commercialized a very long time ago, certainly well before the colonial era and probably before extensive cassava and maize cultivation. This had been a yam and egusi-melon system.

Own-account farming, however, was quite rare amongst women in 1968, although not unknown. Of the sixty farms I visited (66 farmers), two belonged to women: middle-aged sisters, living on their father's land, and farming in ways that differed in only a couple of major ways from the men of the same village. Their farms were slightly smaller, and they never grew yams in more than a few heaps. Another woman had an onion garden in wetlands in the dry season. They hoed, planted, harvested and generally carried out most of the tasks done by men. Land clearing could be done by hired labour, which both men and women employed.

There was no cultural injunction or moral objection to women farming on their own account. It was more a question of whether bending over in the sun all day was desirable for a woman in the childbearing and nursing years. Farming is said to be aesthetically problematic. People age quickly and become thin working when farming. Their skin becomes dry and dark rather than shiny and supple. In pragmatic terms, since women's labour was a substantial and important contribution to men's farming, any conflict of seasonal peaks on one's own and men's farms might lead to awkward bottlenecks if women were farming on any scale. So farming for women was inadvisable and awkwardly timed rather than frowned on; any woman to whom the conditions did not apply could easily become a farmer. The two women farmers I knew then were probably past childbearing, were marginally married, living on their fathers' land rather than their husbands' land, providing food for their children as well as a cash income. They were entering the stage of life where the gender constructions around sexuality and reproduction lose some relevance and they were choosing to veer closer to a male pattern of life.

Here one should extend the time-frame and add that gender in Yoruba culture and history is more a secondary than a primary characteristic. A person is a person first, a member of a kinship-political unit, and thereby a woman is eligible in principle for many activities normally considered male. In the history of this community, for example, there were not enough drummers in the early years after settlement and so women from a drumming compound practised their family craft. Such a conception allows for what we might perhaps term situational flexibility in the gender division of labour as well as giving women ritual and socio-political obligations.

Because of these aspirations and obligations, all Yoruba women, like men, need money. Money (*owo*), children (*omo*), and well-being (*ati alaafia*) are the basic components of the good life for everyone. A woman has her own obligations, both to her natal kin group and her children, that cannot be met without cash. Evidence for women's demand for independent cash income goes back well into the early years of the nineteenth century. All able-bodied women have an occupation, usually more than one over a lifetime and generally, in a farming community, different ones for different seasons. In 1968, women's occupations were mainly concentrated in trade, primary processing, cooked food preparation and harvest work.

In 1988, *agbe* (farmer) is an occupational title claimed by women. In a sample of 222 women of all ages, over two thirds (69 per cent) said that they have farms of their own. Extrapolating from my studies of men's and women's farms, perhaps 20 per cent of the total arable acreage is now farmed by women, a growth that has developed at the same time as men's farms have also grown in size. Taking 1968 as an arbitrary but useful baseline, I would estimate that – without accounting for demographic and occupational shifts for the moment – the small farm sector in this town and its environs has increased its acreage by about 50 per cent over twenty years, over half of that increase due to the entry of women into farming, and the rest due to the expansion of the farms of men already farming and having started farming since 1968. So this shift of women into farming is not a reallocation of tasks and responsibilities between the sexes, but part of a quite major expansion in farming in general.

Seeing both the figures on change and the apparent ease of the transition – which is now taken largely for granted – I mistrusted my earlier inference that women were rare farmers in the past. In fact, my survey in 1988 did confirm that women's farming had been a minority affair of somewhat older women. Nine per cent of the 222 women interviewed had been farming for twenty years or longer, and the youngest age at which they had started farming was 26, an age at which a woman would have been ten years into her marital career. While these numbers impressed me that the stereotype of 'male farming' had been substantially correct in the 1960s, they also highlighted the already existing cultural and economic viability of women's own account farming, which only the magnetism of the central tendencies – cultural and statistical – implicit in the concept of custom, had relegated to so minor a place in the ethnography of the time. The existence of women's farming way back in time makes sense of the apparent lack of contention about their entry in much larger numbers during the past twenty years. Women's farming fits into a conceptual and pragmatic niche already created.

But the change is not simply quantitative growth. When one moves back and forth from the frame to various foci within it, some striking qualitative shifts emerge, which suggest neither an absolute departure from custom, nor a simple continuation and expansion of an old customary sub-theme, but something else: an elaboration and a creation of a new configuration.

The key concept for this analysis is the temporally-centred conception of the cohort, that is, a category of people engaging in a particular activity for the first time at a particular moment and therefore under particular historical conditions. Although it is a well-known concept in demographic and social research, its use in anthropology has been limited, and its enormous utility as one method of understanding collective, rather than individual biographical, historical experience presented itself to me initially through the data rather than through theory.

Working with both my survey of 222 women, and a more intensive study of 41 women farmers (40 farms), I initially thought in the anthropological terms of generation, that women of different ages and life stages would have characteristic farming patterns. This approach was quite revealing for the male farmers for whom farming had been their main life's work. The key variables are farm size, the proportion of land initially cleared by tractor, and the proportion of the land in cassava cultivation. Each of these variables contrasted male and female patterns of farming: men's farms were bigger, used commercialized inputs differently, and were more diversified in cropping pattern. Cassava, of course, has tended to be a more female crop in Africa as a whole, as I suggested earlier with respect to the long history of female farming.

Figures 2 and 3 summarize the results of an age-generation approach to women's farming, drawing on my sample of 41 farmers (40 farms). First farm size and proportions cleared by tractor.

Figure 2: Labour Sources for Farm Clearing by Age of Women Farmers. Idere, Nigeria, February 1988

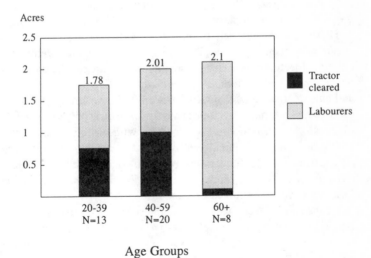

Age Groups

The variation in farm size by age/generation is quite narrow and rather surprising; the largest category is only 18 per cent larger than the smallest, and there is no peak in the middle years as one might expect. Tractor use perhaps fits with expectations, that the younger generation might be more likely to use newer inputs.

Now cropping patterns:

Figure 3: Proportion of Farm in Cassava by Age of Women Farmers.   Idere, Nigeria, February 1988

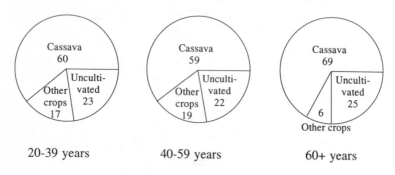

20-39 years   40-59 years   60+ years

Again there is a substantial similarity in the proportion of land devoted to different crops. Women are particularly focussed on cassava production, with a ten-percentage point variation from lowest to highest.

These results are both illuminating and puzzling. They show a specifically female pattern of farming that corresponds well with the cultural objections; women have smaller farms, hire substantial amounts of the labour and tractors to do the hard, exacting labour in the fields, and tend to grow crops that afford flexibility in the timing of work. But the apparently limited variations amongst women is puzzling, since they range in age from under 20 to over 70, with all the variation in life condition that that entails. Again the static, typological approach to 'women' as a single category turned out to conceal the most interesting dynamic processes and hid, *a priori*, any ways in which female and male farming actually resembled one another.

Trying another tack I went back to the year of entry into farming. And here a certain pattern appeared that corresponded roughly with regional economic conditions. Taking the sample of 153 women now farming (out of the 222 in the sample), the following distribution emerges, which I felt justified in dividing into three steps.

Figure 4: Women now Farming by Year Started.
4 compounds, Idere, 1988   (N=153)

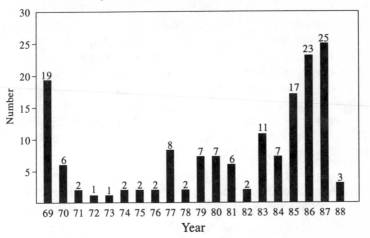

First column includes 1969 and before. Total sample 222 women, the resident female population of four Idere compounds on a festival weekend, one compound from each town quarter.

The large peak at 1969 represents the fact that I have grouped all those farming longer than twenty years. Between 1969 and about 1976, the entry of women into own-account farming was probably well below 1 per cent a year, a rate that would maintain a steady participation level of about 10 per cent. Around 1976, the rate of entry picks up to about 3 or 4 per cent per year, and plateaus at that level until around 1984, when it leaps upward to between 10 and 12 per cent per year for three years.

Now these phases of Nigerian history have some quite different characteristics. The period before 1976 sees the end of the Biafran War, the gradual revival of urban demand, some transport improvement and so on. During this period, the older pattern prevailed: a few women went into farming each year but largely for idiosyncratic reasons.

By 1976, the conditions of the oil boom had really taken over: demand was high, transport was enormously improved, the occupational structure diversified, urban consumption patterns shifted and many commentators argue that the population grew dramatically.

1984 marks the beginning of the current economic crisis during which urban demand has stayed high, positive prices for farmers have been offset by dramatic increases in all consumer prices and the restoration of payment for services such as schooling and medical care.

Women's farming expanded during *both* these latter two phases, under widely varying conditions, suggesting that farming became an answer to several agendas, not a single response to a single condition. By looking at each *cohort* one might be able to link these conditions with women's changing constructions of a workable productive life.

Going back to farm sizes and my three variables analysed by cohort, a variation in pattern of farming jumped out. As Figure 5 shows, farm size varies by cohort by a factor of 2.6; the women who started farming before 1976 have farms 260 per cent of the size of those starting in the most recent phase, with those in the 1976-83 phase falling in between. That first cohort is closer to the male farm size than the others, 81 per cent of the mean for the male sample.

Figure 5: Labour Sources for Farm Clearing Cohorts of Women and All Men. Idere, Nigeria, February 1988

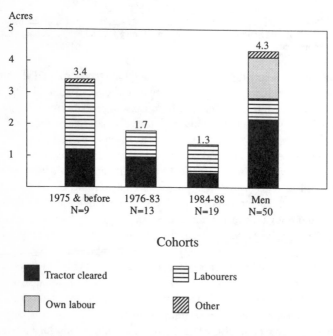

Farm size for small-scale male farmers
Mean: 4.3 acres
Median: 3.4 acres
C.V.:   65%

Farm size for female farmers
Mean: 1.9 acres
Median: 1.5 acres
C.V.:   86%

Labour mobilization in clearing for all the women's farms differs from the men, in that women hardly ever do their own clearing (note the dotted section of the male column). Otherwise, what one sees for the women is an increasing use of tractor hire, but a more striking increasing proportional use of hired labour which requires somewhat more bargaining skill. If we look at farming style represented in Figure 6, complementary variations emerge. Cassava cultivation varies from 54 per cent of total area for the earlier cohort, through 61 per cent for the middle cohort, to 79 per cent of the most recent cohort. Diversification increases directly with the time spent at farming, inversely with the recency of the era – and conditions – of entry.

Figure 6: Proportion of Farm in Cassava. Cohorts of Women farmers. Idere, Nigeria, 1988

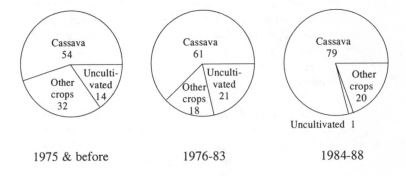

1975 & before   1976-83   1984-88

This variation amongst cohorts makes sense, the aspects fit together; economic conditions, farm sizes, and crop diversity produce the same pattern. The three short time-frames have their own characteristics.

The next element to explore is the experiential one using person-centred time, consisting of each cohort of women's own explanations, constructions, ambitions and changing patterns of activity. With the former analysis done, I looked at my interviews in cohorts rather than taking the whole female category or dividing it up by age and generation.

Again I found patterns. In the more intensive study of 41 women and their farms, I had asked about former and present occupations, life situation and the reasons for taking up farming. Before going into farming, those in the oldest cohort, with one exception, had been either traders or doing no other occupation. Their reasons often included the need to bring up children alone: to provide food and an income but without doing the amount of travelling required by trade. Their situation reflects my more general sense that the minority of women who took to farming in the past were embarked into middle-age, marginally married, and needing to support dependents in food as well as purchased items.

The middle cohort was markedly different. Most had been very active in some kind of fairly substantial business such as trading food crops to urban centres. The comparative profitability of their current occupations had suddenly been affected after 1976 by the intersection of personal difficulties with the intensification of urban demand and the extension of the road network that made trade and processing much more competitive. Those who had been in trade found it difficult to replenish capital at a certain point, and those buying cassava to process for sale had found their supplies drying up as male farmers either did it themselves or turned to larger-scale bulk selling to transporters with pick-up trucks and lorries. Own-account farming became a potentially profitable enterprise that – unlike trade – one could enter without much capital, that could be kept to a low labour input if cassava were the main crop, thus allowing continued work at other things that might bring good returns if prices lurched upwards, and in any case provided food for a growing family population.

The most recent cohort, by contrast, had been predominantly in the cooked food, small-scale processing sector working the local market; only two had been in some sort of fairly substantial trade. This cohort included more of the quite old and very young, trying out farming as a small-scale experiment. Only in this cohort did anyone give as a reason for farming that they were emulating others. Their small farm size and predominance in cassava suggests a limited and focussed orientation and perhaps limited farming skill.

One sees, then, two things: that farming by women becomes increasingly plausible as it comes to answer an increasing variety of female agendas, and that those agendas are still amenable to differentiation from one another. For the older cohort, farming was an avocation and a solution to unstable support from men; for the middle cohort, it was a way of sourcing one's own needs for trade and processing under conditions of expanding competition in trade and transport; and the last cohort, working in the context of the increased cost of living and the past modicum of female success in farming, brings all these reasons forward to 'try it out'. None of these conditions has disappeared.

Each new stage adds a further element to the configuration, making farming an attractive, possibly increasingly necessary, proposition for further elements in the female population as the regional division of labour, male and female, shifts.

One can now begin to pose questions about the social and cultural implications, the emerging images and dilemmas for the immediate future of Yoruba women farmers. The fact that there is a powerful motivation and a collectively constructed configuration around it, does not mean that conditions and institutions will support its optimal development or growth. If the newest cohort gradually expands and diversifies to resemble the older one, pressure will be placed on land tenure; 'present ethnography' therefore needs to focus on key cases involving a wife's long-term access to good land in a system where plots have to be put into bush fallow. If prices remain as volatile as they have been in past years, women's farming will be much more vulnerable than men's because of the disproportionate dependence on hired labour for clearing and heaping; ethnography needs to focus on the dynamics of failure and insolvency. If the middle, more ambitious, farming cohort makes money, they might try to go back into trade; ethnography would look at investment and the juggling of several occupations and income sources (Berry 1985). If farming remains possible but not profitable, the key issue to explore is whether women give up farming and take on an expanded role in – for example – agricultural wage labour, or perhaps increasingly use their farms to take over the formerly male activity of family provisioning, resulting in a fundamental shift in family responsibilities. Women's conceptions of those responsibilities will figure prominently in the solution. However infrequent at present, cases illustrating people's emerging thoughts and actions on these points can indicate the geography of their immediate future.

People themselves do not usually try to predict the future in comprehensive terms, but a 'present ethnography' needs to include – in a manner different from the distant vantage point of history and the close analytical perspective of practice – the ways in which the various paths forward are prefigured.

Conclusion: Present Ethnography with Multiple Temporal Frames

At present the patterns of farming in Africa – and in particular in Nigeria – are quite volatile. The volatility of the end of the twentieth century is as much a challenge to anthropology as the evolutionary trends, the timeless structures and the long-term transformations on which we used to concentrate. An anthropology adequate to understanding the motifs of late twentieth-century African dynamics needs to be experimental with time, self-consciously varying the length of time-frame, trying out framing versus centring conceptions of time, and exploiting already existing concepts such as the cohort, which can bring history and biography, culture and situation together. Neither the past nor the future of women's hoe cultivation is yet clear.

Looked at in this experimental way, the surge of women into farming in this small Yoruba community is not a paradox of evolutionary change – evolution going backwards as it were – nor a transformation of the culturally defined division of labour, nor unambiguously a linear trend (a rise or decline) in female status. We draw on those models but avoid applying them with *a priori* conviction. The past twenty years of re-appraisal – with ourselves, colleagues, farmers and a whole host of others – has conveyed the danger of turning too quickly to familiar models with their own implicit judgements about temporal framing and significance, hidden presumptions or old intellectual connections. Untested assumptions shortcut the understanding of both men's and women's, separate and joint, construction of plausible ways of living in the present and of envisaging possible futures, using the experiential and cultural legacies of the past. But the very close view afforded by current practice theory cannot define the parameters of inventiveness, and we do need the more distant views that capture large movements and macro-forces. So we are only part way towards rethinking the powerful propositions of evolutionary and structural theory in the light of late twentieth-century dynamics. Until new syntheses may be worked out, the logic of enquiry has to be multiple, experimental and ultimately participatory.

Notes

* This paper is a slightly revised version of the Hans Wolff Lecture for 1989, of the African Studies Program, Indiana University. I am grateful to my colleagues there for their comments on it and for copyright permission.

The fieldwork was undertaken with grants from: the National Institute for Mental Health (1968-9), the Joint Committee on African Studies of the Social Science Research Council/American Council of Learned Societies (summer 1987) and the National Science Foundation (1988). In 1968-71, I was a graduate student in the Department of Anthropology, University of Rochester and an Occasional Student in the Sociology Department, University of Ibadan. In 1988, I was affiliated with the Institute of African Studies, University of Ibadan and with the International Institute of Tropical Agriculture, Ibadan. I am grateful for all this support.

References

Baumann, H., 'The Division of Work according to Sex in African Hoe Culture', *Africa*, vol. 1, 1928, pp. 289–319

Berry, S., *Fathers Work for Their Sons*, Berkeley, University of California Press, 1985

Boserup, E., *Woman's Role in Economic Development*, London, St. Martin's Press, 1970

di Leonardo, M., 'Gender, Culture and Political Economy: Feminist Anthropology in Historical Perspective', in M. di Leonardo (ed.), *Gender at the Crossroads of Knowledge: Feminist Anthropology in the Postmodern Era*, Berkeley, University of California Press, 1991, pp. 1–48

Gluckman, M., 'The Utility of the Equilibrium Model in the Study of Social Change', *American Anthropologist*, vol. 70, 1968, pp. 219–37

Goody, J. (ed.), *The Developmental Cycle of Domestic Groups*, Cambridge, Cambridge University Press, 1958

Guyer, J. I., 'Food, Cocoa and the Division of Labor by Sex in Two West African Societies', *Comparative Studies in Society and History*, vol. 22, 1980, pp. 355–73

—'Naturalism in Models of African Production', *Man* (N.S.), vol. 19, 1984, pp. 371– 88

—'The Multiplication of Labor. Historical Methods in the Study of Gender and Agricultural Change in Modern Africa', *Current Anthropology*, vol. 29, 1988, pp. 247–72

—'Female Farming in Anthropology and African History', in M. di Leonardo (ed.), *Gender at the Crossroads of Knowledge: Feminist Anthropology in the Postmodern Era*, Berkeley, University of California Press, 1991, pp. 257–77

—'Small Change: Individual Farm Work and Collective Life in a Western Nigerian Savanna Town, 1969–1988', Africa, vol. 62, no. 4, 1992, pp. 465–89

Guyer, J. I. with O. Idowu, 'Women's Agricultural Work in a Multimodal Rural Economy, Ibarapoa District, Oyo State, Nigeria', in C. Gladwin (ed.), *Structural Adjustment and Transformation: Impacts on African Women Farmers*, Gainsville, University of Florida Press, 1991, pp. 257–80

Idowu, O. and J.I. Guyer, 'Commercialization and the Harvest Work of Women. Ibarapa, Oyo State, Nigeria', Women's Research and Documentation Centre, Occasional Paper No. 2, Institute of African Studies, University of Ibadan, 1991

Mills, C. Wright, *The Sociological Imagination*, Oxford University Press, 1959

Peel, J., *Ijeshas and Nigerians*, Cambridge, Cambridge University Press, 1983

Richards, A., *Land, Labour and Diet in Northern Rhodesia. An Economic Study of the Bemba Tribe*, Oxford, Oxford University Press, 1939

3

Down to Fundamentals: Women-centred Hearth-holds in Rural West Africa

Felicia I. Ekejiuba

Introduction

Significant influences on my intellectual development and my theoretical orientation derive as much from my graduate work in anthropology as from my roots in rural Nigeria, and my perceptions of gender relations both during my childhood and during my research in the rural areas. I grew up in an environment in which the 'working' mother was the norm. Women routinely shared costs and responsibilities of household welfare. Children, women and men worked side-by-side to produce food for the family and to sell the surplus to buy what they could not produce. With the development of wage labour and the commoditization of production, women became increasingly concerned with family food security as well as with diversifying their sources of income to contribute to family income, thereby supplementing the below-subsistence wages their spouses earned from the formal sector. My mother, for example, a pioneer of women's education in eastern Nigeria, gave up her pre-marriage occupation as a school teacher on the grounds that she did not earn enough income from it nor did it leave her with enough time to devote to her family. She went back to farming as well as selling cooked food – fried black bean balls and corn pudding. But she kept up her role in education through offering adult literacy classes for women in the parish where my father was an Episcopal minister.

After my father retired to his natal village, my mother further developed her interests and skills in organizing women by initiating community self-help projects for building maternity/health clinics, roofed market stalls, and improving village drinking water sources. These activities earned my mother the title '*isi njin*', literally the prime mover. I also watched her and other women punish men who repeatedly battered their wives or who made disparaging comments about women and their reproductive anatomy, what Van Allen (1972) described as 'sitting on a man' and Ardener (1975) dubbed '*titi ikoli*' with reference to Cameroonian women.

In the community where I grew up, rape was considered a heinous crime and rapists were severely punished. Repeated violence against a woman was decried and was sufficient grounds for divorce and the return of bridewealth. Kinsmen often avenged such violence. Many women of my mother's generation survived childless marriages by manipulating the flexible gender division of labour. My maternal aunt, for instance, emerged from a 'failed', childless marriage to re-establish her 'hearth-hold'. She was discouraged by her kinsmen from remarrying. She had her first and only son a year after she left her husband who was perceived as abusive and impotent. She later became a 'female husband' (Amadiume 1987) by 'marrying' her own wife who increased the 'hearth-hold' by producing four more children for her. As a trained midwife, she established and operated a very successful, privately owned maternity home. This enabled her to support and provide shelter for members of her 'hearth-hold'.

One of the main problems I had as a graduate student of anthropology at Harvard in the 1970s was reconciling my childhood experiences of women as initiators of development and active participants of social and economic processes in their communities with their image in much of the existing literature as 'marginalized', 'downtrodden' and 'exploited' by patriarchy and motherhood. The literature emphasized an attitudinal discrepancy between rural women and educated, urban-based women and men of my mother's generation. Fortunately, studies by Green (1947), van Allen (1972), Ardener (1975), Pala (1979), Mba (1980), Sudarkasa (1987) and Amadiume (1987) provided welcome alternative perspectives to that of Little (1973) and others, convincing me that my earlier perceptions of rural West Africa were neither biased nor localized.

One of my intellectual goals as a graduate student, as a field researcher in rural West Africa, and as a professor of anthropology, was to attain a greater degree of fit between anthropological concepts and the realities of West African societies. This motivated me to join other African women scholars in forming the Association of African Women for Research and Development (AAWORD) to address the problems of conceptualization and prioritization in the study of African women. AAWORD eventually gained a consultative status at the United Nations and its studies, as well as those by its members, have influenced, to a great extent, the direction of subsequent research on African women.

My dissatisfaction with the adequacy of the household concept relative to my perception of West African rural society underpins this chapter. The following revisits the ongoing debate on the usefulness and limitation of the household as a unit of data generation and analysis. Based on the realities of rural West African societies, the paper argues for a woman-centred unit of social analysis, which focusses on women's activities and organizations and perceives their responsibilities and roles as both catalysts and full beneficiaries of development.

Poor-fit Category: 'Households' in Rural West Africa

Recent literature from development and feminist studies as well as from participatory, action-oriented field experiences all suggest that women's voices should be heard and that gender-disaggregated statistics and data should be generated to facilitate the mainstreaming of gender issues. The search for means of increasing the visibility and audibility of rural African women demands, among other things, a rethinking of the concept of the household hitherto used as the basic unit of data collection and analysis of gender. The *a priori* definition of the household and the assumption that women are passive or secondary production and procurement agents are largely responsible for women's silence as perceived in western development literature (Guyer and Peters 1987). We need to revisit the long-standing debates on the limitations of the household as a socio-economic unit for data collection and analysis and the nature of allocational behaviour of the household.

Smith, Wallerstein and Evers (1984) have described the household as an 'income-pooling, co-residential and joint unit of production and consumption' within which the 'reproduction of human labour or the individual is assured through the consumption of a collective fund of material goods'. Stauth's (1984) definition of the household as a 'capitalist institution that secures and guarantees the reproduction of commodified labour, capitalist reproduction being characterized by shared income' projects middle-class, western capitalist gender relations on pre-capitalist and non-western emerging capitalist systems. Indeed, as Goody (1976) and Guyer (1984) have demonstrated, the assumptions of a simple household model do not fit African residence, production, decision-making and consumption patterns, particularly as the household model was imported from the West and East Asian social contexts where 'millennia of religious, legal and fiscal measures have given the household a corporate character'.

The continuing debate on the household clearly indicates that many of the basic assumptions have become obsolete and unrealistic, even for advanced capitalist societies (Smith et al. 1984; Guyer and Peters 1984). The concept is even less accurately applied to those societies which are based on an entirely different gender ideology, where the capitalist mode of production is only just beginning to converge with the non-capitalist societies. The debate has focussed mainly on the definition, boundaries, authority, resource allocation and pattern of decision-making within the household. The view that the household consists of a father, mother(s) and children with the man as the head and sole provider has been universalized and has informed government policies pertaining to rural areas. For example, wage and tax policies have allowed the male 'head of household' to collect allowances for the wife and children. This perspective has also informed the design of project intervention (Guyer 1984; Elwert 1984; Guyer and Peters 1987).

Attempts to re-conceptualize the household, making it more theoretically relevant should include examining the historical processes which have transformed African gender ideology. The gradual transformation of gender ideology has driven a material wedge between men and women, a process of gender stratification is underway, characterized by differential access to production resources, notably education, technology, credit, land, capital and sources of income. The concept of the household, as it is currently applied, is itself part of the subtle ideological transformation which has facilitated the assertion of colonial power nationally and male power domestically. The concept clouds the true pattern of gender interaction and power relations, portraying the impression of men as sole providers and of female dependence and passivity, as opposed to their active participation in socio-economic processes. The negotiated relationships that result in interdependence and relative autonomy between the sexes are conveniently swept aside for want of suitable analytical constructs.

Colonial policy displaced women from their place in the social structure. The colonial denial of women's active participation in socio-economic and political processes prevailed, despite the reality of women's active economic production in agriculture, and their role in processing and distributing products through trade. In some places, women challenged the colonial policies of exclusion, organizing a series of cooperative credit and/or work groups aimed at increasing performance in the face of externally imposed constraints (Okonjo 1976; Afonja 1985). They were behind a series of social movements in various parts of Nigeria which resisted the impositions (Afigbo 1977; Mba 1980).

In the post-colonial period, the myth of women's invisibility and inaudibility continues to be perpetuated through 'household' data collection and through development theory and planning exercises. The gap between reality and theory has had disastrous consequences for women's livelihood, national well-being and food security since women have hardly been targeted as beneficiaries of mainstream development, nor have they been involved in different stages of planning and follow-up implementation. Thus, the theoretical debate on the usefulness of the household as a unit of analysis parallels practical attempts by African women to press for adequate recognition and accounting of their contribution to national wealth and family well-being.

Hearth-hold Defined

The search for a more gender-sensitive analytical framework leads quite naturally to a recognition of the importance of female-directed social units, what I term, hearth-holds (Ekejiuba 1984). Hearth-holds can either have an independent existence of their own or can be the most intimate, clearly discernible subset nestled in the household. In other words, hearth-holds are an extension of the mother-child bond. The unit is centred on the hearth, or stove (in Igbo, *ekwu, mkpuke*) and is a concept that men and women themselves employ in their daily lives. The unit is demographically made up of a woman and all her dependents whose food security she is either fully or partially responsible for. The dependents include all her children, her co-resident relatives and non-relatives who, in one way or another, assist her in provisioning, caring for and nurturing members of her hearth-hold who share in the food cooked on her hearth for a significant part of their lives. The male spouse can be either a full member of the hearth-hold, but in most cases he oscillates between several hearth-holds, that of his wives, mother and mistresses.

The hearth-hold is primarily a unit of consumption and also a unit of production. Its function as a reproductive and socializing unit usually depends in part on transfers from other hearth-holds or households. It is not necessarily a co-residential unit since members may temporarily reside in places other than that occupied by other hearth-hold members.

The woman (mother) and the hearth are physical symbols of the unit.

The mother-child bond structures the relationship. Even when there is only one hearth-hold in the household, there is an observable pattern of interaction and reciprocal exchanges between the head of the household (male) and the head of the hearth-hold (female). Each has a different set of dependents and clearly defined responsibilities, which in turn gives rise to gender-specific patterns of production, investment and incentive responses. Recognition of these patterns is essential to understanding the complex interplay of autonomy and dependence of household members.

There are different ways the hearth-hold is linked to other social units, namely other households, their component hearth-holds or the community at large. Such links are necessary for the hearth-hold's access to labour – through informal work groups or hiring of labour – and other resources. Awareness of these links is relevant to an understanding of rural production strategies and the gender-differentiated impact of planned intervention.

The hearth-hold head may be a farmer, a trader, a craftswoman, a wage earner or a professional in the formal sector, or any combination of these. A multiple production base and the search for additional sources of income, including urban and international migration, are part of a woman's strategies for maximizing her ability to meet her various obligations both to her hearth-hold and to her kin and community networks.

The male head of the household acts on his own account, and has his own barn, land, labour, etc. He contributes to, but is never solely responsible for, the total expenditure of the component hearth-hold(s). When the household spans several hearth-holds, as is common in a polygamous marriage situation, he is entitled to periodic but assured access to food, labour and sexual services from the hearth-hold heads. His primary responsibility to each of the hearth-holds is to provide a dwelling unit and some access to resources such as land, cattle, and fruit trees that support hearth-hold productive activities. He also supplements school fees and hospital bills of hearth-hold members and is expected to provide some meat for each of the hearth-holds.

In recent times, high commodity prices, low stagnant incomes, unemployment, forced retirement and retrenchment of workers and repeated devaluation of currencies, all induced by structural adjustment programmes, have dramatically reduced or even eliminated the household head's contributions to the hearth-holds and added greater pressure on the earnings of the hearth-hold heads. Correspondingly, the demands on the time and labour of women have increased as they search for additional sources of income so as to ensure the survival of their hearth-holds.

Trading, crafts, such as cloth or mat weaving, hair plaiting, formal sector jobs and other kinds of off-farm enterprises afford women opportunities to acquire cash and maintain a more independent position. Indeed, most women try to combine different sources of income and are constantly exploring ways of diversifying these sources. The harsher the economic situation, the less likely they are to get the statutory contribution from their husbands and the more they strive to combine many informal sector activities. The increased incomes guarantee women an independent means of physical reproduction. They are able to buy foodstuffs if their husbands do not produce or provide enough. They can also accumulate money for hard times so as to pay school and hospital fees.

Some women are able to transform cash into prestige, as men do, by taking titles and becoming members of illustrious or secret societies. The additional income also enables women to extend their personal influence, in the family and community by participating in political activities, paying fees, making voluntary donations to community development projects, and buying imported luxury goods and real estate property for themselves. The resulting independence and power increases women's chances of competing for and holding public offices, or initiating divorce or separation from abusive, impotent or lazy husbands. Many are known to have invested part of their wealth in paying bridewealth which entitles them to wives through whom the strength of their hearth-holds is increased (Amadiume 1987; Ekejiuba 1992).

Nonetheless, these women are the exception to the general rule. It has been shown that hearth-hold heads tend to invest more on basic needs in the form of food, health, and schooling, while men tend to spend more on capital-intensive and prestige commodities such as bicycles, building materials, meat, as well as extra-household expenses to secure status in their communities. It is ironic that while the demands of basic needs provisioning have increased as a result of commoditization and most recently, structural adjustment, a woman's access to the resources that had in the past enabled her to produce goods and earn income to meet her hearth-hold's welfare needs, have diminished.

Nested Hearth-holds in Household and Lineage Matrices

In Nigeria, amongst rural dwellers, educated and uneducated alike, a number of circumstances give rise to a multiplicity of female-directed hearth-holds nested in a household. These include: first, polygyny or multiple spouse marriage systems as are prevalent among Moslems and farmers practising shifting cultivation; second, leviratic unions, in which a man takes over the social responsibility of protection and care of his deceased brother's wife (or wives) in addition to his own wife; woman-to-woman marriage (Amadiume 1987); third, three or more generational 'households' of parents (male and/or females) and their married children (as in the Hausa *gandu*); and fourth, joint family households of either: brothers in a patrilineal system, sisters in a matrilineal system, or brothers and their unwed/divorced sister(s) in a patrilineal system. In all these instances, several hearth-holds can form subsets which are nested in the larger household usually, but not always, headed by a male (Guyer 1986). On the other hand, the divorce, migration or death-induced absence of males may result in the unity of the household and the female-headed hearth-hold.

The household has common resources – land, cattle, fish ponds, fruit trees – which are controlled and managed by the household head. Some portion of these resources are subdivided among the hearth-hold heads as a means of income-earning to enable them to provision their dependents. A hearth-hold is generally co-resident, occupying and controlling its own space, i.e. a house, room, etc. It has its own water storage facilities, cooking utensils, cooking fuel, yam or grain storage facilities, traction or farm animals, and land, held independently of other hearth-holds.

Each hearth-hold head is primarily responsible for providing members of her hearth-hold with food, clothing, school fees and caring for children, the elderly and sick. Women have provisioning agendas separate from men. Their material resources, time and labour are not always subsumed under that of the male spouse. Often, but not always, there is a partial pooling of resources. Many studies have demonstrated different patterns of expenditure for husbands and wives. Separate ownership of property, dwelling space and labour, the basis of a woman's autonomy and independence, is enshrined in the ideology and structure of the hearth-hold. In addition to her contributions and the obligatory contributions from the male spouse, transfers from other hearth-holds and households, mostly from members of a woman's natal hearth-hold or patrilineage, enable women to cope with the demands of ensuring her hearth-hold's well-being.

The relationship between hearth-hold heads – wives, co-wives, mothers-in-law – and household heads is marked by solidarity and conflict. Competition between a wife and mother-in-law often occurs over weaning the male spouse from his membership in the mother's hearth-hold so that he becomes fully identified with the wife's hearth-hold. Conflict between co-wives arises over the male spouse's obligatory contributions of labour and resources to the component hearth-holds, and can be greatly exacerbated by conflict between siblings from different co-wife mothers. Conflict between spouses centres mainly on material factors, namely resource allocation, support to relations, etc.

In spite of hearth-hold heads' well-known need for sufficient land for food production, the household head can and sometimes does sell or pawn land to raise the capital to marry more wives, or engage in conspicuous consumption, such as buying a radio, betting, building a house or taking a chieftaincy or other titles to enhance his prestige. Gender-differentiated responses to incentives means that hearth-hold heads are eager to exploit new opportunities for earning additional income by trading instead of, or in addition to, farming. A hearth-hold head may combine wage work with trading and/or farming, migrating to the city or across national and international boundaries. Such migration can be undertaken either with the entire hearth-hold or by making arrangements for their care *in situ*, using kin, friendship or other network ties until it becomes possible for the unit to be co-resident once more.

In summary, intra-household relationships may be, and often are, made invisible by a singular focus on the household or on individual adult males and females in the household. Household/hearth-hold interaction, largely determines responses to externally injected incentives, such as new technology, capital, credit or additional avenues for income generation. Hearth-hold/household interaction involves some pooling of the means of subsistence, some autonomy of constituent units, and some conflict over allocation of resources and consumption goods. In Wong's (1984) words: 'The extensional character of network ties is as crucial to the reproduction of the individual as the exclusion principle of a bounded unit.'

Both the hearth-hold and the household depend on resource transfers from similarly constituted, but semi-autonomous, family units for their reproduction. It can be argued, however, that the hearth-hold creates a more internally coherent, tightly bound entity with more clearly defined and hence less contestable social relations. Thus, it is more socially, economically and emotionally stable over time. The incidence of divorce, separation, and vertical or horizontal multiple marriages makes the household a more volatile unit.

Predicament of Virilocal Hearth-holds

Although a great number of African societies are patrilineal, patrilineality is not as much at issue as virilocality, i.e. when women physically move to the location of their husband's patrilineage at marriage. In so doing, women are isolated from their natal support systems (Elwert 1984). Before Christianity and western middle-class ideology changed gender relations, a woman was not expected to change her family name when she got married. In spite of marriage, women were still considered members of the patrilineage of their birth, even after their death. In matrilineal societies, women remained in their lineage of origin while the husband moved out of his lineage of birth into that of the wife.

In patrilineal societies, unmarried women, i.e. never married, separated, divorced and widowed, often lived in their birthplace together with their peer group based on the long established ties they had to their patrilineage of birth. In all these cases, the woman received as much respect and resources as men within the patrilineage. She was respected for her age; age being an important criteria for establishing one's position in the social hierarchy. She was also respected as a patrilineal mother, aunt, and sister by her brother's children, and patrilineal cousins, all of whom were considered her children. On the other hand, her own biological children by her husband belonged to her husband's lineage.

Traditionally, within her household and the patrilineage of marriage, a woman was considered to be a stranger, particularly at the time of the death of her husband, and especially if she was childless. She was not expected to inherit his property. His brothers and adult offspring had the first claim to these. Thus, within her marital home, a woman had to strive to accumulate and keep her own property, namely that which she brought into a marriage and that which she acquired during the marriage through agricultural production, marketing and other enterprises (Elwert 1984). Economic and cultural links with her lineage of origin were important to her and were maintained through her periodic visits and financial contributions to relatives' funerals, weddings, etc.

Both the man and woman had obligations within their lineages of origin: the married woman to her brothers, sisters and kinsmen, the man to his. They also had obligations to each other. The man was obliged to provide a hearth-centred living space, some cattle and/or a plot of land for the wife's gardening and agricultural production on her own account. The size of the plot was determined mainly by the land available to the lineage, as well as the time, energy and labour she could mobilize.

Among many Nigerian groups such as the Urhobo of southern Nigeria, a woman could 'retire' after completing her marital assignment of reproducing and socializing her children and thereafter only periodically visited her husband's patrilineage at her children's invitation (Onoge 1992). In most other areas, even when she did not statutorily retire, a woman's corpse was normally taken back to her natal village to be buried among her kinsmen and women, symbolizing her continued membership in this group, which neither marriage nor death severed.

In recent times, especially under the influence of Christianity and its insistence that 'a man and a woman are joined in holy matrimony until death do they part', women have become more strongly identified with the 'household' as their husband's spouse. Their position within their patrilineage of birth as well as their patrilineage of marriage has become more ambiguous, often operating to the detriment of women's status in both cases. The cultural stipulations about 'retirement' and burial are sometimes negotiated and waived or modified, based on the nature of the relationship between the conjugal pair. Negotiations are often mediated by the intervention of adult offspring of the woman (Uzoka 1992).

In other areas, traditional cultural practices are still strictly adhered to as a strong statement about women's social status. Whether old or new practices are followed, it is primarily virilocality rather than patrilineality which isolates a woman from unambiguous resource rights and a firm support base. Christianity, colonial policy, modern bureaucratic systems, and development praxis, promoting the notion of male household headship and life-long virilocality, have contributed immensely to women's loss of material security from her kin.

Hearth-hold Concept's Utility to Development Work

A focus on the hearth-hold as an independent unit of analysis, or as a subset of the household in which it is nested, enables us to understand the significance of male and female adults as independent agents of development and change. The shifting boundaries and size of households and the complex pattern of inter- and intra-household relationships vis-à-vis goods and service transfers, time allocation, and mobility can be better understood by focussing on female-directed hearth-holds. The gender-specific division of responsibilities within domestic units, gender-differentiated needs, resource access and factor allocation and their implications for effective development programming will become evident.

Efforts to generate gender-sensitive data that will facilitate macro-planning and mainstreaming of women's issues so as to arrest their declining quality of life should focus on the dynamics of the relationship between the household and the hearth-holds. This would include a consideration of: first, the ways in which hearth-hold heads take turns to include the household head as a consumer within their unit; second, inter-hearth-hold competition for the household's expected contributions to the hearth-hold; and third, how households strive to protect their autonomy and financial independence and yet cooperate to ensure access to production factors and the survival of the total unit.

More information is needed on the complex interplay of cooperation and conflict. For example, to what extent is labour pooled across household and hearth-hold boundaries for childcare, for production, and for processing and distribution of agricultural products? Such data could enrich farming systems research projects and other participatory, action-oriented programmes aimed at improving the living standards of women and children, e.g. water projects, food security programmes, land reforms, income-generating activities, measures to improve health and modernize agriculture.

The distinction between the hearth-hold and household proves particularly useful when carrying out socio-economic surveys and community sensitization. I can illustrate this with reference to a water project in 77 rural Nigerian villages that I was involved in. At the pre-project stage, the priority that villagers attached to having safe, piped water relative to other needs such as electrification was assessed. Furthermore, the willingness and ability of villagers to contribute to the operational maintenance of the water scheme, as well as the organizational form of such maintenance was assessed. Many of the goals of the project made a focus on the hearth-hold as a unit of data collection imperative.

Women and children had responsibility for fetching water, often over long distances ranging from 2 to 8 kilometres. Women's need for water – for cooking, cleaning, washing clothes, bathing themselves and their children and drinking – differed from that of men who needed water primarily for bathing and drinking. Each hearth-hold owned its own small containers for storing water and only the more affluent in the communities could purchase larger water storage containers, of 500-1000 gallon capacity, through either collective or individual expenditure of the hearth-hold and household heads. Women were responsible for ensuring that water was clean and safe, by boiling or adding alum. Women's actions were critical to the prevention of water-borne diseases.

The survey collected data on the basis of female hearth-hold and household units. Income, education and water use of the household head was distinguished from that of the hearth-hold heads. The findings revealed significant differences in the priority placed on water. Women listed water and health centres as a number one priority in contrast to men who mentioned roads, community banks and electricity. The responses indicated that more women than men were prepared to contribute money and labour to keep the surroundings of the water tap clean. Some were prepared to serve on the village water committee and a few were prepared to undergo the training necessary to maintain the water pumps to prevent the breakdown of the amenity.

The hearth-hold/household distinction was also relevant in implementing income-generating activities in the rural communities. A pilot project was geared to organizing rural women into a development-oriented cooperative through which informal education and income-generating activities could be pursued. The project stressed members' participation in needs identification, project planning, implementation and project monitoring. During the first two months such basic issues as who qualified to be a member of the cooperative, what the least cost of each share was, and the minimum and maximum number of shares to be bought by an individual, were discussed and agreed upon. The definition of those qualified to be members was based on hearth-hold rather than household headship. Any woman who had set up a hearth independent of her mother-in-law or any co-wife was considered qualified to be a member. She was expected to buy the specified minimum number of shares, contribute labour, water and sand for the building either through her own labour or that of a representative from her hearth-hold.

Overall, the women appreciated that their opinions were being sought and their participation solicited as revealed in one woman's particular observation: 'People [in previous development projects] in the past treated us as if we did not exist, as if our opinions were not seen as necessary. So we ignored the team and later there was nobody to keep the piped water clean, that is, if there was any drop of water left in the tap.'

In this water project, the 'hearth-hold' proved to be both conceptually useful and organizationally practical for project implementation. Focussing on the hearth-hold enhanced our comprehension of the village economy with its gender- and age-based distribution of labour and resources. The villagers' livelihood system consisted of a mix of hearth-hold and household survival strategies developed over time. The respective heads of the two units mobilized available resources and exploited opportunities for the benefit of their respective units, a pivotal fact often ignored in development planning and policy-making.

Conclusion

The hearth-hold/household distinction can facilitate more effective analysis of gender and intra-household relations. It enables us to see women, not as appendages to the household, but as active, often independent actors who shoulder responsibilities and take risks, make different contingency plans, and strive to maximize their livelihood options and the positive impact of their efforts on their dependents.

The interaction between hearth-holds and households is too important to be relegated to footnotes and caveats. Using the 'hearth-hold', a female-centred unit of analysis, for sampling, data collection, analysis, development planning and project implementation, could prove to be a more direct way of reaching women. It could help prevent the off-target project outcomes that are all too frequent in the field of women and development. In so doing, there is a better chance of making women and their dependents true beneficiaries of educational, technological and economic development.

References

Afigbo, A., 'Revolution and Reaction in East Nigeria 1900-1920', *Journal of the Historical Society of Nigeria*, vol. III, no. 3, 1977, pp. 539–57

Afonja, S., 'Changing Modes of Production and the Sexual Division of Labour among the Yoruba', *Nigerian Journal of Economic and Social Studies*, vol. 22, no. 1, 1988, pp. 85–105

Amadiume, I., *Male Daughters, Female Husbands,* London, Zed Press, 1987

Ardener, S., *Perceiving Women*, New York, Bent and Halsted, 1975

Elwert, G., 'Conflicts Inside and Outside the Household: A West Africa Case Study', in J. Smith, I. Wallerstein and H.-D. Evers (eds), *Households and the World Economy,* Beverly Hills, 1984

Ekejiuba, F., 'Contemporary Households and Major Socio-Economic Transitions in E. Nigeria', in J. Guyer and P. Peters (eds), *Workshop on Conceptualising the Household*, Cambridge (Mass.), 1984

—, 'Omu Okwei, the Merchant Queen of Osomari', in B. Awe (ed.), *Nigerian Women in Historical Perspectives*, Lagos, 1992

Geerhart, J.D., 'Farming Systems Research, Productivity and Equity', in J.L.

Moock (ed.), *Understanding Africa's Rural Households and Farming Systems*, Boulder, Westview Press, 1986

Goody, J., *Production and Reproduction*, Cambridge, Cambridge University Press, 1976

Green, M.M., *Ibo Village Affairs*, New York, Praeger Press, 1947

Guyer, J., *Family and Farm in Southern Cameroon*, Boston, African Studies Centre, 1984

—, 'Intra-household Processes and Farming Systems Research: Perspectives from Anthropology', in J.L. Moock (ed.), *Understanding Africa's Rural Households*, 1986

Guyer, J. and P. Peters, 'Introduction, Conceptualizing the Household: Issues of Theory and Policy in Africa', Special Issue, *Development and Change*, vol. 18, no. 2, 1987, pp. 197–214

— (eds), 'Conceptualizing the Household: Issues of Theory, Method and Application', Workshop Proceedings, Cambridge (Mass.), Harvard University, November 1984

Jones, C.W., 'Intra-household Bargaining in Response to the Introduction of New Crops: A Case Study from N. Cameroons', in J.L. Moock (ed.), *Understanding Africa's Rural Households*, 1986

Little, K., *African Women in Towns*, London, Cambridge University Press, 1973

Mba, N., *Nigerian Women Mobilized*, California, 1980

Moock, J.L. (ed.), *Understanding Africa's Rural Households and Farming Systems*, Boulder, Westview Press, 1986

Okonjo, K., 'Rural Women's Credit Systems: A Nigerian Example', in S. Zeidstein (ed.), 'Learning About Rural Women', *Studies in Family Planning*, Nov./Dec., vol. 10, no. 11, 1976

Onoge, O., personal communication, 1992

Pala, A., 'Women in Household Economy: Managing Multiple Roles', *Learning about Rural Women*, New York, The Population Council, 1979

Peters, P., 'Household Management in Botswana: Cattle, Crops and Wage Labor', in J.L. Moock (ed.), *Understanding Africa's Rural Households*, 1986

Rogers, B., *The Domestication of Women*, New York, Tavistock Publications, 1980

Smith, J., I. Wallerstein and H.-D. Evers (eds), *Households and the World Economy*, Beverly Hills, Sage, 1984

Stauth, G., 'Households, Modes of Living and Production Systems', in J. Smith et al. (eds), *Households and the World Economy*, 1984

Sudarkasa, N., 'The Status of Women in Indigenous African Societies', in Terborg-Penn (ed.), *Women in Africa and the Africa Diaspora*, Washington D.C., Howard University Press, 1987

Uzoka, F.A., personal communication, 1992

Van Allan, J., 'Sitting on a Man: Colonialism and the Lost Institutions of the Igbo Women', *Canadian Journal of African Studies*, vol. 6, no. 2, 1972, pp. 165–212

Wong, D., 'The Limits of Using the Household as a Unit of Analysis', in Smith et al. (eds), *Households and the World Economy*, 1984

4

Myth of the African Family in the World of Development*

Bridget O'Laughlin

Introduction: From Modernization to African Modes of Production

When I first became interested in the relationship between the sociology of the African family and economic development, modernization theory dominated academic approaches to development. All social processes were conceptualized in polar terms: the extended African family was giving way to the nuclear family; status was becoming achieved rather than ascribed; kinship ties were being dissolved by the solvent of the market.

My objections to this literature were twofold. First, in the Cameroonian highlands where I was teaching, a labour reserve area that was also an important coffee growing region, kinship ties of very diverse and complex kinds were of continuing importance to people in the towns and migrants to the cities as well as to peasants. Second, since most of the modernization studies had very predictable conclusions as to the imminent demise of African kinship systems, it hardly seemed worthwhile to read them. Rather than sitting back to watch the inevitable happen, I turned to anthropology. It seemed to grapple better with the lives of African people as actually lived and thought.

In veering toward anthropology, however, I encountered different problems. Many ethnographic studies, including my own first fieldwork on collective work groups in southern Tchad, were so particularistic that it was difficult to draw conclusions that were relevant for development policy. Further, anthropological studies in Africa generally abstracted from the world of imperialist exploitation and national oppression that was part of everyday life for African peasants and workers. Finally, anthropological theory was rooted in a structural-functionalist theoretical

63

framework that contributed little analytically to understanding class and gender conflicts in African society.

Throughout the 1970s, various writers, sociologists and economists as well as anthropologists, struggled to clarify the links between economic development and African social organization. They used myriad case studies and comparative material in the attempt to theorize in a general way the specificity of African history and modes of production. Here, I would mention particularly Ester Boserup, whose work inspires this volume, Jack Goody, Goran Hyden, the French historian Coquery-Vidrovitch, and Marxist anthropologists such as Rey, Meillassoux and Terray who wrote on 'the lineage mode of production'. They emphasized the contrasts between forms of class and property in Africa and those of Asia or Latin America. They explored the relationship in Africa between extensive hoe-based agriculture, the absence of a landed agricultural class and landless proletariat, the importance of women and children's labour for the reproduction of households, the imperative for demographic expansion and the dominance of descent group organization.

If we piece together various strands of this work, we can construct a coherent image of a pre-colonial Africa which, though ahistorical, nonetheless captures much that is true. Shifting rainfed farming with hoes supports low population densities and corresponds to communal ownership of the land and unstable territorial communities. The most important determinant of differences in wealth is the amount of productive labour that a household controls; there is no class that holds a monopoly over land or other means of production. Rights to labour are organized through lineages, groups based on lines of descent. Control over rights in women, who both farm themselves and bear the children who are future workers, are central to male lineage authority. The conjugal family is weak in African societies compared to larger kinship units like the lineage.

The scientific work lying behind this image was not, of course, so coherent. Boserup wrote within a modernization framework and was little concerned with the class questions and specificities of capitalist development that preoccupied Hyden and the Marxists.[1] Boserup tended to treat population density as a determinant of the dynamics of African farming systems, whereas Goody and the Marxists saw population as a dependent variable. The anthropologists were generally uncomfortable with the abstraction from history implicit in Boserup's view of Africa. Within the Marxist group, there was discomfort with the analytical dualism that seemed to be implied by the articulation of modes of production approach.

Most of these theoretical debates were not resolved. They just died. While we debated African modes of production, in Africa ploughs and fertilizers were spreading, many people lost access to land, new national bourgeoisies were using the state to establish a basis for private accumulation, and single mothers were hiring themselves out as workers on the farms of rich peasants as well as on plantations. I do not mean that modernization theory was therefore right, only that the attempt to pin down the specificity of African social life was overtaken by economic and political processes common to many developing countries.

I myself withdrew from the formal debates around African modes of production and spent thirteen years teaching and doing applied research in Mozambique. The context of theoretical discourse changed radically. Eduardo Mondlane University in Maputo was polarized around different traditions of Marxist analysis, with sharply different theoretical conceptions of how to analyse African societies and hence of what socialism should mean in Mozambique. The research I did violated the techniques of total immersion and participant observation I had been trained to follow. It was collective, rapid, and generally responded to specific government research requests. It could never have been done without a sharp theorization of research questions, and our theoretical premises clearly limited our range of questions and possible answers.

As the Renamo guerrillas gnawed away at the fabric of rural life, research concerned with problems of socialist transition lost its political and ideological legitimacy in Mozambique. A new generation of foreign consultants appeared, concerned with the development of the private sector in agriculture and opposed to state-farms and cooperatives. Some consultants were nearly messianic in their espousal of the smallholder model for Mozambique, and many drew attention to the need to focus on women farmers, usually in an appendix.

Given that I belonged to a group labelled 'peasant-lovers', one might think that this new emphasis would have made me happy. In fact I was deeply disturbed. The new wave of consultants failed to recognize how deeply wage labour was integrated into the organization of smallholder production in many areas of Mozambique. I also objected to discussions of women farmers that treated the large number of women-headed households in Mozambique as a given and failed to discriminate analytically among the very different market positions of rural households. Whatever the failures of socialism in Mozambique, it included a strategy of assault on the colonial structure of the economy that relegated many rural women in Mozambique to scratching out a very partial subsistence on sandy infertile soils.

Presently, I have returned to western academic life, teaching in a population and development programme. It is apparent that the superficiality I found in many World Bank consultants' analysis of rural life in Mozambique has a certain intellectual legitimacy in demographic circles. Curiously, this legitimacy derives partly from the anthropological debates around African pre-colonial production systems that I left behind in the 1970s. Whereas most anthropologists have retreated from generalizations on the specificity of African social life, in some corners of the world of applied development studies, particularly in the field of population and development, there is no such reticence. Creative theoretical attempts to understand the specificity of social processes in Africa have now hardened into dogma. The search for useful generalizations has turned into a distorting oversimplified account, often with little empirical base. It attributes the failures of economic development projects in Africa to the legacy of traditional pre-colonial patterns of family organization.

Initial optimism about the process of demographic transition in Sub-Saharan Africa gave way, with the economic failure of the 1980s, to a Malthusian emphasis on the instability caused by rapid population growth (Hyden 1990). Given the failure of post-independence development strategies in Africa, the World Bank's concern with limiting population growth seems to be commonsensical. The demographic theory of the 'African Family System', provides an explanation rooted in African tradition for Africa's exceptionally bad economic performance.

Because this theory recognizes the importance of women's farming in African production systems, it also has some legitimacy in the literature on women and development. The 'African Family System' is now taking on the status of a popular myth in the world of development consultants, repeated without serious attention to its assumptions, implications or empirical basis. Like all powerful myths it captures part of reality, but also hides from analytical view political and economic forces that Africa shares with the rest of the world.

Myth-making: The Demographic Specificity of Africa

The demographic discourse on Africa is dominated by the Caldwells' polemical view of the distinctive culture of fertility in Africa (Caldwell and Caldwell 1987). More reasoned and reasonable arguments for the demographic specificity of Africa are, however, presented by other mainstream demographers.[2] I shall rely principally on McNicoll and

Cain's (1990) essay on rural development and population to illustrate present conventional wisdom on the impact of rural social organization regarding fertility patterns and economic development in Africa.

McNicoll and Cain seek to remedy the reductionism of neo-malthusianism by analysing the social and political institutions that link economic development and fertility. They see variation in family systems as one of the most important determinants of patterns of population development and economic growth. Most of the developing world, they argue, has joint household systems with partible inheritance encouraging early marriage, but limiting the demand for children. Sub-Saharan African joint family systems are, however, quite different.

Their distinctive features as identified by McNicoll and Cain (1990) are: households integrated into lineages, larger descent-based corporate groups; a weak conjugal bond relative to ties with one's natal family or lineage; and lineage groups serving as the locus of control over the demographic and economic behaviour of individual members.

The African family system is thought to inhibit economic development in a number of different ways. First, the 'unfavourable family system' motivates continuing population growth and thus environmental instability and general poverty (McNicoll and Cain 1990). Second, lineage rights hamper the development of the market. Third, because of the importance of lineages, territorially based local communities are weak and do not act to promote demographic restraint and environmental stability as a countervailing force to the 'unfavourable family system'. Finally, the uniqueness of the African family system, namely the weakness of conjugal ties, has been used to explain why economic development has led to a large number of households headed by women in contemporary Africa (Lesthaeghe 1989b).

There is a certain theoretical affinity here with earlier studies on the matrifocal family in the Caribbean and challenges to Moynihan's analysis of African-American family life presented as part of a culture of poverty. Deviations in family form from the nuclear family model are treated not as social pathology, but rather as the expression of 'traditional' forms of family life in new contexts.

The demographers' image of weak conjugal bonds in African family systems draws support from a broader women and development literature, anchored in Boserup's work, emphasizing the specificity of the gender division of labour in rural Sub-Saharan Africa. To slightly overstate the case, in rural Africa women hoe and men talk, whereas in Asia and Latin America women are restricted to the domestic domain.

The implications of African women's role in farming for the process of development vary with different views of the authority structure of African families. In her work on African farming systems, Boserup (1990) sees the African family not only as patriarchal but also as very autocratic. Men want large families because women and children are free labour. Men leave women to grow subsistence crops on inferior land, and oblige women and children to help with the production and processing of cash crops. Because men determine what women do, development has meant more work and less control for women.

Others have argued that the importance of African women's work in farming and trade and the relative weakness of the conjugal bond give women more power than in the rest of the developing world. The World Bank (1989) report, *Sub-Saharan Africa – From Crisis to Sustainable Growth,* develops the notion that because African women are such important workers, they have access to areas of decision-making prohibited to women elsewhere. African women are 'lead managers' within the household:

> African women are the lead managers within the household for providing food, nutrition, water, health, education and family planning to an extent greater than elsewhere in the developing world. They have always been active in agriculture, trade, and other economic pursuits. Women are guardians of their children's welfare and have explicit responsibility to provide for them materially.

Nonetheless, the World Bank report also sees African women's economic capabilities and their ability to manage family welfare as threatened by patriarchy in the 'modernization' process itself. Gender bias in legal systems, education, and access to credit and agricultural services has meant that women cannot take advantage of the better income earning opportunities that have emerged in Africa. The increasing scarcity of fuel and water increase domestic pressure on women's time.

Emphasis on women's farming and Africa has recently been integrated by Palmer (1990) with the demographic arguments on the specificity of African family systems to produce a new diagnosis of the problems of African agriculture. Palmer (1990) argues that gender bias is the weakest link in Sub-Saharan African economies. She conjures up the spectre of increasing misery and spiralling population growth, suggesting that if the problem of gender bias is not resolved, African economies may have 'a comparative advantage only in lines of production based on the super-exploitation of women and a demand for children's assistance'. For

Palmer, the risk in World Bank structural adjustment programmes is that by concentrating on tradables they will draw African women away from own-account farming and reinforce survival strategies for women that emphasize fertility and dependency. She contends that 'a package of programmes and policies that improves and secures women's own account farming' could alter this 'recipe for demographic disaster' (Palmer 1990). African women farmers must now be targeted as the principal clients of agricultural development projects.

There is a certain coherence in this set of arguments, which is why I have called it the 'Myth of the African Family'. It is easy to see why some feminists have been sympathetic towards the knitting together of women's fertility and women's farming in the analysis of the problems of agricultural development in Africa. Certainly, the importance of women as farmers in Sub-Saharan Africa has been overlooked in development projects. Certainly, gender discrimination shapes the structure of rural African households and marks the forms of intervention by the state in agriculture.

Yet, I would dispute the critical point in the myth, the notion that in Africa the conjugal bond is 'traditionally' weak, reflecting the predominance of women's labour in farming systems and the importance of lineage ties. In the following section, I shall look critically at the theoretical debates underlying the analysis of African family systems. Here, I shall argue that weak conjugal ties cannot be derived *a priori* either from the structure of African lineage systems, or from the pre-colonial gender division of labour. In the last section, I shall use some of my own research experience in Tchad and Mozambique to show why I think that assuming the weakness of conjugal ties and focussing on women's own-account farming creates a distorted and partial view of the problems confronting women in rural Africa.

Theoretical Basis of 'The African Family System'

What then is the scientific power of the notion of the specificity of the African family system? Is there any way to criticize it without retreating into anthropological particularism? First, we should note that although many of the elements of the myth would not stand up to empirical verification, the principal question is theoretical clarity. The image of the African system is a comparative one, i.e. it is different from family systems of northern Europe, Latin America or South Asia, without a clear specification of the basis of comparison. To argue that the conjugal bond is weaker in Africa than it is in the rest of the developing world, or to say that women have more autonomy from men, implies that we have some analytical apparatus for looking comparatively at rural social life in Africa, Asia, the Americas, Europe.

Analytically, what I am calling the myth of the African family derives its legitimacy from two major theoretical enterprises. Both have contributed immensely to our understanding of rural society, in Africa and elsewhere. The first, descent theory, was constructed by British social anthropologists working under colonial regimes and seeking to understand the coherence of rural societies not integrated into centralized state political systems.[3] The second is the feminist critique of household models, in both sociology and economics, which took the structure of authority in the household as natural, given, and benign or inevitable. Both have captured important aspects of social process in rural Africa. Yet their theoretical ambiguities leave space for the ideological distortion characteristic of much World Bank rhetoric on economic development in Africa.

Descent Theory

British social anthropology saw the basic elements of traditional African society as closed corporate groups defined by lines of descent. These groups were exogamous, shared some forms of common property, and were based on the authority of male elders who controlled rights in women and children through the exchange of bridewealth. The constituent domestic units of African lineages were 'houses', the mother and children who lived and ate together. Polygyny, correspondingly, was an ideal, though not a demographic practicality, for all men. All descent groups were hierarchically defined nesting groups, broken down into segments that united at a higher level. Political unity was defined by these groups rather than by territorially based communities.

Jack Goody's (1976) work enriched descent theory by attempting to specify more explicitly the technological and economic basis and political implications of descent group organization in Africa. He argued that the absence of the plough and the relative openness of agricultural resources in Sub-Saharan Africa made access to labour, and hence people, the primary source of wealth and power. This contrasted with the importance of the inheritance of productive property and hence with the sharply defined class divisions of Asian and European systems. The difference is reflected in regimes of marriage. In the African systems, the passage of bridewealth allocates reproductive powers over women. In Eurasia, the dowry distributes parental property to a daughter at the time of marriage.

Kuper (1988) observes that the classical enthnographies of descent theory in Africa, Evans-Pritchard's *The Nuer* of the Sudan and Fortes' work on the Tallensi, relied heavily on subordinating the messy details of everyday life to the model of descent theory. I think that Kuper underestimates the extent to which descent theory really does reflect the ideological image that many African religions/sciences draw of how the social world *should* be constructed. My respect for Evans-Pritchard's analytical powers, as opposed to his literary skill, was considerably diminished during the course of my own fieldwork when the male elders and oracles of the village where I was living sat me down to make sure I understood how lineages were supposed to work, despite the various abuses practised by their wives, sons and daughters. Their emphasis on the provocations of their wives made clear just how important were conjugal ties to the functioning of the lineage system.

Descent theory did, however, overemphasize the coherence and corporateness or closure of lineage groups. Kuper (1988) cites an insightful critique by Audrey Richards, one of the best of the British ethnographers of Africa, of Evans-Pritchard's *The Nuer*, based on her own field research in Africa:

> ... nothing is more remarkable than the lack of permanence of particular lineages or 'segments'; the infinite variety there is in their composition, their liability to change owning to historic factors, the strength of individual personalities and similar determinants. Such societies, in my experience, are not divided into distinct and logical systems of segments, but rather owe their being to the existence of a number of different principles of grouping.

Richards' observation corresponds to much of what the ethnographic literature on Africa describes, for patrilineal as well as matrilineal societies, for West Africa as well as for central, eastern and southern Africa. Lineages tend to be shallow, each extended family is potentially a new lineage segment, long ancestral lines are identified with political power, social ties of kinship are forged bilaterally, people are often tied to more than one descent group in irregular (i.e. not kinship based) ways. In other words, African kinship systems provide a flexible language for forging social ties, not the fixed organic language imposed by the structural-functionalism of descent theory.

At a political level, descent theory also underestimates the importance of communities and durable territorial ties between people of different lineage groups. In much of rural Sub-Saharan Africa, whether residence was dispersed or in nucleated villages, a set of descent groups, linked over time by marriage, neighbourhood and friendship, occupied different sections of common residential and farming land. Rights to land were acquired through residence in this community, not through membership in a lineage *per se*, and land in fallow could be redistributed between groups within it. In politically stratified systems, one of the lineages would be considered the owners of the land, and a chief or king chosen from it. In less stratified systems, one of the lineages might be ritually responsible for the land. In either case, at a local level the formal or informal council of elders is usually composed of the senior members of all associated lineages, not just those of the royal or ritually privileged group.

Descent group theory under-emphasizes the importance of conjugal ties in African production and reproduction. This problem is illustrated in a short and very cogent discussion by Elizabeth Colson of patterns of family change in Africa. She wrote in 1962, during the first years of African independence, and did not retreat, as anthropologists are wont to do, from the murky waters of generalization.

Colson challenged the assumption referred to at the beginning of this chapter and common to many modernization studies that in Africa the conjugal family was being detached from wider kinship groupings (Colson 1970). She argued that in traditional African family groups the primary or nuclear domestic group is the woman and her dependent children, with men acting as intercalary elements, linking women to wider kin groups. I would note here that Colson is primarily concerned with the jural definition of domestic groups; intercalary or not, men are linked with women in a conjugal bond. Questioning the assumption that matrilineal organization was giving way to patrilineal principles, Colson suggested that cash cropping, land shortages, wage employment, labour migration and changes in legal codes tended to strengthen matrilateral ties at the expense of patrilineal ties and gave new independence to nuclear families based on a woman and her children rather than the conjugal tie.[4]

Colson was one of the first to suggest that male labour migration did not necessarily represent increasing misery for rural women left behind. Because African women were active agriculturalists, the absence of men often meant increasing independence and autonomy for women in the management of their households. She also noted that the opportunity of doing wage-labour was used by rural women who ran away to factory work in towns to escape oppression.[5]

There was much that was both perceptive and iconoclastic in Colson's argument, but there were also important social processes that slipped from view. The first is the social cost of the migrant labour system. Colin Murray (1981) has made this point very sharply:

> ... there is some substance to criticism of kinship analyses based on the imposition of western categories such as that of the nuclear family, but such criticism is quite gratuitous if it leads the critic either to insist by contrast but without appropriate evidence on the importance of the 'extended family', or to undermine the credibility of evidence – now surely overwhelming – that the enforced separation of spouses generates acute anxiety, insecurity and conflict. The latter tendency implies an alternative, distinctly African, view of marriage and the family which does not presuppose intimacy between husband and wife and which is not therefore undermined by the separation of spouses.

Secondly, by abstracting from class relations that cross-cut town and country, Colson, like descent theorists more generally, did not deal with the differentiation of women's experience implicit in the increasing proportion of woman-headed households in the labour reserve areas of southern Africa. Many women-headed households, when not supported by remittances from wage-earning men, were desperately poor.

The forms of the conjugal family were both shaped by wage-labour relations and themselves shaped by the process of class differentiation in the countryside. Households of either a nuclear or extended type that integrated men on a regular basis were more likely than mother/child units to establish title to prime commercial land through regular use and sometimes through formal registry. Such households were more likely to be able to pay school fees and to withstand the loss of their children's labour through school attendance. Their children commanded better wages or took over positions in state employment that gave them access to economic as well as political resources. The strength of conjugal ties thus came to have important consequences for the class position of women and men.

Descent theory could not deal with the dynamics of changing gender and kinship relations and rural class formation because it remained trapped in analytical dualism. It accepted as given the difference between traditional and modern Africa based on abstraction from the very world whose creation was nurtured by anthropological research. The economic, social and political dualism of colonial Africa was constructed by a state that sharply controlled the movement of African working people, men and women, in country or town. Principles of descent were enshrined and rigidified in customary law codes applied only to Africans, and particularly in customary marriage laws based on the sharp objectification and subordination of women. These codes were administered through traditional authorities, but behind them was the power of the colonial state, and a world of pass laws, forced labour, forced cash cropping, displacement from land, a world without African rights to political organization or franchise. Dualistic systems of land tenure and the absence of any system of pension or reform for African workers linked future security to the continuing presence of women in rural production in communal tenure areas. A theoretical understanding of capitalist development, in Asia, Europe, and Latin America, as well as in Africa, would immediately have brought these mechanisms to view.

Feminist Critique of the Household Model

The demographic elements of the myth of the African family are clearly borrowed from an eclectic reading of the ethnography of Africa with special emphasis on descent theory. There is another important theoretical underpinning for the economic references of the myth. This is the critical literature on the contradictory gender structure of households in general and African households in particular.

Feminist research in the social sciences has led to a new consensus around the conceptualization of gender relations which has important implications for the way we look at economic development in Africa. I will distinguish some of the major propositions of this new consensus in order to trace where certain theoretical ambiguities and lacunae give ground to the emergence of myth.

The central proposition of the gender consensus is that the sexual division of labour in society is not natural and hence not necessarily universal.[6] It is historically and socially shaped. The conceptual distinction between sex and gender captures the difference between what is biologically given and that which is socially defined. There is also no natural or fixed form of the family, and hence no universal form of the household (Harris 1984). The ties of conjugality and filiation that define the nuclear family have no natural priority in the constitution of social groups. In short, the family, conceived of as man, wife and their children, is not a universal basic unit of society. It has, therefore, no analytical priority in the analysis of social groups.

These propositions ground a powerful theoretical critique of the premises of household economics (Evans 1989; Sen 1990; Koopman 1991). Development economists applied the neo-classical theory of the firm to the analysis of non-wage labour forms, particularly smallholder family-based agriculture. This meant assuming a unity of interests among members of the household, maintained either by the reasonableness or authority of the household head. It also required treating households as units of production, consumption and exchange. Once the universality of the sexual division of labour and the conjugally based nuclear family is challenged, these assumptions are no longer tenable. Men, women, and children may have contradictory and conflictual as well as cooperative interests within households. Production, consumption and exchange, as well as residence, sexuality and childbearing, may be organized by different kinds of units.

The gender-based critique of household economics has been particularly important for clarifying studies of family and household in rural communities in Africa. Guyer and Peters (1987) observe that in Sub-Saharan Africa there are not necessarily any isomorphic relations between units of production, consumption and investment. Recognition of the complicated nature of relations of gender and generation within African rural households has helped clarify problems met by agricultural projects. There are now numerous accounts of agricultural projects that failed in Africa because they were negotiated with men whereas their success depended on women working more while reaping no return from it (e.g. Staudt 1982; Chipande 1987). Boserup stressed the ways in which modernization intensified women's work and marginalized them. The newer literature on women and development shows that women also resist and defend their interests.

Not only do women do the greater part of everyday agricultural tasks in many parts of Africa, but they also have considerable autonomy over how they use their time and their resources. The economic inter-dependence of wives and husbands appears to be particularly weak in parts of West Africa. Fapohunda (1987) lists a number of ways in which domestic units in southern Nigeria, for example, deviate from the colonial household model of co-residential units with commonly held economic resources and joint budgets: first, many women are not economically dependent on their husbands and many are *de facto* or *de jure* household heads; second, spouses do not pool incomes, do not hold joint bank accounts and rarely hold joint assets; third, spouses have separate allocative priorities rather than a common budget; and fourth, financial commitments are not limited to conjugal units but extend to larger families of origin.

Here we enter, however, one of the areas where a certain theoretical imprecision has led to distortion in the applied literature on women and development. The last three points establish that there is a sharp gender division of labour in the organization of households and that there are realms where women have significant power of decision. They do not, however, imply that there is hence no cooperation between spouses. To the contrary, though incomes may be held separately, allocative priorities can be, but need not be, complementary. Similarly, assistance and commitments from and to each partner's kinship network influence patterns of work and expenditure of each of the spouses.

Only Fapohunda's first point implies absolute independence of women from their spouses. Here it is significant, however, that the point applies to many but not *all* women. It implies a socially differentiated society. It is precisely the relationship between social differentiation and the options open to different groups of women within the household that needs to be clarified. For some, conjugal ties have never been established. For others, autonomy is the outcome of a social process in which conjugal ties have been ruptured through death and divorce. We know that in many parts of Africa a high proportion of those who are *de jure* or *de facto* heads of households are in fact desperately poor. Maintenance of conjugal ties is often economically and socially advantageous to all members of the household. Among other things, it permits access to the wider web of non-conjugal support that each partner's ties of kinship, friendship and clientage weave.

Even for West Africa, then, I think that the concept of relative autonomy is not analytically useful. Since 'relative to what' is not clearly specified, the concept becomes the opposition autonomy/dependence. The bonds of interdependence, as well as conflict and difference, that unite conjugal families in Africa, as well as in the rest of the world, are given too little analytical attention. Theoretically, it leads to a kind of methodological individualism which begins with women's interests, rather than with the ways in which different gender interests are socially and historically shaped. At a practical level, it gives rise to development theories that assume women's economic independence, such as Palmer's (1990) conviction that promotion of women's own-account farming represents the way forward for African agriculture.

Conjugal Terms in Women's Farming

In this section I shall argue both that conjugal ties are important in the organization of production and reproduction in Africa and that analysing *variation* in the forms of conjugal relations in Africa is crucial to understanding the nature of the crisis of agricultural production and hence the possibilities open to women farmers. If we assume that weak conjugal relations and the autonomy of women in production are inherent in African family systems, then we are theoretically blocked from analysing the ways in which conjugal relations are the variable product of historical forces that act upon different strata of African women and men in different ways.

To illustrate what I mean, I want to look at women's agricultural strategies in two quite different situations, in place, time and social context. The first is based on two years of very conventional anthropological fieldwork that I did in Mbabao, a village in a smallholder cotton-growing area in southern Tchad, in the period from 1969 to 1971. The second was with the women who made up the majority of members in agricultural production cooperatives in southern Mozambique in the early 1980s. Neither case is representative. I am not trying to show that there is a universal set of conjugal relations in Africa. I want to demonstrate that in both cases we miss important determinants of women's farming strategies if we assume that conjugal relations are unimportant, or if we assume one particular variant of conjugal relations, i.e. the weak conjugal bond.

Conjugal Negotiations in Tchad

In its internal political and social organization, Mbabao was a typical central African village, with the idiom of descent defining people's relations to each other as well as to the ancestors. The village was made up of various co-resident patrilineage segments that had lived together and often intermarried for several generations. Hence, most people had both maternal and paternal kin living in the village. Most disputes were arbitrated without recourse to government administrative structures, through an informal council of lineage elders and village-wide ancestral ceremonies. Everyone had access to land within the land area associated with the village. Village residents participated in each other's collective work groups and hunted together. Normatively, the patrilineage was supposed to be the unit of ownership of enduring forms of property: money accumulated through bridewealth, livestock, canoes, hunting nets, ritual titles. In fact, most patrilineage segments were divided into smaller bridewealth pools.

There were two central units of labour cooperation in Mbabao: the conjugal family, consisting of husband and wife and unmarried children; and the granary group, normally composed of a group of conjugal families, a localized descent group segment, under the authority of the senior male. In practice, some granary groups were reduced to a single conjugal family. This generally meant less flexibility and security because of the smaller pool of labour and lesser absolute size of food surpluses controlled by small granary groups.

All adult members of the granary group cultivated individual plots, but their principal crops, cotton and sorghum, were always cultivated in rotation in a common group of fields. Sorghum, the principal staple food, was harvested and pooled in a common granary. The head of the granary group decided what should be kept for seed, what could be sold or given, what should be used for brewing beer for collective work and when grain should be distributed to the women of the group for current consumption.

Within the granary group members of the constituent conjugal family cultivated adjoining plots and cooperated regularly, without concern for reciprocity, in everyday tasks. Men assisted their wives in clearing large trees and couples often helped each other to finish tardy weeding and picking cotton. Men carried home large logs for firewood. The gender division of labour within the conjugal unit was, however, highly imbalanced. Women cared for children, nursed the ill, fetched firewood and water for daily consumption, pounded grain, provided wild and cultivated vegetables and seeds for sauce and oil, cooked food, swept the houses and courtyard, brewed beer, and did petty vending. Men built and repaired houses, granaries and fences, repaired tools, and were responsible for providing meat or fish for regular consumption, either by hunting or purchase.

Every cultivator's cotton was weighed and paid for separately by the cotton company. All women could tell me down to the cent how much they had received for their cotton in the preceding year. Yet in most conjugal families, money from the sale of cotton was pooled and controlled by the husband. How cotton money was actually spent was an area of discussion and/or conflict in most conjugal families. Unmarried men over sixteen preferred to hold on to at least a part of their own money. Some married women also kept back cotton money and paid their own taxes, but this was considered perilously close to breaking the cooking pots, the last thing a woman did before leaving her husband. It was an option most often exercised by childless women or those whose children were already grown.

Crops such as beans, peanuts, okra and cassava that were grown in mixed association with cotton and sorghum were individually controlled by each cultivator. Small plots of subsidiary crops, such as maize, sweet potatoes, sesame, rice or cucumbers were cultivated separately by both men and women, both for consumption and for sale or barter. These crops and any proceeds from their sale were controlled by the cultivator. Each woman controlled her own granary and prepared food at her own discretion for her husband, children and herself, but meals were generally shared within the granary group and often with other kin and friends as well.

Keeping an extended family granary group together required constant compromise and diplomacy on the part of the head. The granary group was often temporarily or permanently restricted to the constituent conjugal families. Ruptures usually resulted from disputes over relative contributions of labour in relation to consumption. These were prefaced by the complaints women made to their husbands and then quarrels between women of the granary group, culminating in their refusal to eat food prepared by each other. These breakdowns of commensality eventually made cooperation in production untenable. In Mbabao there was no inverse relation between the strength of descent-based groups like the granary group and bridewealth pool and that of conjugal families. To the contrary, weak and conflictual conjugal relations corresponded to shallow descent groups.

Standing back from this system, we can see that the women of Mbabao indeed had control over how they organized their work, consumption, and money from subsidiary production and vending. They were aware of inequality in the organization of production and consumption and prepared to do something about it. The yields from women's fields were consistently lower than those of men. Would it not make sense, then, in extension programmes to target women's own account farming, to improve the productivity of women's plots? To answer this we have to look at why the yields of women's fields were lower than those of men.

Contrary to the stern recommendations of the cotton extension agents, everyone in Mbabao planted cassava plants in their cotton plots, as 'famine food', subsistence security for the following year. But women planted more cassava, planted it earlier and also inter-cropped okra, shading the developing cotton pods. All cultivators felt the conflict between weeding cotton and weeding sorghum plots, and cotton yields were very responsive to the timing of weeding. Whereas men sometimes gave priority to their cotton fields, women favoured food crops.

At first glance, this may appear to be a classic male/female specialization in cash versus subsistence farming, with women attending particularly to the variety and security of everyday consumption. In Mbabao, men thought about this opposition differently. They said that money was a man's thing, durable, going forward like the patrilineage in time, whereas women's things got used up. In fact, men not only produced more cotton than women did; they also produced more sorghum, the basic staple.

How then could men grow both more cotton and more sorghum than women? The most obvious answer would simply be that men spent more time than women did on agricultural tasks, because women had so many other kinds of work to do. In part this is true. Time budgets showed that women often came home earlier from the fields than did men in order to cook, they lost time caring for small children in the fields, they stayed home to take care of the ill, and they cut back time in the fields in the last month of pregnancy and in the period after childbirth. Yet much of women's extra work was done when men were at rest. The village woke to the sound of women pounding grain, water had to be fetched early before going to the fields, and women worked as men sat chatting around the fire at night.

The other underlying determinant of differences in yields was the organization of collective labour, skewed in favour of men who were the head of granary groups. The head of the granary group could allocate grain to be used to prepare a meal for small collective work groups in which members of the granary group or patrilineage segment participated. Or he could allocate grain for a beer party, in which case people from other lineage groups in the village would attend. Work groups were called when work was falling behind, particularly for weeding. Given the impact of timely weeding on yield, use of collective labour meant a better harvest. Although beer parties were normatively a form of reciprocal labour, much of the labour was done by young men without grain surpluses sufficient to sponsor work groups themselves. Beer parties were called for the sorghum plots of any member of the granary group, and for men's cotton plots, but generally not for the cotton plots of women. Women on their own organized small reciprocal work-groups for agricultural tasks, but could not mobilize enough labour to make a beer party worthwhile.

Despite considerable areas of control by women over their time and resources, occasional labour cooperation was so important in Mbabao that it would not make sense to aim extension projects at women's own-account farming without directly confronting the structure of patriarchal authority that gave men control over collective labour. The subsistence position of a woman on her own with small children would be very insecure. Women's space in the system of labour cooperation within the granary group was negotiated through conjugal relations. Decisions about agricultural innovations requiring a reorganization of labour would necessarily have implications for the granary group that would first have to be arbitrated between wife and husband in the conjugal unit.

Correspondingly, as many have already shown for male-centred development projects in Africa, to focus on the husband or the head of the granary group would also mean increasing tension between women and men. This was, in fact, the central flaw in a 'productivity' scheme introduced by the cotton company in Mbabao. The male heads of ten of the most productive granary groups were assigned cotton plots along the road and advanced credit to grow stand-alone cotton with regular insecticide spraying and frequent weeding. Although these men did obtain much higher yields with the new techniques, most retreated from the scheme the following year. They felt that too much labour was diverted from grain to cotton and were criticized by their wives for the pressure of work at weeding time. Sorcery charges were brought, by women, against a man who was said to have improved his cotton income by organizing many beer parties without providing reciprocal labour. Any successful extension project in Mbabao would have to work with both women and men cultivators, and deal with both the conflicts and interdependence inherent in the gender and age relations of the conjugal family and granary group.

Mababao is not, of course, a 'typical' African farming system. Men are heavily involved in everyday cultivation tasks like field preparation and weeding. Located in a dedicated cotton-growing area, distant from major urban, plantation or mining centres, Mbabao had little labour migration. No women of reproductive age lived outside of a conjugal family. What about the vast numbers of women-headed households in other parts of Africa, especially Africa of the labour reserves? Are they not precisely the group that can be reached by extension programmes aimed at the development of women's own-account farming? The next sub-section will address these questions using case study material from Mozambique.

Conjugal Disruptions in Mozambique

Male labour migration to the plantations and mines of South Africa began in southern Mozambique in the last century, but the migrant labour system was institutionalized by the 1914 accord between the colonial Portuguese and South African governments that established the Save river as the northern limit for South African mine recruitment.[7] Contracts on the mines were for twelve or eighteen months, and miners worked repeated contracts with short periods of home leave. For the period on the mines, the migrant worker was effectively withdrawn from family farming, and sometimes even from management of the farm. With the oscillating emigration of men, women expanded the kinds of labour they did. They gradually took on felling, clearing, milking and even ploughing and caring for cattle.

Settler farming in fertile valleys and mixed ranching began in southern Mozambique early in this century, but became an important part of Portuguese colonial policy with the development of the Limpopo river irrigation scheme and the construction of the Limpopo rail-line in the 1950s. Late in the colonial period sugar plantations began to operate in Maputo province. The structure of capitalist agriculture was thus varied: Portuguese smallholders in the irrigation scheme, middle and large-scale settler farmers and plantations in other valley areas.

Cash crop production became an important source of income for some peasant households in southern Mozambique. Both cotton and rice were cultivated by women as obligatory crops until the 1960s and smallholder production of these crops continued to be important until independence. In the 1960s, the colonial state moved toward the promotion of specialized smallholder production of rice and wheat, even in areas where land was being taken over by settlers.

Late colonial labour policy in southern Mozambique may appear to be contradictory, integrating as it did the growth of settler farming, the opening of new plantations, continued export of labour to South Africa and the promotion of peasant marketing. It worked, however, for two reasons. First, peasant differentiation meant that some households recruited external labour to produce marketed surpluses. Second, the intensity and depth of proletarianization made a cash fund for purchasing consumer goods, a precondition for the reproduction of rural households.

As in other labour reserve areas of southern Africa, generations of migrant labour led to increasing instability in conjugal relations. The number of households headed *de jure* by women was about 30 per cent for Gaza and Maputo provinces by the time of Independence. The percentage of women actually managing their households alone was, of course, larger. The number of households made up of only one person, mainly widows and divorcees on their own, also increased. Households headed by women really on their own were poor and stayed poor. Without access to remittances, they had no possibility of investing in agriculture or increasing the scale of their production.

With deepening proletarianization and social differentiation, the nature of women's work came to depend increasingly on what kind of households they belonged to. The agricultural tools that they owned signified their class standing. Some women ploughed the heavy soils of the more fertile valleys or wetlands and earned income from crop sales. These were generally women who belonged to households that owned draft animals and ploughs and had sufficient labour for herding cattle and doing extra weeding at peak periods. These households tended to have permanent adult male members working in agriculture. Alternatively, if a woman maintained close ties with a well-paid migrant husband or son sending regular remittances, she could rent a plough and hire casual workers to help with seasonal tasks.

Other women continued to rely on the hoe, growing cassava and peanuts on sandy marginal but easy to weed land. Their households did not own draft animals and ploughs, had little labour to help with weeding, and not enough money to rent draft animals. Even their subsistence production was uncertain, and they often had to buy food or work in neighbours' fields for it. Some of these women and their children turned to casual labour on settler farms, on plantations, and in the fields of their neighbours. In 1970, in Gaza province, with the largest acreage of irrigated settler farming, 55 per cent of all casual labour was done by women and 18 per cent by children under fifteen years. Most of these women were divorcees or widows or women whose sons and husbands simply did not maintain any real economic link with the family in the countryside. Reasons for this could be personal and idiosyncratic, but very often reflected the male migrant's lack of success in finding well-paid employment.

For rural households, different ways of working and levels of consumption came to reflect differences in access to irrigable land, cattle, ploughs, and labour. They were also determined by wage differences among migrant members of the household whose remittances were used to buy cattle and ploughs and to hire casual labour. For rural women, barred from ownership of cattle and ploughs, and restricted to the meagre wages and labour-exchanges of casual farm labour, access to productive resources depended on establishing and maintaining conjugal relations.

After Independence in 1975, Frelimo's policy was to 'deconstruct' the migrant labour system by reorganizing agriculture. Abandoned settler farms and plantations were transformed into socialist units of production, either state-farms or cooperatives. Independent smallholder farming was to be gradually marginalized. Any embryonic development of a Mozambican rural bourgeoisie was to be blocked. Producer cooperatives were thought to be the best way to develop peasant production. Rather than some individual small-scale producers developing their own-account farming, all would advance together. This policy was applied with particular rigour in the two southernmost provinces of Gaza and Maputo, each of which had large areas of irrigated commercial agriculture, and sharp differentiation of the peasantry in some regions.

In the 1980s, both the rural and peri-urban cooperatives in southern Mozambique had a distinctive pattern of sexual composition: most of their members were women. Data on the sexual composition of the cooperatives were collected in a series of case studies of seventeen cooperatives in Gaza and Maputo provinces, done by the Centre of African Studies in Maputo and other researchers. In fifteen of these cooperatives, more than two-thirds of the members were women. Both male and female members also tended to be old, though variation was greater here. The overall composition of the cooperatives thus reflected the intense proletarianization of men in the migrant labour system: men of productive age were seeking wage-labour.

Cooperative members in Gaza and Maputo came from distinct economic strata. Most members of cooperatives were women from poor families with marginal agricultural production. A minority of the members produced regular marketed surpluses on individually worked irrigated plots. These were invariably men, the prototypical prosperous peasant, though often with a recent history of migrant labour. The cooperatives' management was usually made up of such men who specialized in planning, organizing, buying and selling, leaving everyday cultivation to the women. Tensions often explicitly emerged between the two groups, interpreted in gender terms. In songs recorded by A. Manghezi in Josina Machel Cooperative in Matutuine, Maputo Province, the women members characterized their cooperative as a house of exploitation where the old women never bother anyone, set off to work at the crack of dawn, never get ill, have no clothes and nothing to eat.

The number of members per hectare worked was extremely high in most cooperatives. Although in theory all members worked a regular shift every day, few careful registers were kept, and most members kept more flexible hours. Despite the large number of workers, yields per hectare were typically lower than in individually worked plots. Although large areas were ploughed, a small proportion of the land belonging to rural cooperatives was actually cultivated collectively.

Production results were almost always poor. It is at first hard to see what held members to the cooperatives. Rural cooperatives accumulated massive debts and were thus unable to distribute any profits to members. Some of them at first paid an 'advance', much like a low monthly wage, but the banks then began to restrict such credit.

The different strata in the cooperative were united not by their collective production, but rather by the access that the cooperative gave them to other resources. Where fertile land was scarce, i.e. in river valleys, most cooperative land was divided into two parts, one cultivated collectively and the other parcelled into individual plots. Membership in a production cooperative meant that members could buy at official prices a special quota of consumer goods, such as cloth, sugar or oil that were traded at much higher prices in parallel markets. Meals were served during the working day. Cooperative produce was also distributed to members, or sold to them at low official prices. Improved seed, fertilizers, and agricultural implements were distributed to the cooperatives in accord with their declared production targets, and then a part sold off to members, again at official prices.

The different economic strata of members used the resources acquired through the cooperative in different ways. For elderly widows with meagre budgets for food and cooking-fuel, the regular meal at the cooperative was very important. Most of the subsidized inputs were purchased by the more prosperous farmers who managed the cooperative. Poor members had neither the extra cash to spend on them, nor sufficient labour to work the irrigated land on which they would be used. One cooperative in Maputo Province, for example, cultivated nine hectares and had 78 members, 12 men and 66 women. In 1983, the cooperative received 19 ploughs, all of which were sold to male members of the cooperative. The president bought three.

The advantages of cooperative membership sometimes lay outside the cooperative itself. Poor members, generally women, were often economically subordinate, through kinship or patronage ties, to the managers of the cooperative. Their work in the cooperative was only part of the labour prestations they offered in return for the loan of a plough or a tin of maize or sweet potatoes at the time of harvest. They sought to reinforce through the cooperative the web of kin and friendship that would have been stronger had they belonged to an established conjugal unit.

Many women on their own, especially widows and divorcees growing old, came to cooperatives in southern Mozambique precisely because they could not develop their own-account farming. They found security in the cooperatives, but they did not become productive workers. The financial results of cooperative production were so bad that most rural cooperatives fell apart or distributed their land among the members as soon as credit was restricted and subsidies reduced with structural adjustment. Many poor women had already lost these irrigated plots because they could not work them efficiently.

The gender and age composition of the cooperatives in southern Mozambique reflected historical patterns of exploitation of labour that produce an increasing number of women-headed households, and sharp differentiation of agricultural production. Cooperatives based on the structure as it is were economically unviable. They were support organizations based on a fragile alliance of interests between different economic strata, held together by the intermittent work of women on their own. The cooperative movement was rooted in the existing class structure of agricultural production, without ever becoming an instrument for its transformation. The only group of women that moved ahead was the prosperous stratum, usually with a strong conjugal base, that was able to use the cooperatives to develop own-account farming.

The obstacles to developing women's own-account farming for the impoverished majority of women-headed households have manifested themselves clearly as Mozambican policy has turned from cooperatives to the smallholder model. Women-headed households that have no regular cash income to pay a wage worker have insufficient labour to organize grazing and watering of draft animals, so they are not helped by oxen distribution schemes. Some irrigated state-farm land has been distributed to smallholders, including women-headed households. But again without hiring on extra workers women-headed households cannot do the intensive weeding that irrigated land requires, so their yields are low and they default on the payment of irrigation fees. They fall behind on canal cleaning, and thus are the focus of complaints by neighbours in the irrigation scheme. They cannot take advantage of credit because their scale of production is so low it will not support administrative costs. The development of own-account farming will not help these women. They will benefit more from attention to the wages, conditions of employment and political organization of agricultural wage workers, and from an organized defence of their rights to land for subsistence plots.

Conclusion

The power of a strategy based in the development of women's own-account farming is its simplicity; it would empower the vast majority of rural women, reduce fertility rates and resolve crisis of agricultural production in Africa. I have argued in this paper that this simplicity is illusory. In parts of Africa, like Mbabao, where there are few women-headed households, even when women have considerable control over their own time and resources, their choices are constrained by the structures of cooperation as well as conflict in conjugal relations.

In parts of Africa, like southern Mozambique, where there are many households headed by women, only a small group of women could benefit from the development of own-account farming, and, ironically, many of these are women with relatively well-paid, though absent, husbands. Here, the real problem is breaking with the migrant labour system that underlies the ever-increasing number of poor women-headed households. This will depend on much more than the restructuring of smallholder production.

It seems to me quite wrong to assume that either lineage organization or women's importance in farming implies that conjugal bonds are weak in rural Africa. To the contrary, despite great diversity in the organization of production and reproduction, enduring conjugal relations of both cooperation and conflict between husbands and wives are common in rural Africa. Where conjugal bonds are weak, this is a result of the forms of exploitation of labour established in the colonial period, not the inherent tendency of African family systems.

Rather than dismissing the importance of conjugal relations in rural Africa, we need to look explicitly at the ways in which variation in conjugal relations are intertwined with class differentiation in rural areas. In many parts of rural Africa, land is not marketed and agrarian class structure is not clearly defined by land ownership. Whether rural families stay poor or develop a basis for accumulation depends on access to labour. Variation in access to labour depends in part on differentiation in conjugal relations and hence on the process of negotiation of contradictory gender relations in conjugal units.

Conjugal relations do not define class structure, but along with other political and social relations they sort out people's positions within it. We need analytical tools that clarify this process. We need to be able to conceptualize, for example, the fact that forms of household and family in rural areas are tied up with the structure of rural and urban labour markets. We cannot begin by assuming one particular form of conjugal relations, 'the weak conjugal bond', as a given in African societies.

The persuasiveness of the 'Myth of the African Family' reflects its simplicity, its power to explain a wide range of phenomena, from patterns of fertility to women-headed households to the failure of development projects. It locates the causes of Africa's present economic crisis in the traditionalism of African rural families, rather than in the complex economic and political relations that tie Africa to the rest of the world. This simplicity is deceptive. African social structures are as complex as those of the rest of the developing world, as are the solutions to its problems of agrarian development.

Notes

* I would like to thank D. Bryceson, L. Hanmer, F. Sheriff, U. Vuorela and M. Wuyts for sharp and generous critical discussion of the first draft of this paper.

1. See Benaria and Sen (1981) for a good critique of Boserup's modernization framework, and its consequences for her analysis of women's role in development.

2. See, for example, the volume edited by Lesthaeghe (1989) on reproduction and social organization in Sub-Saharan Africa. There is, of course, critical debate around the specificity of African family systems and demographic transition in Africa within demography as well (c.f. Robinson 1992).

3. Kuper (1988) is particularly useful in showing how descent theory emerged from a concern with different political systems, rather than from the theorization of household and family organization *per se*.

4. Here, Colson foreshadowed Mary Douglas' (1969) later discussion of the resilience of matriliny in contemporary Africa.

5. This theme of the liberating possibilities of wage-labour for African women has been polemically developed by Sender and Smith (1990) in their study of plantation and peasantry in Tanzania. Mbilinyi's study of runaway wives (1989) also deals with the ways in which gender contradictions within households shaped different responses to colonial oppression.

6. I will not attempt to recognize all the work, by many women, that led to this new consensus. For a good discussion of the gender division of labour, see Mackintosh (1984). Margaret Mead's Samoa work represented an early challenge to the notion of natural sex roles. Within twentieth-century anthropology, the notion of a universal family was always contested, though often reaffirmed.

7. See First (1983) for a detailed analysis of migrant labour and its consequences in southern Mozambique.

References

Benaria, L. and G. Sen, 'Accumulation, Reproduction and Woman's Role in Economic Development; Boserup Revisited,' *Signs*, vol. 7, no. 2, 1981, pp. 279–98

Boserup, E., 'Population, the Status of Women, and Rural Development', in G. McNicoll and Mead Cain (eds), *Rural Development and Population:*

Institutions and Policy, New York and Oxford, Oxford University Press, Supplement to *Population and Development Review*, no. 15, 1990 (1989), pp. 45–60

Caldwell, J. C. and P. Caldwell, 'The Cultural Context of High Fertility in Sub-Saharan Africa', *Population and Development Review*, vol. 13, no. 3, 1987, pp. 409–37

Chipande, G., 'Innovation Adoption among Female-headed Households', in J.I. Guyer and P.E. Peters (eds), 'Introduction, Conceptualizing the Household: Issues of Theory and Policy in Africa', Special Issue, *Development and Change*, vol. 18, no. 2, 1987, pp. 315–27

Colson, E., 'Family Change in Contemporary Africa', *Annals of the New York Academy of Sciences*, vol. 96, no. 2, pp. 641–52, reprinted in J. Middleton (ed.), *Black Africa*, New York, Macmillan, 1962, reprinted 1970, pp. 152–8

Douglas, M., 'Is Matriliny Doomed in Africa?', in M. Douglas and P. Kaberry (eds), *Man in Africa*, London, Tavistock, 1969

Evans, A., 'Gender Issues in Rural Household Economics', IDS Discussion Paper No. 254, Institute of Development Studies, University of Sussex, Brighton, UK, 1989

Fapohunda, E.R., 'The Nuclear Household Model in Nigerian Public and Private Sector Policy: Colonial Legacy and Socio-Political Implications', in J.I. Guyer and P.E. Peters (eds), 'Introduction, Conceptualizing the Household: Issues of Theory and Policy in Africa', Special Issue, *Development and Change*, vol. 18, no. 2, 1987, pp. 281–94

First, R., *Black Gold: The Mozambican Miner, Proletarian and Peasant*, Sussex, The Harvester Press, 1983

Goody, J., *Production and Reproduction: A Comparative Study of the Domestic Domain*, Cambridge, Cambridge University Press, 1976

Guyer, J.I., 'Household and Community in African Studies', *African Studies Review*, vol. 24, nos 2/3, 1981, pp. 87–137

Guyer, J.I. and P.E. Peters, 'Introduction, Conceptualizing the Household: Issues of Theory and Policy in Africa', Special Issue, *Development and Change*, vol. 18, no. 2, 1987, pp. 197–214

Harris, O., 'Households as Natural Units', in K. Young, C. Wolkowitz and R. McCullesh (eds), *Of Marriage and the Market: Women's Subordination in International Perspective*, London, CSE Books, 1984 (1981), pp. 136–55

Hyden, G., 'Local Governance and Economic-Demographic Transition in Rural Africa', in G. McNicoll and M. Cain (eds), *Rural Development and Population: Institutions and Policy*, New York and Oxford, Oxford University Press, Supplement to *Population and Development Review*, vol. 15, 1990 (1989), pp. 193–211

Koopman, J., 'Neoclassical Household Models and Modes of Household Production: Problems in the Analysis of African Agricultural Households', *Review of Radical Political Economics*, vol. 23, nos 3&4, 1991, pp. 148–73

Kuper, A., *The Invention of Primitive Society*, London, Routledge, 1988

Lesthaeghe, R., 'Production and Reproduction in Sub-Saharan Africa: An Overview of Organizing Principles', in R. Lesthaeghe (ed.), *Reproduction and Social Organization in Sub-Saharan Africa*, Berkeley, University of California Press, 1989a, pp. 13–59

—, 'Social Organization, Economic Crises, and the Future of Fertility Control in Africa', in R. Lesthaeghe (ed.), *Reproduction and Social Organization in Sub-Saharan Africa*, Berkeley, University of California Press, 1989b, pp. 475–505

Mackintosh, M., 'Gender and Economics: The Sexual Division of Labour and Subordination of Women', in Young, Wolkowitz and McCullesh (eds), *Of Marriage and the Market: Women's Subordination in International Perspective*, London, CSE Books, 1984 (1981), pp. 3–17

Mbilinyi, M., 'Women's Resistance in "Customary" Marriage: Tanzania's Runaway Wives', in A. Zegeye and S. Ishemo (eds), *Forced Labour and Migration: Patterns of Movement within Africa*, London, Hans Zell, 1989, pp. 180–210

McNicoll, G. and M. Cain, 'Institutional Effects on Rural Economic and Demographic Change', in McNicoll and Cain (eds), *Rural Development and Population: Institutions and Policy*, New York, Oxford University Press, Supplement to *Population and Development Review* 15, 1990 (1989), pp. 3–42

Murray, C., *Families Divided*, Cambridge, Cambridge University Press, 1981

Palmer, I., *Gender and Population in the Adjustment of African Economies: Planning for Change*, Geneva, International Labour Office, Women, Work and Development, vol. 19, 1991

Robinson, W.C., 'Kenya Enters the Fertility Transition', *Population Studies*, vol. 46, 1992, pp. 445–57

Roesch, O., 'Socialism and Rural Development in Mozambique: The Case of Aldeia Comunal 24 de Julho', Ph.D. Thesis, University of Toronto, 1986

Sen, A., 'Cooperation, Inequality and the Family', in G. McNicoll and M. Cain (eds), *Rural Development and Population: Institutions and Policy*, New York and Oxford, Oxford University Press, Supplement to *Population and Development Review*, vol. 15, 1990 (1989), pp. 61–76

Sender, J. and S. Smith, *Poverty, Class and Gender in Rural Africa: A Tanzanian Case Study*, London, Routledge, 1990

Staudt, K., 'Women Farmers and Inequities in Agricultural Services', in E.G. Bay (ed.), *Women and Work in Africa*, Boulder, Westview Press, 1982

Tibana, R., 'Pequena Produção Familiar e Cooperativas nas Zonas Verdes de Maputo: Que Caminhos?', Maputo, Universidade Eduardo Mondlane, Faculdade de Economia, 1986

White, C.P. and A. Manghezi, *The Role of Cooperative Agriculture in Transforming Labour Relations and Gender Relations: Experiences from the Green Zones*, Research Report for the Centre of African Studies, Maputo, Mozambique, n.d.

World Bank, *Sub-Saharan Africa: From Crisis to Sustainable Growth*, Washington, D.C., IBRD/World Bank, 1989

Tinker and M. Bramsen (eds), *Women and World Development*, Washington, D.C., Overseas Development Council, 1976

Vaughan, M., 'Which Family? Problems in the Reconstruction of the History of the Family as an Economic and Cultural Unit', *Journal of African History*, vol. 24, 1983, pp. 275–83

Yousseff, N. and C. B. Hefler, *Rural Households Headed by Women: A Priority Issue for Policy Concern*, Geneva: ILO, Rural Employment Policies Branch, 1982

5

Uses and Abuses of the Concept of 'Female-headed Households' in Research on Agrarian Transformation and Policy

Pauline E. Peters

In this brief review of the emergence and use of the concept of 'female-headed households', I draw on a burgeoning literature as well as my own research experience in Botswana and, currently, in Malawi. I set out both the contributions and the perils of the concept and, on the basis of what we have learned so far, indicate some new conceptual and methodological directions.

Emergence of the Concept

The concept of the 'female-headed household' emerged in the course of the feminist critique of an ungendered analysis and practice of 'economic development'. Through the 1960s, the growing documentation of the myriad 'failures' of development was linked to the critique of over-simple liberal economic projections based on a 'trickle-down' theory and to the rise of the oppositional theses of under-development and dependency. In addition to the examples of development policies and projects worsening rather than improving people's welfare, feminist scholars, activists and policy practitioners made the further point that women had suffered disproportionately more than men (Boserup 1970; Tinker 1976). In the United States, an active group of feminist critics lobbied Congress on behalf of a 'women in development' approach, resulting in the 1973 Percy Amendment to the US Foreign Assistance Act, which mandated special attention to improvement of 'women's status' in the course of US-aided development

(Moser 1989).

The research documenting the unequal benefits received by women from development posited that one cause was the uncritical reliance on 'the household' as the major unit of surveys, projects and delivery of services. In practice, the household became equated with the 'male head' who, as 'principal respondent' provided the information requested in surveys, and, as 'head of the household', received the information, technology, or services provided by development projects and became the named holder of cooperative membership, land titles, or other benefits issued to the household. Feminist research showed that this conflation of household and male head resulted in gross under-counting of female work, reduced access for women to new technologies and services such as credit, and sometimes weakened women's rights to land (Staudt 1978; Okeyo 1980; Beneria 1981; Dey 1981; Cheater 1981).

This line of research also revealed that, contrary to the unstated premise of research and policy models, not all households were 'male-headed'. Furthermore, the category of 'female-headed households' proved to be disproportionately disadvantaged relative to other households. National or other large-scale surveys as well as intensive local studies showed that female-headed households had less land and other resources and lower incomes (Kossoudji and Mueller 1981; Yousseff and Hefler 1982; Buvinic, Lycette and McGreevey 1983; Staudt 1985; ICRW 1988; Rosenhouse 1989). Moreover, female-headed households were actually increasing, partly due to high levels of male out-migration (Murray 1981; Bush, Cliff and Jansen 1986; also see former references), partly to increasing socio-economic differentiation (Cliffe 1978), and partly to shifts in family and kin relations, such as the decline in 'inheritance' of widows (Guyer 1986; Potash 1986).

Feminist research on the processes of agrarian transformation, commercialization and economic development produced critiques of simplistic notions derived from Engels that women's status would improve once they were able to escape the limits of the conjugal family and enter the 'productive' economy. The research documented the structural discrimination suffered by women in 'segmented' labour markets, the 'double burden' produced by the failure of gendered divisions of labour to change significantly, and the persistent ideologies constraining women in the 'domestic domain'. These proved to be highly relevant to understanding the particular problems of female-headed households.

Similarly, the phenomenon of female-headed households was relevant to research by social historians and others on the variation in family and household organization over space and time, on the role played by different family structures in capitalist development and historical process more generally, and the question of the relation between the 'nuclear family' and socio-economic change (Goody 1972; Laslett 1972; Anderson 1980; Meillassoux 1981). The insights from these and other lines of research have influenced the way in which 'female-headed households' are understood in the context of past and contemporary political economies and cultures. Finally, understanding the ways in which systematic patterns of gender differentiation are linked to the emergence and reproduction of the category of female-headed households has influenced gender theory more broadly.

In short, the emergence of the concept of female-headed households contributed to and benefited from policy analysis and research on agrarian change and economic development. On the other hand, several analytical distortions have emerged from the use of the concept of female-headedness. Both the uses and abuses are reviewed below. The ensuing debates have served not only to clarify the particularities of the phenomenon of female-headed households, but also to suggest new directions in research and policy concerned to take serious account of the role of gender differences in socio-economic processes.

Uses of the Concept

A primary contribution of the concern with 'female-headed households' has been to reveal the problems of abstract, un-situated concepts used in research and policy formulation. Analysis and action conducted with concepts such as 'the household' or 'farmers' or even 'small' or 'poor' farmers have been shown to be insufficiently discriminating since they fail to take account of significant differences between, for example, male-headed households and female-headed households or between small male farmers and small female farmers. The recognition of gender as a principle of differentiation with effects similar to differentiation by 'farm size' or 'income' has been slowly growing. The literature on female-headed households has been an important part of the effort to develop methods for analysis and practice which take account of gender and other social differences. The large, and related, literature on the shortcomings of household models, including the so-called 'new household economics', draws on and, in turn, feeds into the debates about female-headed households (Jones 1983; 1986; Folbre 1984; 1986; 1991; Goldschmidt-Clermont 1985; Kabeer 1992). Both literatures contribute to the knowledge about 'intra-household' patterns of social relations and about negotiations over rights and responsibilities (Guyer and Peters 1987; Carney and Watts 1990).

The attempts to understand why female-headed households were, on average, more disadvantaged and faced greater difficulties than male-headed households also contributed to the literature on patterns and sources of gender differentiation. That female-headed households were less able to obtain credit, agricultural advice or other services revealed, for example, the ways in which women more generally suffered the liabilities of being 'invisible' within male-headed households. Greater understanding of strategies followed by female-headed households also 'provided a prod to reappraise how women in male-headed households spend their time and money' (Dwyer and Bruce 1988, cited by Bruce and Lloyd 1992). Similarly, deciphering the dynamics of female-headed households' disadvantage brought to light differences among the latter, leading to the development of distinctions between 'female-headed' and 'female-maintained' (i.e. supported primarily by a woman's efforts whether or not the household is formally 'headed' by a man), and between 'de jure female-headed' (where the woman has no current husband and is recognized as the legal 'head') and 'de facto female-headed' (where the husband is absent for much of the time in labour migration, other work, or where he is polygynous).

The reasons that policy analysts have found female-headed households interesting include the following: they provide 'a means of identifying vulnerable households', 'a way of learning more about the extent of women's economic contribution to families' in terms of income and work, and a window onto the effects on children's welfare of being brought up 'without the [regular] support of their fathers' (Bruce and Lloyd 1992). A focus on female-headed households has also raised important questions about the process and outcomes of class differentiation (Murray 1981; 1987) and the production of poverty.

Abuses of the Concept

As knowledge has grown about female-headed households, a number of shortcomings in using them as a way of discussing gender differentiation and of investigating the processes of economic development and agrarian change have become more obvious.

First, there has been a tendency to equate female-headedness with poverty and disadvantage. Yet research has shown that female-headed households are quite heterogeneous (Izzard 1979; Kerven 1979; Peters 1983; Lloyd and Brandon 1991; Kennedy and Peters 1992). Not all are 'poor and vulnerable'. A policy decision to 'target' female-headed households in some fashion, therefore, is unlikely to solve the perceived problems of *some* female-headed households and *some* women since the particular reasons for the problems will include other factors in addition to the status of being a female household head.

The second point, then, is that household structure is not the only dimension that needs to be taken into account when differential advantages and burdens are found between men and women. The most dangerous consequence of the degree of attention paid to female-headed households in the world of development policy is to *equate* this attention with taking account of gender differences. On more than one occasion, I have found that some officers in donor agencies and governments jump, in one sentence, from expressing interest in or concern with 'women-in-development' to 'female-headed households' in the next, obviously equating the two.

One of the most paradoxical consequences of a focus on female-headed households is to obscure the constitution of gender relations. This is because of an analytical asymmetry between the two main categories of male-headed and female-headed, which I once referred to as the paradox of 'the empty box' (Peters 1985). Designating a household 'female-headed' signals the absence of an economically active adult man and, by definition, indicates the presence of a woman, the female head. Designating a household 'male-headed', however, signals only the presence of the normatively assumed male head; it is silent about the presence of an adult woman or women. I have shown elsewhere that, just as the use of 'farmers' or 'households' without attending to crucial differences within such categories misdirects agricultural or other policy, so does a simple opposition between male-headed and female-headed. This is because the opposition obscures the important role of women in agriculture and other activities *within* male-headed households (Peters 1984; 1986). Moreover, as pointed out by Murray (1987), to see 'female-headed households, single women and "matrifocal" households ... as ... deviations from the "nuclear family" household obscures recognition of the fact that the inequalities, the tensions, the conflicts, the pressures of dissolution associated with such "deviant" forms are strongly manifest within the "nuclear family" [or male-headed] household also.'

Relatedly, too close a focus on household type (whether female-headed or not) may obscure the way in which the characteristics of the household are defined and influenced by relationships outside the household. This is the aspect of inter-household or supra-household relations that is as essential as the question of intra-household relations in analysing the organization and dynamics of households. One of the main lessons emerging from the various debates about 'the household' and the 'female-headed household' in relation to gender and social process is the need to recognize the interactions *among* levels of social organization and *between* social units and social processes.

Arguably, one of the most important contributions made by African studies to the literature on gender has been on just this issue. While not peculiar to Africa, an essential lesson from research on the continent has been that 'households' or 'domestic units' cannot be understood in terms of their internal dynamics alone, but only in relation to the broader social groups, networks and categories in which they are embedded. 'People ... draw on ... extra-domestic ... structures and networks ... for resource access' (Guyer and Peters 1987). In short, the household, female-headed or not, must be situated within its social matrix (Stack 1974; Lewis 1981; Vaughan 1983; papers in Moock 1986; Mackintosh 1989). The household may be one in a series of 'nested' units, ranging from the unit of a woman and children (the 'hearth-hold', as defined by Ekejuiba in Chapter 3) through compound, lineage and so forth; or it may overlap with other social units (as when a consumption unit overlaps but does not completely coincide with the production unit (Gastellu 1987)). These structural links and the flows and channels between persons and between social units are all influences on the structure and organization of a household.

Such a conception entails understanding social dynamics over varying time-frames. The lack of attention to dynamic change is evident in the way female-headedness is often equated with 'matrifocality'. Matrifocality is itself a bundle of features rather than a single characteristic and may refer to household composition (Gonzalez 1970; Murray 1981), the pattern of affectivity or interaction among members or between linked households, the cultural value placed on the role of 'mother' (Smith 1973), the economic and social marginality of male conjugal partners, or any combination of these (Gonzalez 1970; Stack 1974). Smith specifically argues against equating matrifocality with female-headedness. In both the Caribbean, where greatest use has been made of the concept of matrifocality, and in working-class Britain, families may be considered 'mother-centred' or matrifocal (Bott 1957) even though a husband-father is present. The comparative cases across a range of countries suggest that, if there is a similarity, it is a correlation between matrifocality and bilateral or matrilineal kinship systems (Geertz 1961; and references cited above).

The populations most associated with matrifocal families are those of the Black diaspora in the Americas (Gonzalez 1981; Moses 1981; Massiah 1982; Bolles 1986). The central role of mother and the prominent part played by women in social and economic life in Black groups in the US and the Caribbean has produced a lively discussion about the interaction among the persistence of cultural models (deriving from West Africa, in which women as wives retain a stake in their natal groups and enjoy a certain semi-autonomy in work, income and decision-making), the experience of slavery and institutionalized racism, and chronic and pervasive poverty (above references and Mintz 1981).

The literature on household and family among the Black diaspora suggests another lesson for consideration of female-headed households in Africa. Although approximately one-third of households in the Caribbean are female-headed (Massiah 1982), most women and men marry (there is a range of marital relations from 'visiting' relations, common-law marriage and legal marriage). Thus, female-headed households represent transient and repeated phases of being without a resident adult man. One consequence important for analysts to recognize is the 'permeability' of household boundaries and the need to place households within broader networks of relations among kin and neighbours (Stack 1974).

Secondly, such female-headed households should be distinguished from those which are female-headed over much longer periods – for example, in the migrant labour societies of southern Africa (Murray 1981) or households of widows. The Caribbean and US female-headed households are more similar to those of matrilineal/matrilocal groups in Africa (such as those in Malawi). Here, most adults have a number of conjugal partners in seriatim. At any one point in time, there is a high proportion of female-headed households, but most women move between 'male-headed' households, during the periods when they have a resident husband, and 'female-headed' households, when they are 'between' husbands.

The superficial identity of household form threatens to obscure the different patterns of intra-household relations and different conceptions of gender, sexuality and conjugality, as well as the social, cultural and political-economic dynamics producing and reproducing typical household forms in particular societies. The broader analytical failing is to assume that attention to female headship is equivalent to enquiring into gendered patterns of family and household organization, work, income, and so forth.

It is important to stress, too, that gendered patterns refer not only to relations between men and women as husbands and wives, which certainly loom large in the topic under discussion here. They include, too, relations between sisters and brothers, between co-wives, between mother and daughter, and others, all of which are mediated in part by gender.

A few examples from Botswana may illuminate the point. Most marriages among Tswana are 'processual': a relationship between a woman and a man becomes a marriage over time (Comaroff and Roberts 1981). Male out-migration is an important factor in this pattern. One consequence is that many women spend many years living with their children in their natal compound, which their 'husband-to-be' visits. In a number of instances, this has led to tension and conflict between the woman and her brother, who has the right to inherit the compound from their parents. The brother is caught between the conflicting needs to support the kin in his natal compound and to support his own wife and children, who may be living in the same compound or in the natal compound of his 'wife-to-be'.

Another site of tension may be between a woman and her adult daughters who leave their children to be cared for by her while they go to town to earn money. One woman in her fifties expressed this as her having become the mother of her daughters' children. On the other hand, solidarity relations between mother and daughter and between brother and sister also exist. One woman explained that she and her brother worked cooperatively 'like oxen yoked together', a relationship that is frequently carried into the next generation as a set of claims and responsibilities between 'mother's brothers' and 'sister's children' (Peters 1983).

In short, analysing the gender dimensions of socio-economic and cultural processes means looking at more than household structure, headship, or husbands and wives. Too myopic a focus on female-headedness has led analysts and policy-makers to ignore the lesson that gender differences intersect with other social differences and these, in turn, with household structure. To fail to conduct such an analysis is to confuse both problem and solution. Again, this point links up with the now extensive cross-disciplinary literatures on the need to analyse the effects of gender differentiation *as it interacts with* other social differences of age, caste, class, race and ethnicity.

Challenges and New Directions

One tension in the literature on 'female-headed households' and on household analysis more broadly is between the need to develop more appropriate typologies, for research and policy purposes, and the need to understand the processes that generate different types of households and other social units. The position of different categories of women cannot be understood only with reference to 'household headship', nor can 'the dynamic processes that are crystallized in particular household forms' be analysed by focussing only on households (Peters 1983). At the same time, 'there is a valid need to define which are the *key* social units in a particular system [and] how they are constituted', since households and other social units 'are major channels as well as outcomes' of social process (Guyer and Peters 1987). In policy contexts, too, key units, like households of different types, must be defined for surveys or services (e.g. Chipande 1987; McMillan 1987). Yet one must also be sensitive to the recursive nature of social process; that is, directing services to a particularly defined category of disadvantage, i.e. unmarried mothers, female-headed households, etc. may merely reproduce those units rather than resolve the disadvantages they face.

One response to the critique of the focus on female-headed households is to urge that one not start with asking what are the types of households, but what are the key units of production, consumption and investment (Gastellu 1987). Moreover, in addition to asking the questions usefully posed by Crehan (1992): what do households do? how do they do what they do? why do these people organize particular activities in those particular ways? how do the households survive and/or change over time?, one also investigates the flows and transfers between households and other social units or categories. In these ways, one is led to enquire simultaneously into both *units* and *processes*. Research has now shown very clearly that households and the relations among persons within a household change and adapt over time, whether seasonal (Jones 1983; 1986), over a project cycle (Dey 1981; McMillan 1987), or over longer periods (Murray 1981; 1987; Martin and Beittel 1987). Research and policy need to build in *time* to their methods of analysis. A particular challenge emerging from this approach concerns the relations between the development cycles of domestic units and the processes of class differentiation. This requires that researchers 'situate cyclical changes within a historical understanding of particular trends and divergences' (Murray 1987). This, in turn, can lead to stimulating comparisons within Africa as well as between the African continent and other regions.

The need to identify key social units for policy purposes has been noted above, as well as the ever-present danger that, by 'targeting' particular units or categories, unintended negative effects are produced. A recent paper points to the way in which attention to 'headship' in population policy analysis has had the quite unintended consequence of deflecting research and policy away from the role of fathers in female-headed households. The authors call for 'a new research focus on the family that transcends the physical and temporal boundaries of the household, and a policy focus that inquires into and seeks to support parents' economic and social responsibilities for children, particularly the neglected father-child relationship' (Bruce and Lloyd 1992). This conclusion is reached because too narrow a focus on 'female heads' has tended, paradoxically, to assume too great an emphasis on mothers' 'investment' in their children and too little on that of the father. Taking a child-focussed perspective, they state 'that children are entitled to the social and economic resources of both ... parents'.

The call by Bruce and Lloyd for 'a new research focus on the family' appears to run counter to the fears expressed a few years ago that a family-centred approach has often proved detrimental to a woman-centred approach (Buvinic 1984). This is not a simple disagreement, since the respective authors have far more in common in their approaches than differences. In fact, an approach seeing women as *only* mothers can have as negative effects as one which posits them *only* as female heads. What is crucially at issue here is the attempt to improve women's lives, but not in ways that deny improvements to the lives of children and men and vice-versa.

These conclusions pertinently raise the ever-present problem faced by research and policy-action, namely, the recursive nature of analysis and practice or, in other terms, knowledge and power. Seeking to understand gender differentiation through identifying, studying and 'targeting' female-headed households has had some unwanted effects in practice and has produced certain analytical blinkers.

In addition, they suggest important differences across regions in gender relations and social organization. The phenomenon of the 'female-headed household', as noted, may differ in significance over space and time for the persons within it and for the society in question. Female-headed households have long been seen as unfortunate deviations from the norm of male-headed households, in statistical and ideal terms. The early work on female-headed households saw them, in most cases, as victims of ill circumstances, namely: death, abandonment, migration, war. Research in Africa is now suggesting that some female-headed households are such by choice. Some young women are either seriously delaying or refusing marriage for a variety of reasons that critically include gender relations (Moore 1988), but probably also entail relations of class, religion, and so on. There are intriguing similarities between the ways in which 'female-headed households' and women choosing to bear children outside marriage are on the increase in both 'third' and 'first' worlds. The use of pre-marital contracts drawn up by couples in the USA is reminiscent of some of the classic negotiated bridewealth marriages in Africa. Differences abound, of course. The point is that households and female-headedness must also be placed within the social context and processes from which they emerge.

A further suggestive example comes from the English-speaking Caribbean where a predominant 'family system' is female-headed households with men moving between them as lovers, husbands, sons and brothers (Bolles and D'Amico-Samuels 1989). A conclusion that 'the biological father [of children in the female-headed households] should or does bear the brunt of breadwinning is not borne out in Caribbean family systems', therefore distinguishes the Caribbean situation from those supporting the conclusion of Bruce and Lloyd, cited above, about the 'father's role'. The authors of this review note that Caribbean matrifocal families and women's relative autonomy must be understood within their 'conditions of poverty and limited choices', a conclusion that echoes work in Africa and elsewhere. At the same time, by asking what might women elsewhere 'learn from the flexibility of Caribbean family systems' in coping with the changes in the modern world, they suggest the 'female-headed household' may have positive dimensions for women and raise the kind of intriguing parallels across regions noted above.

Here, as elsewhere, anthropologists try to follow the fine line between an insistence on the historical and cultural specificity of social forms and a comparative approach that draws out similarities and contrasts across the multitude of specifics. The 'female-headed household' is another example which requires both.

The conclusion to be drawn from the debates about female-headed households and what they imply for gendered patterns of change is simply stated though far more difficult to practise: we need, as researchers and practitioners, to be self-critical about the categories and approaches we devise for analysis and practice. In particular, surveys and other research methods should not take 'the household' as the only unit of enquiry and analysis. To address 'intra-household' relations, both men and women adults must be interviewed. To address 'supra-household' relations, research cannot rely solely on random sample surveys in which the household or the individual is the unit, but must complement such surveys with (a) intensive, ethnographic analysis to identify key social units, networks and categories within which households and individuals are situated; and (b) longitudinal analysis in which the *same* individuals and social units are restudied over time in order to identify key social processes. These multiple approaches, which I am currently using in a study in Malawi, facilitate clearer understanding of socio-economic process and the role of gender relations, as well as provide the basis on which policy frameworks premised on 'the' household can be carefully scrutinized to identify potential unfair discrimination against women, or other social categories.

References

Anderson, M., *Approaches to the History of the Western Family, 1500–1914*, London, Macmillan, 1980

Beneria, L., 'Conceptualising the Labour Force: The Underestimation of Women's Economic Activities', in N. Nelson (ed.), *African Women in the Development Process*, London, Frank Cass, 1981, pp. 10–28

Bolles, A.L., 'Economic Crisis and Female-headed Households in Urban Jamaica', in J. Nash and H. Safa (eds), *Women and Change in Latin America*, South Hadley (Mass.), Bergin and Garvey, 1986, pp. 65–83

Bolles, A.L. and D. D'Amico-Samuels, 'Anthropological Scholarship on Gender in the English-speaking Caribbean', in S. Morgen (ed.), *Gender and Anthropology. Critical Reviews for Research and Teaching*, Washington, D.C., American Anthropological Association, 1989, pp. 171–88

Boserup, E., *Women's Role in Economic Development*, London, George Allen and Unwin, 1970

Bott, E., *Family and Social Network*, London, Tavistock, 1957

Bruce, J. and C.B. Lloyd, 'Beyond Female Headship: Family Research and Policy Issues for the 1990s', Paper presented at the Conference on Intrahousehold Resource Allocation: Policy Issues and Research Methods, 12–14 February 1992, International Food Policy Research Institute, Washington, D.C., 1992

Bush, R., L. Cliffe and V. Jansen, 'The Crisis in the Reproduction of Migrant Labour in Southern Africa', in P. Lawrence (ed.), *World Recession and the Food Crisis in Africa*, London, James Currey, 1986, pp. 283–99

Buvinic, M., 'Projects for Women in the Third World: Explaining their Misbehavior', Washington, D.C., ICRW, 1984

Buvinic, M., M. Lycette and W.P. McGreevey (eds), *Women and Poverty in the Third World*, Baltimore, Johns Hopkins University Press, 1983

Carney, J. and M. Watts, 'Manufacturing Dissent: Work, Gender and the Politics of Meaning', *Africa*, vol. 60, no. 2, 1990, pp. 207–41

Cheater, A., 'Women and their Participation in Commercial Agricultural Production: The Case of Medium-Scale Freehold in Zimbabwe', *Development and Change*, vol. 12, no. 3, 1981, pp. 349–77

—, 'Formal and Informal Rights to Land in Zimbabwe's Black Freehold Areas: A Case Study from Msengezi', *Africa*, vol. 52, no. 3, 1982, pp. 77–91

Chipande, G.H.R., 'Innovation Adoption among Female-headed Households: The Case of Malawi', *Development and Change*, vol. 18, no. 2, 1987, pp. 315–27

Cliffe, L., 'Labour Migration and Peasant Differentiation: Zambian Experiences', *Journal of Peasant Studies*, vol. 5, no. 3, 1978, pp. 326–46

Comaroff, J.L. and S. Roberts, *Rules and Processes*, Chicago, The University of Chicago Press, 1981

Crehan, K., 'Rural Households: Making a Living', in H. Bernstein, B. Crow and H. Johnson (eds), *Rural Livelihoods: Crises and Responses*, London, Oxford University Press, 1992, pp. 87–112

Dey, J., 'Gambian Women: Unequal Partners in Rice Development Projects?', in N. Nelson (ed.), *African Women in the Development Process*, London, Frank Cass, 1981, pp. 109–22

Dwyer, D. and J. Bruce (eds), *A Home Divided: Women and Income in the Third World*, Stanford, Stanford University Press, 1988

Folbre, N. 'Household Production in the Philippines: A Non-Neoclassical Approach', *Economic Development and Cultural Change*, vol. 32, no. 2, 1984, pp. 303–30

—, 'Hearts and Spades: Paradigms of Household Economics', *World Development*, vol. 14, no. 2, 1986, pp. 245–55

—, 'Women on their Own: Global Patterns of Female Headship', Population Council/ICRW Working Paper Series, 1991

Gastellu, J-M., 'Matrilineages, Economic Groups and Differentiation in West Africa: A Note', *Development and Change*, vol. 18, no. 2, 1987, pp. 271–80

Geertz, H., *The Javanese Family*, New York, Humanities Press, 1961

Goldschmidt-Clermont, L., *Unpaid Work in the Household: A View of Economic Evaluation Methods*, Geneva, ILO, 1985

Goody, J., 'The Evolution of the Family', in P. Laslett and R. Wall (eds), *Household and Family in Past Time*, Cambridge, Cambridge University Press, 1972, pp. 103–24

Gonzalez, N., 'Toward a Definition of Matrifocality', in N. Whitten and J. Szwed (eds), *Afro-American Anthropology: Contemporary Perspectives*, New York, Free Press, 1970

—, 'Household and Family in the Caribbean: Some Definitions and Concepts', in F.C. Steady (ed.), *The Black Woman Cross-Culturally*, Cambridge (Mass.), Schenkman Publishing Co., 1981, pp. 421–30

Guyer, J. I., 'Beti Widow Inheritance and Marriage Law: A Social History', in B. Potash (ed.), *Widows in African Societies*, Stanford, Stanford University Press, 1986, pp. 193–220

—, and P.E. Peters, 'Introduction, Conceptualizing the Household: Issues of Theory and Policy in Africa', Special Issue, *Development and Change*, vol. 18, no. 2, 1987, pp. 197–214

ICRW (International Center for Research on Women), 'Women-Headed Households: Issues for Discussion', Paper prepared for Joint Population Center/ICRW Seminar on the Determinants and Consequences of Female-headed Households, Washington, D.C., 1988

Izzard, W., 'Rural-Urban Migration of Women in Botswana', Report, National Migration Study, C.S.O., Gaborone, 1979

Jones, C., 'The Mobilization of Women's Labor for Cash Crop Production: A Game-Theoretic Approach', *American Journal of Agricultural Economics*, vol. 65, no. 5, 1983, pp. 1049–54

—, 'Intra-household Bargaining in Response to the Introduction of New Crops: A Case Study from North Cameroon', in J.L. Moock (ed.), *Understanding Africa's Rural Households and Farming Systems*, Boulder, Westview Press, 1986, pp. 105–23

Kabeer, N., 'Beyond the Threshold: Intrahousehold Relations and Policy Perspectives', Paper presented at the Conference on Intra-household Resource Allocation: Policy Issues and Research Methods, 12–14 February, 1992, International Food Policy Research Institute, Washington, D.C., 1992

Kennedy, E. and P. Peters, 'Household Food Security and Child Nutrition: The Interaction of Income and Gender of household Head', *World Development*, vol. 20, no. 8, 1992, pp. 1077–85

Kerven, C., 'Urban and Rural Female-headed Households' Dependence on Agriculture', Central Statistics Office, Gaborone, Botswana, 1979

Kossoudji, S. and E. Mueller, 'The Economic and Demographic Status of Female-Headed Households in Rural Botswana', Research Report No. 81–10, Population Studies Center, University of Michigan, 1981

Laslett, P., 'The History of the Family', in P. Laslett and R. Wall (eds), *Household and Family in Past Time*, Cambridge, Cambridge University Press, 1972, pp. 1–89

Lewis, J. van D., 'Domestic Labor Intensity and the Incorporation of Malian Peasant Farmers into Localized Descent Groups', *American Ethnologist*, vol. 8, no. 1, 1981

Lloyd, C.B. and A.J. Brandon, 'Women's Role in Maintaining Households: Poverty and Gender Inequality in Ghana', Population Council, Research Division Working Paper No. 25, New York, 1991

Mackintosh, M., *Gender, Class and Rural Transition*, London and New Jersey, Zed Books, 1989

Martin, W.G. and M. Beittel, 'The Hidden Abode of Reproduction: Conceptualizing Households in Southern Africa', *Development and Change*, vol. 18, no. 2, 1987, pp. 215–34

Massiah, J., 'Women who Head Households', in *Women and the Family*, Barbados, WAND, 1982, pp. 62–130

McMillan, D.E., 'Monitoring the Evolution of Household Economic Systems over Time in Farming Systems Research', *Development and Change*, vol. 18, no. 2, 1987, pp. 295–314

Meillassoux, C., *Maidens, Meal and Money*, Cambridge, Cambridge University Press, 1981

Mintz, S.W., 'Economic Role and Cultural Tradition', in F.C. Steady (ed.), *The Black Woman Cross-Culturally*, Cambridge (Mass.), Schenkman Pub. Co., 1981, pp. 515–34

Moock, J.L. (ed.), *Understanding Africa's Rural Households and Farming Systems*, Boulder, Westview Press, 1986

Moore, H.L., *Feminism and Anthropology*, Minneapolis, University of Minnesota Press, 1988

Moser, C.O.N., 'Gender Planning in the Third World: Meeting Practical and Strategic Gender Needs', *World Development*, vol. 17, no. 11, 1989, pp. 1799–825

Moses, Y.T., 'Female Status, the Family, and Male Dominance in a West Indian Community', in F.C. Steady (ed.), *The Black Woman Cross-Culturally*, Cambridge (Mass.), Schenkman Publishing Co., 1981, pp. 499–514

Murray, C., *Families Divided: The Impact of Migrant Labour in Lesotho*, Cambridge, Cambridge University Press, 1981

—, 'Class, Gender and the Household: The Developmental Cycle in Southern Africa', *Development and Change*, vol. 18, no. 2, 1987, pp. 235–50

Okeyo, A.P., 'Daughters of the Lakes and Rivers', in M. Etienne and E. Leacock (eds), *Women and Colonization*, New York, Bergin Publishers, 1980, pp. 186–213

Peters, P.E., 'Gender, Developmental Cycles and Historical Process: A Critique of Recent Research on Women in Botswana', *Journal of Southern African Studies*, vol. 10, no. 1, 1983, pp. 100–22

—, 'Typologies and Empty Boxes: Gender Analysis in Research on Agrarian Change', Presentation to a Seminar on Beyond the International Decade for Women: Roles for Social Scientists, Graduate School, Columbia University, New York, 1985

—, 'Women in Botswana', *Journal of Southern African Studies*, vol. 11, no. 1, 1984, pp. 150–3

—, 'Household Management in Botswana: Cattle, Crops and Wage Labor', in J.L. Moock (ed.), *Understanding Africa's Rural Households and Farming Systems*, Boulder, Westview Press, 1986, pp. 133–54

Potash, B. (ed.), *Widows in African Societies*, Stanford, Stanford University Press, 1986

Rosenhouse, S., 'Identifying the Poor; Is "Headship" a Useful Concept?', LSMS Working Paper No. 58, World Bank, Washington, D.C., 1989

Smith, R.T., 'The Matrifocal Family', in J. Goody (ed.), *The Character of Kinship*, Cambridge, Cambridge University Press, 1973, pp. 121–44

Stack, C., *All Our Kin: Strategies for Survival in a Black Community*, New York, Harper and Row, 1974

Staudt, K., 'Agricultural Productivity Gaps: A Case Study of Male Preference in Government Policy Implementation', *Development and Change*, vol. 9, no. 3, 1978, pp. 439–57

—, *Women, Foreign Assistance, and Advocacy Administration*, New York, Praeger, 1985

Tanner, N., 'Matrifocality in Indonesia and Africa and among Black Americans', in M. Rosaldo and L. Lamphere (eds), *Woman, Culture and Society*, Stanford, Stanford University Press, 1974, pp. 129–56

Tinker, I., 'The Adverse Impact of Development on Women', in I. Tinker and M. Bramsen (eds), *Women and World Development*, Washington, D.C., Overseas Development Council, 1976

Vaughan, M., 'Which Family? Problems in the Reconstruction of the History of the Family as an Economic and Cultural Unit', *Journal of African History*, vol. 24, 1983, pp. 275–83

Yousseff, N. and C. B. Hefler, *Rural Households Headed by Women: A Priority Issue for Policy Concern*, Geneva ILO, Rural Employment Policies Branch, 1982

III

MIXED BLESSINGS OF MOTHERHOOD: FERTILITY, SEXUALITY AND AGRARIAN LIVELIHOOD

6

Women's Workload and Reproductive Stress

Han Bantje

Introduction

In retrospect, it is remarkable one could ever be taught social science without bothering much about people. But that's how it was. Dutch anthropologists took their cues from the empirical tradition of British functionalism and the more abstract and intellectual French structuralism, which stressed the analysis of cultural constructs. Socio-cultural entities were seen as essentially self-contained and governed by their own structural rules, therefore difficult to compare over space or time. The authenticity of other cultures was seen as an intrinsic good that should be safeguarded from western interference as much as possible. Given enough time, each human group would be able to work out an optimal equilibrium between its resources and the physical and intellectual needs of its members. This being so, one studied abstractions such as 'culture' or 'social organization' rather than the well-being of separate categories of people. The rather narrow interpretation of structural coherence as a closed set of relations between the elements of a system made it hard to account for social change other than as emanating from external disturbances.

World events since the middle of the century have rendered such perceptions obsolete. The fiction of the static ethnographic present was not able to account for the emergence of an all-embracing world system to which formerly isolated societies had to accommodate themselves for better or worse. In the hope of avoiding major calamities, mainstream thinking turned to survival, health, and economic development rather than cultural idiosyncrasy. Societies were, in a sense, made comparable

111

by universalizing a conceptual framework based on essentially western values, and relegating concerns about social and cultural identity to the realm of folklore. It was thought that the application of western economic and hygienic principles would generate world-wide prosperity.

At the personal level, my confrontation with the daily reality of African society did not benefit much from acquired academic theory. Even in a remote part of Zambia I found a society far more dynamic and subject to outside pressures than could be accounted for by the relatively harmonic concepts of structural-functionalism. Like many others, I became intrigued by what I had not been taught: how to register, describe, and analyse processes of change. Although I had the good luck of being able to study several societies for a rather long time, my understanding of them was limited until I encountered the much more flexible concepts of systems analysis.

Systems analysis offered me a coherent conceptual framework encompassing both human and biological processes. Through its representation of linkages between sub-systems as feedback processes, social change can be seen as human adaptation to natural phenomena and the unforeseen results of human actions. Thus, the introduction of certain crops, or animals, or techniques, may have far-reaching consequences for working routines, social habits, residence patterns, and ultimately health and reproduction. The primary unit of social analysis should be the household production system rather than the 'society' or 'culture', as it is the basic locus of social reproduction and environmental adaptation.

Not unrelated to the gradual shift of my perceptions was the fact that much of my work was concerned with nutrition, that is, the interaction of consumption and production, of people and the land. Through the 1970s and 1980s, the study of the causes of malnutrition in societies progressed rapidly, and was increasingly understood as a problem of ecology, rather than just knowledge and availability. This led to concerns about population, reproduction, and the condition of women in general. Any nutrition studies pointed to the central role of women in food production and biological reproduction.

The study of social change is dependent on the availability of suitable data series. Given their limited duration, the traditional micro-studies of anthropologists were very unsuitable, even when repeated at intervals. Collecting time series data on a long-term basis is demanding work for which most researchers simply have neither the time, nor the facilities. Routine data recording of any kind is still a new phenomenon in most Third World countries. Data series are typically brief and unreliable.

Nevertheless, where they exist they can be a powerful tool for detecting processes of change.

Having tried for some time to collate and understand data series on weather, agricultural production, and settlement patterns in a rural area of Tanzania, it was a pleasant surprise to discover that birthweights had been recorded and were kept in quite a number of health institutions throughout the country. Birthweight data has the advantage of being an important indicator of the physical condition of women, and in so doing offers insight into the social and biological conditions of the society. It responds to a wide range of biological, social and economic factors, and has also been found to have a strong predictive value for later biological and intellectual development of children. The relevance of birthweight as an indicator for socio-economic development has been explored. More specifically, with reference to the subject of this book, it is a variable which sheds some light on the material circumstances of women hoe cultivators in Sub-Saharan Africa.

Decades of concern over the welfare of rural African women and children have resulted in a widely accepted picture of them as being overworked, exploited, powerless, sick and malnourished, a picture that is reinforced almost daily by reports arriving from disaster-struck parts of the continent. In contrast with health statistics suggesting a positive impact of primary health care in Africa, production statistics show a decline in overall food availability over the past decades. The harsh realities of life translate into a high incidence of disease, low life expectancy, low birthweights, undernutrition and high infant mortality.

It seems unwarranted to relate such observations to women without taking into account their social background. Women are affected, but so are men and the whole pattern of social relationships. Concern has been expressed about the growing burden on women of biological reproduction and agricultural production, and it is one of the aims of this book to explore that issue.

This chapter reviews a number of studies of maternal health and nutrition for evidence of a deterioration in the condition of women. Women's labour tasks and reproductive behaviour are discussed. Observed trends suggest that both have become progressively more demanding. The combination of heavier tasks and poor nutrition can be assumed to result in a deteriorating energy balance, ill health, and poor reproductive performance. The chapter highlights the findings of studies of maternal energy balance and birthweight which have aimed to produce objective measurements of changes in the bio-social situation. The examples cited are mainly based on experiences from Tanzania.

Women's Role in Agriculture

African smallholder hoe agriculture is a labour-intensive mode of production. In most cases, field operations and concomitant activities are carried out manually, requiring three to six months intensive field labour each year. Partial mechanization, e.g. cultivation with ox ploughs, only shifts the problem, as the resulting larger fields require more labour for weed control and harvesting.

Most current farming systems have evolved from shifting cultivation, i.e. the clearing and burning of vegetation to improve soil fertility. The advantages and limitations of such systems have been described in detail (e.g. Allan 1967). Their labour requirements are relatively small. Once the trees have been cut, generally a male task, fire takes care of fertilization, weed control and pest control all at once. Sowing is done by broadcasting, and the need for hoeing and weeding is minimal. As long as the population density is low enough to allow for lengthy regeneration of the forest (20-25 years) the system is sustainable.

However, with increasing population densities, the cycle has been shortened, forest has given way to bush fallow, bush to grass fallow, and grass to semi-permanent cultivation. Soil fertility is no longer restored, and people have to cultivate larger fields in order to feed themselves. Other changes have contributed to areal expansion of agriculture as well, notably the need to raise money for basic commodities, which is mostly satisfied by growing cash crops.

These changes have had unequal implications for male and female roles in agriculture. The need for cutting trees has greatly diminished, but field preparation and weeding have become much more laborious. In addition to growing food crops under more difficult conditions, women now also take part in the production of cash crops. This has considerably increased their workload.

Although there are societies where men and women share agricultural tasks fairly equitably (e.g. the Wasukuma of Tanzania), and a few where women hardly cultivate at all (mainly pastoral societies), on the whole, crop production is mostly women's work. Predominantly, men have not responded to the shifting balance in agriculture by doing more farm work. Frequently they are engaged in other activities such as trade, and wage-labour. In agriculture, their interests focus on the management and marketing of cash crops. The modern elements associated with these, such as ox ploughs, fertilizers, and pesticides, are not normally extended to the women's fields. On the contrary, the weeding and harvesting of the ploughed fields make a heavier demand on women's labour.

Education, commercialization, and changing opportunities have led to a rejection of the old concepts of parental control, and resulted in a fragmentation of the former extended family households. In Tanzania, this trend has been reinforced by government decisions taken in the context of socialist policies. While nuclear households have the advantage of being more flexible in their response to modern developments, the functions of farm management and collective support have suffered. Women who used to work in groups under the guidance of experienced elders, are now left to struggle alone without the advantage of the economy of scale of a larger household. A newly-wed wife, young and inexperienced, perhaps pregnant with her first child, who is given an unrewarding piece of land in a strange village, may find it difficult to produce enough food for the family.

Other changes have to be taken into account as well. Progressive deforestation has made it harder to find firewood, a task that may now absorb many hours a week. The shifting of villages from along streams to roads has made drawing water also a harder job. Existing water sources are often too small to serve the larger population concentrations, whereas the modern facilities that were foreseen have not been provided, or do not function well. In the new situation, suitable soil for vegetable gardens may also be unavailable or too far away.

Field studies abound with examples of women carrying water and firewood over long distances, or spending many hours a day cultivating their fields, in addition to domestic tasks. Attempts at quantification have in some cases yielded extreme findings (White, Bradley and White 1972). While illustrating how bad things can get, such extremes are not a good basis for generalization. By and large, people prefer to settle in areas where water and firewood are within easy reach. Collecting them is tedious, but in areas of ecological balance, this is not usually out of proportion with labour resources.

In summary, the progressive loss of soil fertility, the introduction of cash crops, the break-up of extended families, and wider ecological changes, have all contributed to make women's agricultural tasks more arduous.

Women's Reproductive Role

The human reproductive cycle, beginning with conception, is complete only when the offspring reach physical maturity. Its phases, notably pregnancy, birth, lactation, weaning, and early childhood, each present particular problems and are subject to further subdivision. Pregnancy and lactation have high energy costs which may not be possible to satisfy adequately from substandard diets. They also entail a certain amount of discomfort for the mother, which may interfere with productive tasks.

From a systems perspective, the biological process is embedded in a socio-ecological setting. At each stage, physiological events are conditioned by interacting environmental, social, cultural and psychological factors. Such interactions involve a number of reproductive hazards, as well as checks and balances protecting the reproductive function. The complexity of these interactions and the time lags involved, are only gradually coming to light. Some authors believe that aspects of reproductive behaviour may be conditioned by factors operating during the mother's own intra-uterine development, i.e. twenty or thirty years earlier (Ounsted and Scott 1982).

Childbirth is a crucial event in a person's life and in the biological and social continuity of the lineage. Awareness of the potential dangers to mother and child during confinement, delivery and early childhood is reflected in many societies by the ritual obligations surrounding childbirth. In most African societies, childbirth is surrounded with customs that offer some degree of effective protection to women. There are notions of rest before delivery, a return to the woman's own circle of relatives, preferably her mother, involvement of experienced old women in the delivery, rest and a special nutritious diet after delivery to stimulate lactation. Secrecy is considered an important protective mechanism. In Tanzania, women theoretically stay inside for 40 days after delivery, and the child is not considered to exist socially until after that period. Such customs differ from one social group to another, and are now more and more replaced by elements of modern health care.

Total fertility in Africa is high. In Tanzania, for example, it is estimated that the average woman delivers seven children (URT 1983). Therefore, within a space of about twenty years, a woman may go through the cycle of pregnancy and lactation about seven times. When lactation is prolonged, as is still often the case in rural areas, nursing is only discontinued with the onset of the next pregnancy. The more fertile women are therefore continuously either pregnant or lactating over a period of some twenty years.

Due to the relaxation of social control, and the need for many women to fend for themselves, the age of first pregnancy is now often lower, and pregnancies are less widely spaced than in the past. This potentially results in higher total fertility rates. Although women still like to return to their mother's home for delivery, there is a tendency for social support functions to deteriorate in the modern situation. On the other hand, ante-natal clinics are now widely available and attended, at least in Tanzania, providing malaria prophylaxis, screening for anaemia and complications of pregnancy, as well as providing some advice on nutrition and general behaviour during pregnancy.

Although the stereotype of effortless delivery is obviously a myth, women in most cases appear to cope well with pregnancy. Because of a generally low weight gain, about 6 kg on average, physical discomfort only becomes noticeable in the last months before delivery. Work often continues until the very day of delivery. The woman who goes to work in the morning and returns with her self-delivered baby at night is proverbial. Women in labour often come to hospitals on foot or on the back of a bicycle. I have observed a pregnant woman climb into my landrover unassisted, only to be stopped seconds later for the delivery en route.

Biological reproduction is central in women's lives. Most rural women view infertility as one of the greatest disasters that can befall them. A woman without a child can feel bereaved and might do anything she can to obtain one. Sometimes she may succeed in 'borrowing' one from a friend or relative with several children. Reports of child-stealing are not uncommon in African newspapers. There are indigenous techniques to reactivate lactation in women who have breastfed before.

Amongst rural women, a baby is considered proof of female accomplishment rather than a burden. The image of the African woman carrying a heavy headload and a baby on her back may be somewhat disconcerting to westerners, but carrying a baby and feeding it, while being engaged in other activities, is commonplace for rural African women. All peasant production systems require a high level of physical effort and it is not easy to draw a line between heavy work and the detrimental effect of too much work.

Demographic Trends and their Implication for Women

Demographic data suggest that on the whole, biological reproduction is relatively unproblematic. Human groups have succeeded in reproducing themselves even under conditions of great environmental or social stress. Within certain limits, reproduction even seems to be more successful under difficult conditions. Everywhere, deprived populations, or lower socio-economic strata have higher birth rates than wealthier populations or higher strata. According to Thomson, 'human reproduction is an astonishingly efficient process: so much so that the largest population increases are to be found in the poorest countries with the worst socio-economic condition' (Thomson 1980).

Biologically, rapid reproduction may be seen as a defence against extinction, and slower reproduction as a reaction to the removal of this threat. In the western world, lower death rates due to improved socio-economic conditions have been followed by a decline in birth rates and it was expected that this process would repeat itself in other parts of the world. However, it is now doubted that this so-called demographic transition is a necessary and automatic phenomenon. Pre-industrial societies universally had mechanisms to limit the number of births per woman rather than to increase it. In modern times, such mechanisms have succumbed to a relaxation of social norms rather than in reaction to greater biological risks. In Third World societies, there are as yet no definitive signs that the western demographic transition will be replicated. The combination of higher birth rates due to changing social norms and better health care, and falling death rates due to better perinatal care, and control of infectious diseases, is responsible for ubiquitous rapid population growth.

African growth rates are amongst the highest in the world. Reproductive success is socially and culturally valued. A woman's sense of dignity and identity depends on her proven capacity to reproduce. National concern about growth rates is only very recent, and the desire to reduce the number of births as yet limited to small, socially mobile minorities.

In spite of its overall success, reproduction in Africa is not a smooth and painless process. The numerical success is achieved at great costs to society and to women in particular. Miscarriages, still births, infant and young child deaths are all far more frequent than in western societies (UNICEF 1990). In such cases, the physical, social and psychological investments in reproduction to that point are lost. In other words, the woman takes the toll of bearing, delivering and nourishing a child who dies before becoming a full grown member of society. In addition, the care for sick, prematurely born, or malnourished infants places a burden on the health care delivery system and society at large.

High morbidity, and low life expectancy are familiar phenomena in the African context. However, detailed longitudinal studies would be needed to relate these to specific causes in individual women. To get actual data, it would be necessary to follow women throughout their reproductive life, combining data on labour output and food intake, reproductive behaviour, health, weight, etc. This would require lengthy and complex research procedures. Failing these, one has to be satisfied with circumstantial evidence.

Many focussed studies have been done on aspects of the reproductive process and women generally, in such areas as nutrition, health, energy balance, and birthweight. These have provided insight into the complex linkages between the maternal, social and environmental systems. The sections which follow review the literature on some of the parameters that have a bearing on women's physical condition.

Reproduction and Work: Impact of the Hunger Season

Agricultural labour effort is not constant throughout the year, and it does not affect all women in the same way. The length of the agricultural season depends on the rainfall pattern. Labour peaks tend to be shorter and more intensive in dry areas than in wetter areas. In very dry areas, seasonal hunger is a recurrent feature and is deemed to have considerable impact on women's nutritional status during pregnancy and lactation.

In wet areas, malaria and the resulting anaemia may be complicating factors. In the Rufiji valley of Tanzania, people live in temporary huts throughout the flood season to watch their rice crop, exposed to wet conditions, swarms of mosquitoes, sometimes hunger, and deprived of health care. On their return to the village, many pregnant women are found to be in poor health, mainly because of anaemia.

If the length of the labour peak is estimated at three months, and a woman has a three-year reproductive cycle (i.e. pregnancy and lactation), then the chance of the labour peak coinciding with the third trimester of pregnancy is only 1:48. At an average of seven pregnancies per woman, only about one woman in seven would be in that situation. But this theoretical calculation may be too optimistic. Prentice et al. (1981) state that all pregnancies in Keneba (Gambia) are affected, for at least some of their course, by food shortages during the wet season.

The chance that lactation coincides with the hungry season is much greater. Due to late and inadequate weaning, breast milk remains a vital element of the toddler's diet for several years. Every lactation cycle, therefore, is potentially hampered by a period of insufficient nutrient supply. There is still no clear evidence of a direct relation between maternal diet and quality and quantity of breast milk. However, there are indications that poorly nourished mothers produce less milk, and lactation can cease altogether in extreme cases of undernutrition

(Hambraeus 1980). Prentice et al. (1981) found that the deterioration of the maternal diet during the wet season was reflected by decreases in the concentration of all the nutrients in the breast milk, with the exception of lactose.

However, seasonal hunger does not affect all households every year. The problem is not so much what happens under normal conditions as what happens in famine years, in difficult local environments, or among disadvantaged socio-economic groups.

Female Stature as an Indicator

Human stature varies a great deal over time and between groups. Average height in Europe has increased over the centuries. In Africa, even casual observation shows that older people from rural areas are considerably shorter than younger people from more urbanized areas. Women are often much shorter in stature than men. Stature appears to be related to nutrition in infancy. When food intake in early childhood is restricted for a long time, growth development is stunted, and smaller stature is the result. Some studies emphasize the role of infections (Stein, Susser, Saenger and Marolla 1975).

Small stature is associated with poverty, and as children from disadvantaged households have a greater chance of remaining disadvantaged through life, short stature can be seen as a signature of socio-economic status. In Rufiji, Tanzania, for example, it was found that women who depended entirely on farming were on average shorter (151 cm) and lighter (49 kg) than those depending on trade and fisheries (Bantje 1981).

Seasonal or chronic low body weight are good indicators of the degree of physical stress. Both low body weights and seasonal weight variations have been documented, showing fluctuations of several kilos in the course of the year, for both men and women. Prentice et al. (1981) report that in the Gambia women at all stages of lactation lost nearly 1 kg body weight per month during the wet season, whereas during the dry season all lactating women gained weight.

Small stature may also be responsible for complications in childbirth if the pelvis is too small to allow free passage of the baby. This is the cause of the very high incidence of caesarian deliveries in Africa. If unattended, the problem can cause death at birth. Certainly, it is associated with low birthweight, although the effect is hard to separate from that of weight. Bergner and Susser (1970) conclude that mothers' height has no effect on birthweight, which is independent of mothers' weight.

Maternal Energy Balance

Conventional nutrition science is based on the thermodynamic law of conservation of energy. Nutrient intake is converted into energy, growth, fat reserves or body heat according to certain conversion factors. These vary with age and gender, type of activity, and possibly climate, but are thought to be constant for specific individuals, and hence populations of a given composition. Such notions rest on a wide range of experience. Famine and food shortages are known to result in starvation, illness and death. Substandard diets impair health and work output. Infant malnutrition results in well-known disease syndromes such as marasmus and kwashiorkor, and eventually death. On this basis, food requirements at given levels of energy expenditure have been defined for individuals, households, and communities.

This mechanistic approach to human energy balance dictates that under severe conditions women either have to reduce their labour output, restrain their reproductive function by spacing pregnancies, or else sustain lower birthweights. Spacing pregnancies is evidently a limited option in African rural life. Reducing energy expenditure is a plausible reaction, but it is difficult to prove, as data on labour output are notoriously hard to obtain with sufficient precision. Birthweight, on the other hand, has been extensively researched and yields some insight into the mechanisms at work.

However, the human body is not a simple machine and appears to be far more resilient than suggested by conventional nutrition theory. A wide range of individual responses to similar conditions have been observed. During famines some survive while others die. Some children thrive while others die on similar diets. Under conditions of duress the human organism appears to adapt itself to levels of intake that are incompatible with accepted standards. Under wartime conditions, and during famines, at least some individuals have survived against all odds. Human reproduction can be maintained successfully even under very marginal conditions. Such observations throw some doubt on the universal applicability of nutritional standards. Psychological factors appear to have an important effect on the human capacity for survival.

Studies of maternal energy balance during pregnancy and lactation are especially relevant. If food consumption is not enough to make up for the increased energy requirements, negative effects on the maternal system should be expected to occur. Protagonists of nutritional causes of low birthweight have hypothesized a stepwise depletion of maternal reserves over a series of pregnancies, due to the fact that women fail to regain their original pre-pregnancy weight before becoming pregnant again. Actual evidence to substantiate this seems to be lacking. Prentice et al. (1981) investigated women in the Gambia, who lose weight in the rainy season due to insufficient food consumption. However, when controlled for birth rank, the analysis showed no decrease in body weight over successive pregnancies. Under very marginal conditions in Papua New Guinea no such depletion was apparent either (Norgan, Ferro-Luzzi and Durnin 1974).

There still is much debate as to how much extra energy the maternal system really needs during pregnancy (Durnin 1987). The concept that energy intake during pregnancy should be the normal requirement plus that of the growing foetus and placenta, i.e. 'eating for two', is under scrutiny. Many believe that the crucial mechanism is increased metabolic efficiency, rather than increased nutrient intake. Even at low but steady levels of intake, satisfactory birthweights are achieved. Only in acute crisis situations, birthweight is really impaired and food supplements seem to help.

Nonetheless, maternal weight gain during pregnancy is considered an important predictor of birthweight. The incidence of low birthweight tends to be higher among those who fail to build up body reserves. The relationships are extremely complex. Different studies have yielded contradictory findings about the importance of maternal weight and weight gain during pregnancy. This is not surprising as they are closely related. As early as 1968, on the basis of almost 12,000 pregnancies in the USA, Eastman and Jackson concluded that progressive increase in weight gain was paralleled by progressive increase in mean birthweight, and decrease in the incidence of LBW (low birth weight). The combination of low pre-pregnancy weight and low weight gain was associated with a high incidence of LBW, especially in Black women. Similar observations have been reported by other researchers. All concur that there is a great deal of tolerance to variations in nutrient intake, except in extreme cases of deficiency.

Significance of Birthweight

The condition of the baby at the moment of birth, represented by its birthweight, has been found to be a powerful indicator summarizing prenatal development. It is influenced by nutritional, health, and socio-economic factors, and should therefore be a good measure of stress on women. Birthweight is also considered to be the most important single determinant of perinatal mortality and infant development (Bergner and Susser 1970), and therefore a good indicator of reproductive success. It has the advantage of being routinely collected in health institutions, even in very remote areas.

The factors affecting birthweight may be divided into intrinsic factors (sex of the foetus, health of the placenta, possibly genetic factors), maternal biological factors (age, parity, height, weight, weight gain, nutritional status, birth interval), and environmental factors (altitude, infections, labour output, health, smoking, drugs, alcohol) (Sri Kardjati 1985). Multiple regression analysis of these factors provides considerable insight into their relative importance, although not always with identical conclusions (Bantje 1986; Stein et al. 1975).

All influences on birthweight are mediated through the length of gestation, which is more readily associated with maternal health, and the foetal growth rate, presumed to be strongly dependent on the maternal energy balance. The factors most extensively studied are dietary intake, anaemia, and the role of infections. Simple interventions are widely employed in mother-and-child (MCH) work, e.g. malaria prophylaxis and iron supplementation to ward off anaemia; growth monitoring and dietary advice to ensure proper foetal development.

Like other biometric data, birthweight displays considerable variation, with an optimum around 3500 grams. Very high and very low birthweights are usually associated with abnormal conditions. Weights below 2500 grams are termed low birthweights, and are associated with a high rate of perinatal mortality and unsatisfactory child development.

Mean birthweight in tropical countries is lower than in western countries. More importantly, the incidence of low birthweight is much higher: about 10–20 per cent in Africa and Southeast Asia, and 20–50 per cent in southern Asia, compared to 4–7 per cent in western Europe and North America (WHO 1984). Maternal weight gain in tropical countries on average is only half that observed in western countries, i.e. about 6 kg. Perinatal mortality is much higher than in the western world. Complications due to anaemia are frequent. All these observations reflect the harsher conditions for women in less developed countries.

Similar comparisons can be made between different social strata of the same society. Everywhere it is found that birthweights are lower, and infant deaths and diseases more frequent, in poorer socio-economic environments. For these reasons, birthweight has been considered by some to be a good indicator of socio-economic development (SAREC 1978).

In rural populations, seasonal variations in mean birthweight may occur, presumably in response to variations in environmental conditions that affect people by way of health factors and nutritional status. Such variations tend to be greater and more regular in dry areas with a short agricultural season, as both labour input and dietary abundance are subject to greater seasonal extremes (Bantje 1987).

Tolerance Limits: Effects of Women's Nutrition and Heavy Work on Birthweight

Because of the strong association of women's labour effort and food availability in African peasant societies, the nutritional component of birthweight variation deserves closer scrutiny. The reproductive process is dependent on the transmission of nutrients from the environment via the maternal system to the foetus and the infant. In wealthy countries, there is a danger of overeating during pregnancy. But in Third World countries the danger of inadequate nutrition during pregnancy is far greater (Eastman and Jackson 1968; Singer, Westphal and Niswander 1968; Bergner and Susser 1970). The pertinent studies are of three kinds:

(1) Studies of birthweight distribution and its relation to nutrition. Many researchers have found an association between the quality of maternal nutrition and birthweight (Frydman, Belaisch, Berardi, Spira and Papiernik 1980; Delgado, Valverde, Martorell and Klein 1982). The question is how relevant such variations are, as there seems little benefit in pushing birthweights above an optimum of about 3500 grams.

(2) Studies of the effects of acute deprivation. The famines during the Second World War in Leningrad and the Netherlands have been extensively studied (Stein et al. 1975). Their severity resembles that of African famine conditions but they are so well documented as to enable detailed analyses of their effects.

(3) Studies of the effect of nutrient supplementation during pregnancy (Lechtig,Yarbrough, Delgado, Habicht, Martorell and Klein 1975; Delgado et al. 1982). Some effect of nutrient supplementation on birthweight is recorded, but it is only significant when conditions are really bad.

All these studies have confirmed the impact of maternal nutrition on birthweight, and this knowledge has guided the actions of nutritionists and nutrition educators. However, in retrospect, the more striking finding was that the impact seemed so small and the results so inconclusive (Bergner and Susser 1970; Sri Kardjati 1985). Even under extreme famine conditions, mean birthweight dropped by only about 350 grams. Food supplementation during pregnancy showed convincing results only when the overall intake level was extremely low. Even then it is suspected the results may reflect an increase of foetal adipose tissue rather than healthier foetal development (Lechtig et al. 1975). Therefore, one now tends to be much more cautious in stressing the crucial importance of nutrition than a decade ago.

Data on the effect of heavy work are even less conclusive, due to the problem of generating adequate measurements of energy expenditure. There is some evidence for the danger of placental infarct due to heavy work in the last trimester of pregnancy, which could trigger off early delivery and hence lower birthweight (Naeye and Peters 1982; Klebanoff, Shiono and Carey 1990). But other studies have yielded inconclusive or negative results (Rabkin, Anderson, Bland, Brooke, Chamberlain and Peacock 1990).

Reasonably detailed studies are so far limited to western countries. In Africa, there is a danger of placental damage or infection due to the habit of maintaining sexual intercourse until very late in pregnancy. When warned against this, women typically express a fear of losing male support: 'If we refuse intercourse, what shall we eat?' A concern that is, of course, more acute for non-farming women.

Studies of the factors influencing birthweight show statistically significant effects in large enough samples, but all studies find that birthweight displays great individual variation. So much so that the causative factors together explain only about 30 per cent of birthweight variation (Bantje 1986; Møller, Gebre-Medhin and Lindmark 1989). This calls into question the somewhat mechanistic interpretation of the relationship between maternal energy balance and birthweight. Delving deeper into the complexity of maternal-foetal nutrient transmission, many observers now emphasize the *adaptability* of the maternal-foetal system to a wide range of conditions.

Hytten (1980) argues that the foetus by and large is well protected from the vagaries of maternal food intake. He attributed the co-variations of nutrient intake and foetal development to the overall social environment rather than nutrient intake *per se*, and surmised that changes in maternal nutrient metabolism protect foetal development under conditions of low food intake. Such changes would be brought about by variations in hormonal levels due to psychological, social and health factors.

Some research findings support the assumption of an indirect relationship between maternal nutrition and birthweight. Studies in the Gambia and in Taiwan have shown that seasonally low food intakes do not interfere with a normal outcome of pregnancy, although mean birthweights were somewhat low (Prentice et al. 1980; Adair, Pollitt and Mueller 1983). Conversely, Briend (1985) found that among well-nourished women in Dakar, birthweights were much lower than among women of similar weight in Scotland, suggesting that genetic rather than nutritional factors are responsible. Recent studies increasingly play down the effect of nutrition on birthweight (Durnin 1987; Langhoff-Roos, Lindmark and Gebre-Medhin 1987; Møller *et al.* 1989).

In some cases, an inverse relationship was found between pre-pregnant weight and weight gain during pregnancy, which suggests the existence of an auto-regulatory mechanism. Such a possibility was already suggested before the wave of studies focussing on the nutritional component. 'The possibility exists that some biological or psychological factor is at work, such that the weight of the mother at term tends to be more constant than the mother's prepregnant weight' (Weiss, Jackson and Niswander 1969).

The theoretical basis of this concept has been worked out by Sukhatme and Margen (1982). They hypothesize that:

> ... the body regulates its energy balance by adjusting either intake or expenditure or both and that consequently the requirements cannot be considered as fixed and equal to habitual intake. Apparently, the specialized environment in which an individual is raised interacts with the genetic component to keep the variance constant. We do not know how this happens, but it appears that some physiological system plays a role in carrying information from the environment and translating it to maintain homeostasis.

Payne and Dugdale (1977) argue that body weight is a much too crude variable and built a model of the balancing mechanism. They argue that there are 'metabolically lean types' and 'metabolically fat types' whose bodies will react differently during food shortages.

Such studies do not invalidate the importance of the maternal energy balance, and hence the need for concern about an excessive workload for rural women. Sukhatme and Margen (1982) concede that:

for those living at the lower border line of homeostasis ... drought and other losses of food producing capacity ... can rapidly precipitate severe malnutrition. Conditions such as these are also prevalent in the developing world among individuals in the lower socio-economic classes who have already made the maximum adaptation and cannot adjust further.

The importance of these studies is that they reveal the ability of the maternal system to adjust its metabolic efficiency to vastly different levels of intake. Thus, they caution against easy generalizations about the debilitating effects of heavy work and poor nutrition. Unfortunately, the more sophisticated studies are invariably carried out among well-fed populations in a hospital environment. Their findings are not necessarily applicable to rural African populations. *Adaptation clearly has its limits.* Seriously deprived populations have an unacceptably high incidence of low birthweights, and food supplementation is obviously beneficial in cases of severe undernutrition. Birthweights do vary with socio-economic level and with seasonal variations in food supply. Poor women during bad times no doubt are under severe physical stress. The problem is to identify the tolerable limits.

Conclusion

The main purpose of this review is to explore the relationship between maternal workload and reproductive performance. The assessment of the impact of maternal energy balance on reproduction is not as straightforward as might be expected at face value. The complexity of metabolic conversion results in a wide range of individual outcomes in response to apparently similar conditions. Public health variables may be confounded by physiological factors that cannot be investigated, and therefore may only partially explain the degree of success of the reproductive process. Because of wide variation in all relevant parameters, a large amount of data is required to investigate any of these relationships with a sufficient level of confidence. Unfortunately, in the societies we are interested in, the mechanisms to collect such data are poorly developed or non-existent.

Until the sociology of human reproduction in rural Africa is more comprehensively understood by combining demographic, physiological and socio-cultural dimensions, our perception remains at a general level of awareness that certain categories of women and infants are more 'at risk' than others. Under these circumstances, there seems to be little benefit, and even some potential harm, in sweeping statements about the presumed suffering of rural African women, especially when these are based on a comparison with western norms.

References

Aebi, H. and R. Whitehead (eds), *Maternal Nutrition during Pregnancy and Lactation*, Bern, 1980

Adair, L.S., E. Pollitt and W.H. Mueller, 'Maternal Anthropometric Changes during Pregnancy and Lactation in a Rural Taiwanese Population', *Human Biology*, vol. 55, 1983, pp. 771–87

Allan, W., *The African Husbandman*, London, 1967

Bantje, H., 'Household Characteristics and Nutritional Status in the Rufiji Valley', BRALUP Research Paper No. 72, Dar es Salaam, 1981

—, 'A Multiple Regression Analysis of Variables influencing Birthweight', *Tropical Geographical Medicine*, vol. 38, 1986, pp. 123–30

—, 'Seasonality of Births and Birthweights in Tanzania', *Social Science and Medicine*, vol. 24, 1987, pp. 733–9

Bergner, L. and M.W. Susser, 'Low Birthweight and Prenatal Nutrition: An Interpretative Review', *Pediatrics*, vol. 46, 1970, pp. 946–66

Briend, A., 'Do Maternal Energy Reserves Limit Fetal Growth?', *Lancet*, vol. I, 1985, pp. 38–40

Delgado, H.L., V.E. Valverde, R. Martorell and R.E. Klein, 'Relationship of Maternal and Infant Nutrition to Infant Growth', *Early Human Development*, vol. 6, 1982, pp. 273–86

Durnin, J.V.G.A., 'Energy Requirements of Pregnancy: An Integration of the Longitudinal Data from the Five-Country Study', *Lancet*, vol. II, 1987, pp. 1131–3

Eastman, N.J. and E. Jackson, 'Weight Relationships in Pregnancy', *Obstetric and Gynaecological Survey*, vol. 23, 1968, pp. 1003–25

Frydman, R., J. Belaisch, J.C. Berardi, A. Spira and E. Papiernik, 'Maternal Nutrition and the Outcome of Pregnancy', in H. Aebi and R. Whitehead (eds), *Maternal Nutrition during Pregnancy and Lactation*, Bern, 1980, pp. 160–6

Hambraeus, L., 'Maternal Diet and Human Milk Composition', in H. Aebi and R. Whitehead (eds), *Maternal Nutrition during Pregnancy and Lactation*, Bern, 1980, pp. 233–51

Hytten, F.E., 'Nutritional Aspects of Human Pregnancy', in H. Aebi and R. Whitehead (eds), *Maternal Nutrition during Pregnancy and Lactation*, Bern, 1980, pp. 27–38

Klebanoff, M.A., P.H. Shiono and J.C. Carey, 'The Effect of Physical Activity during Pregnancy on Preterm Delivery and Birth Weight', *American Journal of Obstetrics and Gynecology*, vol. 163, 1990, pp. 1450–6

Langhoff-Roos, J., G. Lindmark and M. Gebre-Medhin, 'Maternal Fat Stores and Fat Accretion during Pregnancy in Relation to Infant Birthweight', *British Journal of Obstetrics and Gynaecology*, vol. 94, 1987, pp. 1170–7

Langhoff-Roos, J., G. Lindmark, E. Kylberg and M. Gebre-Medhin, 'Energy Intake and Physical Activity during Pregnancy in Relation to Maternal Fat Accretion and Infant Birthweight', *British Journal of Obstetrics and Gynaecology*, vol. 94, 1987, pp. 1178–85

Lechtig, A., C. Yarbrough, H. Delgado, J.P. Habicht, R. Martorell and R.E. Klein, 'Influence of Maternal Nutrition on Birth Weight', *American Journal of Clinical Nutrition*, vol. 28, 1975, pp. 1223–33

Møller, B., M. Gebre-Medhin and G. Lindmark, 'Maternal Weight, Weight Gain and Birthweight at Term in the Rural Tanzanian Village of Ilula', *British Journal of Obstetrics and Gynaecology*, vol. 96, 1989, pp. 158–66

Naeye, R.L. and E.C. Peters, 'Working During Pregnancy: Effects on the Fetus', *Pediatrics*, vol. 69, 1982, pp. 724–7

Norgan, N.G., A. Ferro-Luzzi and J.V.G.A. Durnin, 'The Energy and Nutrient Intake and the Energy Expenditure of 204 New Guinean Adults', *Phil. Trans. R Soc. Lond.*, B, vol. 268, 1974, pp. 309–48

Ounsted, M. and A. Scott, 'Social Class and Birthweight: A New Look', *Early Human Development*, vol. 6, 1982, pp. 83–9

Payne, P.R. and A.E. Dugdale, 'A Model for the Prediction of Energy Balance and Body Weight', *Annals of Human Biology*, vol. 4, no. 6, 1977, pp. 525–35

Prentice, A.M., 'Variations in Maternal Dietary Intake, Birthweight and Breastmilk Output in the Gambia', in H. Aebi and R. Whitehead (eds), *Maternal Nutrition during Pregnancy and Lactation*, Bern, 1980, pp. 167–83

Prentice, A.M., R.G. Whitehead, S.B. Roberts and A.A. Paul, 'Long Term Energy Balance in Child-bearing Gambian Women', *American Journal of Clinical Nutrition*, vol. 34, 1981, pp. 790–9

Rabkin, C.S., H.R. Anderson, J.M. Bland, O.G. Brooke, G. Chamberlain and J.L. Peacock, 'Maternal Activity and Birth Weight: A Prospective, Population-based Study', *American Journal of Epidemiology*, vol. 131, no. 3, 1990, pp. 522–31

SAREC, *Birth-Weight Distribution – An Indicator of Social Development*, SAREC Report R:2, Stockholm, 1978

Singer, J.E., M. Westphal and K. Niswander, 'Relationship of Weight gain during Pregnancy to Birth Weight and Infant Growth and Development in the First Year of Life', *Obstetrics and Gynaecology*, vol. 31, 1968, pp. 417–23

Sri Kardjati, M., 'Maternal Nutrition Profile and Birthweight in Rural Villages in Sampang, Madura (Indonesia)', Ph.D. thesis, Airlangga University, 1985

Stein, Z., M. Susser, G. Saenger and F. Marolla, *Famine and Human Development*, New York, 1975

Sukhatme, P.V. and S. Margen, 'Autoregulatory Homeostatic Nature of Energy Balance', *American Journal of Clinical Nutrition*, vol. 35, 1982, pp. 355–65

Tafari, N., R.L. Naeye and A. Gobezie, 'Effects of Maternal Undernutrition and Heavy Physical Work During Pregnancy on Birth Weight', *British Journal of Obstetrics and Gynaecology*, vol. 87, 1980, pp. 222–6

Teitelman, A.M., L.S. Welch, K.G. Hellenbrand and M.B. Bracken, 'Effect of Maternal Work Activity on Preterm Birth and Low Birth Weight', *American Journal of Epidemiology*, vol. 131, 1990, pp. 104–13

Thomson, A.M., W.Z. Billewicz, B. Thomson and I.A. McGregor, 'Body Weight Changes during Pregnancy and Lactation in Rural African (Gambian) Women', *Obstetrics and Gynaecology British Commonwealth*, vol. 73, 1966, pp. 724–33

UNICEF/Government of the United Republic of Tanzania, *Women and Children in Tanzania*, Dar es Salaam, 1990

United Republic of Tanzania, *Population of Tanzania* (1978), 1978 Population Census, vol. VIII, Dar es Salaam, 1983

Weiss, W., C. Jackson and K.R. Niswander, 'The Influence on Birthweight of Change in Maternal Weight Gain in Successive Pregnancies in the Same Women', *International Journal of Gynaecology and Obstetrics*, vol. 7, 1969, pp. 210–23

White, G.F., D.J. Bradley and A.U. White, *Drawers of Water*, Chicago, 1972

WHO, 'The Incidence of Low Birth Weight: An Update', *Weekly Epidemiological Review*, no. 27, 1984

7

'Children are Our Wealth and We Want Them': A Difficult Pregnancy on Northern Mafia Island, Tanzania

Pat Caplan

Introduction

In 1985, I returned to Kanga village, northern Mafia Island Tanzania for a third spell of fieldwork in a twenty year period.[1] The focus of my study on this occasion was the relationship between food production and consumption, health and fertility. It had become clear that food production in much of Sub-Saharan Africa was dropping, even as population was rising. The recently published work of Mascarenhas and Mbilinyi (1983) on women in Tanzania suggested that here, as elsewhere, there were important links between women's reproductive activities and their productivity, and hence the levels of food production. I was interested in looking at the dynamics of this situation at the village level.

In the case of northern Mafia, there have been some recent changes which have had important repercussions on food production. During the 1980s, there was a resurgence of cultivation of coconut trees because of the high price fetched by nuts in the markets of Dar es Salaam. Men spent a great deal of time focussing upon their cash crops, including the planting of new trees, much of the work of which was done by immigrant labour. The result of this was that women, left with even more of the responsibility for food production, had yet heavier work burdens. It was thus scarcely surprising that the villagers appeared to be producing less food in 1985 than when I had first carried out fieldwork two decades earlier.[2]

In this article, I consider the effects of a pregnancy not only on the woman herself, but on her kin. The main protagonist, Amina, moved to her parents' house for the latter part of her pregnancy, during which time she became unwell and was cared for by her mother and sister until she was finally hospitalized some time prior to the birth. The article considers the nature of ties between women, especially mothers, daughters, and sisters, and the extent to which their burdens are both relieved and increased by such ties. The second theme considered is that of workloads. Although women's role in subsistence production is crucial and indeed outweighs that of men, few men, and not all women, recognize this. Women do, however, recognize that having children is hard work, which raises the question of why women have many, or bear them even in difficult circumstances. The third theme is thus women's attitudes to childbearing and optimal family size. This theme leads to the issue of sexual preferences of women and men, and questions about gender politics, including women's sexual and reproductive autonomy.

I have chosen to utilize a narrative style in making these points, which are allowed to emerge from the diary which I kept at the time and conversations which I had with the protagonists. In this way I hope to enable the latter's voices to be heard more clearly than is often the case in anthropological texts.

Kanga Village, 1985

Kanga is a large nucleated village lying in the north of Mafia Island, some thirty miles off the Rufiji Delta in southern Tanzania. The economy is a mixture of subsistence (rice, cassava and sweet potatoes) and cash crop (coconuts) farming, together with some fishing. Women do much of the agricultural work in the subsistence sector, for once men have cut down and fired bush to make a field, most of the planting, weeding, guarding of ripening crops and harvesting is done by women. Men do, however, play a significant role in the production of cash crops. They own many more coconut trees than women and are more likely to plant new ones.

One of the major methods utilized in the 1985 research was an in-depth study of a limited number of households, which I visited for long periods on a regular basis, often becoming involved in whatever activities were going on. During the two months of fieldwork from June to July, the harvest was being gathered. Many families move out to live in small huts in their fields during this period, but the household on which I focus in this chapter had remained living in the village, as their rice field was part of village meadow land (*dawe*) and was only a few minutes walk from their house.

The household consisted of Mwalim Ali, a Koran school teacher, and his wife Hadija. They had living with them four grandchildren, whom they were fostering. It is not uncommon for grandchildren to be fostered by grandparents, particularly in cases of divorce or death of parents. In this case, two of the grandchildren were the son and daughter of Ali and Hadija's older daughter, Saida, who had been divorced a few years earlier, and remarried. One child remained with her, and one with the father, while the maternal grandparents took the remaining two. Hadija and Ali's younger daughter Amina, in the last stages of pregnancy, was also staying with them temporarily. It is usual for a woman to return to her mother's home around the seventh month of pregnancy and to remain there to give birth and to recuperate afterwards, at least until the fortieth day purification ceremony. Amina had brought her youngest son with her, leaving her two older sons with her husband's mother. Thus the following are the dramatis personae of this story:

- Ali and Hadija, older middle-aged couple
- Resident grandchildren in Ali and Hadija's household:
  - Bibi, girl aged 15, daughter of divorced elder daughter Saidia
  - Bibi's brother aged 11
  - boy aged 8, child of a deceased son
  - girl aged 6, his sister
- Non-resident relations visiting Ali and Hadija's household:
  - Amina, younger daughter staying with her parents during the final stages of pregnancy
  - Amina's son, aged 2
  - Saidia, older daughter, mother of Bibi and her brother, now living in neighbouring village
  - Saidia's daughter, a toddler
- Non-resident relations:
  - Kombo, who is Ali and Hadija's only living son, working on the Tanzanian mainland.

Scene 1: 5 June, early evening

'Children are Our Wealth, and We Want Them'

Hadija is peeling cassava for supper, the two girls are pounding rice, and one of the boys is gutting some fish. The girls complain about the hard work of pounding and are briefly relieved by the boys. Everyone complains about fasting for Ramadhan. Amina is sitting on the verandah splitting raffia in a desultory way. She is heavily pregnant and tells me that she has high blood pressure, for which she is taking some medicine obtained from the village clinic. Nonetheless, she too is fasting for Ramadhan since 'it is easier to fast now than make up for it later'. I have already seen the family briefly since my arrival, but we have not talked at any length.

Hadija (to me): 'Why do you only have two children?'

Pat : 'Because that was the number I wanted.'

Hadija: 'And why is your second child adopted?'

Pat: 'Because I didn't want to bear another child, and his parents couldn't look after him.'

Hadija: 'Children are our wealth and we want them. We don't have other wealth. If someone has only two or three children, we will pity them. If you have five or six, that's better. They'll look after you. I have heard that you can get sterilized in Dar (the capital city) after bearing a few children, but we don't have that here. It's nice to have a lot of children. You say, today I'll go and see this one, tomorrow I'll go and see that one. Or they come and see you and you are very pleased.'

Pat: 'So is it better to have boys or girls?'

Hadija: 'Both are equally good. But men want boys and women want girls. It is best to have some of each. For there is the work of the bill-hook (nyundu, used by men) and that of the hoe (jembe, used more by women than men), so you need both, don't you? But in your country, since the work is that of the pencil, I suppose it doesn't matter which you get.'

Commentary: Even had I not intended to examine the topic of fertility, it would have been difficult to avoid, because the first question people asked me on my return was how many children I had. When I replied that it was still the same number as on my previous visit several years earlier, many were scathing: 'What's the matter with you? Are you afraid of this work? Who do you think will look after you when you get old? You need at least two of each sex, then each one will have a companion (*mwenzake*).' Fertility rates in the village were high; a sample of 53 women averaged 4.84 children still alive and 1.4 children lost.[3] It was very clear that both men and women desired children, yet as Hadija points out in the above comments, they do not always agree about sex preference, and, as we shall see, they do not always agree about how many children they want, or how frequently.

Scene 2: 9 June, late afternoon

'If Men Only Knew the Trouble we Women Have'

Amina is the only person in the courtyard behind the house, although her father is praying the evening prayer on the front verandah. All of the rest, Hadija and the children, are in the field, harvesting rice.

Amina: 'Do you use hot water after childbirth like us?'

Pat: 'Yes, we do.'

Amina: 'Do you think it has to be exactly nine months before one gives birth? I wish it could be sooner – I feel so heavy.'

Pat: 'It might be a bit earlier or a bit later. But can you sleep at night?'

Amina: 'Yes, sometimes, but I hurt here under my abdomen.'

Pat: 'Will you go to the clinic to have the baby?'

Amina: 'Yes, I hope so.'

Pat: 'But the midwife is away at the moment isn't she?'

Amina: 'Yes, but the paramedic can deal with childbirth. The problem is whether I'll be able to get to the clinic (which is about 5 minutes walk away). If I can walk, I'll go.'

Pat: 'Did you have problems with your previous labours?'

Amina: 'The first time, I had a very long labour. The second was much quicker. One of my pregnancies was twins, but I lost one of them. Men do not know the trouble women get, if they were the ones to give birth ...'

Pat: 'So when you do you plan to go back home to your husband?'

Amina: 'I don't plan to move for quite a while yet. I can't manage all those children on my own. Here I get plenty of help.'

The children return and the younger girl starts pounding. I offer to help her, whereupon Amina tells the boys to lend a hand. We all help, with Bibi, the fifteen-year-old, doing most of the work.

Commentary: Several points emerge from the above conversation. Amina articulates the problems women face in giving birth to children – not only the discomfort of pregnancy, particularly acute in her case, and the pains of birth, but also the sorrow of losing children, although she had lost fewer than most village women. Secondly, she is well aware that men do not realize what women go through. She leaves unfinished her sentence about what might happen if they did, but the implication is that they would be less insistent on having so many children. A third point is the extent to which women who are pregnant (or sick) depend upon kin, especially mothers, to help out not only in caring for them personally, but also in helping with other children.

Scene 3: 11 June, 3 p.m.

'Women Have a Lot of Work ... but Men are Busy with their Own Affairs'

I go to Hadija's field to find her there alone, harvesting. We work together for a while, cutting each rice-stalk separately with the sharp edge of a shell. Some of the grains drop off as one cuts the stalk, and are lost. This labour-intensive method is hard work, bending under the hot sun.

Hadija: 'Did you go by the house? What was Bibi doing?'

Pat: 'Yes, I did. She had already started cooking.'

Hadija: 'I was late starting to harvest this morning, because Amina felt so unwell. Also some people dropped in. So it was 10 a.m. before I could get away. I am really worried about her and don't like to leave her, but I have to get this rice in. Some of it is already spoiled.'

Pat: 'Do men help in the harvesting?'

Hadija: 'Some do, some are even as quick at it as women. But my husband doesn't like to do it. Men are busy with their affairs. Women have a lot of work. I can't do everything – I can't pound or fetch wood or water because of the headaches I get. So that's why I need someone to help. Maybe my daughter Saidia will come and help me harvest.'

Pat: 'So how on earth will you manage when Bibi (who is already engaged) gets married?'

Hadija: 'That's what I ask myself – but what can I do when she is already a grown girl and her in-laws want her? I thought of asking my son Kombo to let me have the young girl he's got living with him, you know, the older sister of our two other grandchildren ... And Bibi's wedding is coming up. I'll have to get some things together for her. I want you to write off for me and order a mattress.'

Pat: 'Why do men like to marry more than one wife?'

Hadija: 'What does it cost them? Often the women pay themselves for their clothes. Mind you, men are responsible for buying things like kerosene, fish and so forth. That is the work of men (*barazani* – literally "of the verandah"). And that's another reason why they don't harvest much – they are busy with their own affairs.'

Pat: 'So when will your older daughter Saidia come and lend you a hand?'

Hadija: 'It's difficult for her to come at the moment, because she hasn't got anyone to guard her field (from pests).'

Pat: 'Can't her husband do that?'

Hadija: 'Does a man guard a field? Never! He's got his own things to do.'

An hour later Hadija's husband appears to help carry the harvested rice back to the house and soon after that she and I leave as well. Two days later Saidia does arrive with her youngest child from the neighbouring village (5 miles away) where she now lives. She was lucky enough to get a lift on a lorry, but, after working in her mother's field all day, she has to walk back, carrying the toddler, in time to prepare the evening meal.

Commentary: In my earlier observations during fieldwork in Mafia, I had frequently been struck by the extent to which women continued to rely upon their mothers for help after marriage. Indeed, I remember feeling quite envious of the ready availability of such help when I was doing fieldwork in the 1970s, a period when my own children were still small and some extra help would have been welcome. But the above conversation shows that this help for daughters carries with it costs for mothers. Women already shoulder disproportionate burdens of work, for they are responsible for almost all domestic labour – fetching wood and water (often from long distances), pounding rice, cooking and caring for children. In addition, they perform more hours of agricultural work than do men.

During this period of harvest, when there are peak labour demands, not all men participate in agricultural work, and those that do tend to work shorter hours. Hadija, for instance, does not expect to get any help from her husband with the harvest. She would like help from her older daughter Saidia, but she in turn cannot leave her own ripening crop to be devoured by such pests as birds, monkeys and wild pigs, nor is Saidia's husband likely to relieve her of the task. The solution for Hadija is to utilize the labour of her resident granddaughter, Bibi, as much as possible, and to replace it with that of another young girl when Bibi leaves to get married.

Hadija refers in our conversation to the obligation on men to provide for the cash needs of the household – kerosene, fish and other bought items. That is why 'men are busy with their own affairs'. But she also notes that, in fact, many women pay for their own clothes (an item which husbands are supposed to supply, but often fail to do) and that she is the one who is responsible for putting together Bibi's trousseau (Caplan 1975).

Scene 4: 19 June, evening

Crops Eaten by the Birds

Amina had been quite unwell when I had called earlier in the day, having coughed all night which kept both herself and her mother awake. That day Amina's mother-in-law had been to visit her, bringing her two older boys to see their mother.

Hadija: 'I've got such a headache, and I've done no harvesting today.'

Pat: 'So who is watching the crop then?'

Hadija: 'No one, it is just being eaten (by the birds). But I can't leave her with the children when she's in this state, I have to stay with her. Have you been to see the new mother yet? (the wife of one of the shopkeepers, and a relative of Mwalim Ali)'

Pat: 'No, I haven't been yet. Have you?'

Hadija: 'Me? No chance. If I can get a woman to sit with Amina, I'll go. She's had a lot of children, that one. Let me see, this must have been something like her eleventh pregnancy – she's got five boys, and she lost three or four daughters.'

Commentary: Here Hadija graphically shows the tension between her obligations to care for her daughter, and the need to guard and harvest the rice. She has had help for one day from her elder daughter Saidia, but it is not enough. Hadija's comments about the wife of the shopkeeper illustrate the fact that some women do bear very large numbers of children, not all of whom survive. In the case she mentions here, as in that of others, there is a greater tendency to lose girl babies than boys, a factor which I have suggested elsewhere is not unconnected with men's preference for boy children, and the extent to which men control household budgets, particularly purchases of food important for weanlings such as eggs and milk (Caplan 1989).

Scene 5: at the house of the shopkeeper

'As Many as God Sends, I'll Receive'

Pat: 'I hear your wife has just had a baby?'

Shopkeeper: 'Yes, now I have ten children (very pleased and proud).'

Pat: 'And are you still planning to go on "working" (a euphemism for having more children) then?'

Shopkeeper: 'Yes, I am.'

Pat: 'How many do you want then?'

Shopkeeper: 'As many as God sends, I'll receive. So far we have enough to eat, thank God.'

Pat: 'So do you prefer to have sons or daughters?'

Shopkeeper: 'Both are good. Daughters don't go far away (when they get married), and so they are at hand when you are old. They'll invite you to live with them. Sons go away (to work on the mainland). They'll bring you presents and money.'

Later, I talk to his younger wife in her courtyard. She has three daughters. One of them wets her pants. As her mother cleans her up she asks me:

Second wife: 'Did you have this work?'

Pat: 'Yes I did.'

Second wife: 'Children are a lot of trouble, but we want them.'

Pat: 'Do you want more then?'

Second wife: 'Yes, I want three more. Six is good. But I want three boys now, all I have is girls.'

I also go to visit the shopkeeper's first wife, the one who has just given birth and is still at her mother's house:

First wife: 'Until now I have only sons. I lost three daughters. One was already walking, another was several months old. So I have called this daughter Hautakiwi ("she who is not wanted").'

Her mother: 'It is like preventive medicine – because the other girls did not stay (alive).'

First wife: 'I still miss the ones who died, and when I see their brothers and think that they might have been here too, I feel very sad. I lost two boys as well, one of them already big enough to go out and play with his friends.'

Pat: 'So are you pleased to have got a girl this time?'

Her mother: 'Of course she is. She will be her friend. A man wants boys and they will be his friends, a woman wants girls, and they will be her friends and talk to her, just as the boys will talk to their father.'

Commentary: These conversations include the view of a father, who, like many men I interviewed, indicates that for him, the more children the better, and attributes agency to God in this matter. This was a not uncommon response, suggesting that the business of fertility is out of human hands. Women too gave similar answers. One woman, who had just given birth to her seventh child, replied in answer to my question about whether she was getting tired of having children: 'How can I refuse to bring my fellow human beings into the world?' In fact, of course, fertility is not entirely in the category of nature (or the hands of God), even in this area where modern contraception is largely unavailable. Women sometimes go away to spend long periods with their natal families in order to avoid getting pregnant for a while. The fact that they have to is indicative of the likelihood that husbands and wives who live together will inevitably have sexual intercourse; indeed, this is seen to be as much desired by women as by men.[4]

The conversations with the two wives show that each wants more children, but of the sex she does not have. The second wife wants boys, and the first wife wants girls. The first wife's mother explains why this is, not only in terms of the different forms of help parents get from sons and daughters, but also in terms of companionship – men talk to other men, women to other women. The word used – *mwenzako* – has the connotation both of someone who is *with* you (a companion) and *like* you. Furthermore, children of the same sex 'belong' to that parent more than children of the opposite sex. As one woman said, 'The boys belong to their father, but the girls are really mine.'

Scene 6: at the mother and child health clinic

'That Operation is a Good Idea'

I am observing at the clinic for a morning, noting the results of the examination of babies and young children by the midwife, who records key indicators, such as weight, on a growth chart.[5] Amina comes in with her mother and is examined by the midwife, who finds her blood pressure has gone up even further. She is told to go and see the paramedic. Hadija is concerned to get back to her harvesting, so I offer to accompany Amina back home later, and then come to the field to report to Hadija. As expected, the paramedic tells her she will have to be admitted to the hospital in the district capital, 30 miles away. Amina and I slowly walk back to her house.

Pat: 'So what will happen now?'

Amina: 'Mother will insist on coming with me. She will have to leave the children at home. Maybe father and his pupils from the Koran school can help with the harvest.'

Pat: 'Have you thought of getting sterilized after the birth? You know they can do that operation in Kilindoni?'

Amina: 'Yes, I think it's a good idea. I think my husband would agree.'

Pat: 'What about the toddler?'

Amina: 'He'll have to go to his other grandmother.'

Commentary: Amina thus considers the possibility of sterilization, but she will first have to get her husband's consent, which is required for all forms of contraception in Tanzania. She thinks he is likely to agree, probably partly because of her difficult pregnancies, and partly because they already have three sons. Other women, however, reported to me that their husbands would refuse to countenance family planning.

Scene 7: Hadija's rice field

'I'll Have to Put my Faith in God'

I go to the field to give the news to Hadija, who is getting some half-hearted help with the harvesting from the boys. One of them wants to go, complaining that it is too hot. She tells him to cover his head so that he won't feel the sun so much. She is very dismayed when I report what the paramedic has said.

Hadija: 'See how much I've still got left to harvest! And I've lost so much time and so much grain by having to delay because of her illness. I think I'll put my faith in God and wait for a few days, rather than going tomorrow, and perhaps I'll get most of this rice in. I just don't have anyone I can call on. Saidia has just started her own harvest. And my husband's sister (who lives next door) is sick and I have to keep an eye on her. If I leave this now, I'll get nothing – and who knows when she'll actually go into labour. She always gets swelling of the legs, but usually it's after she has given birth, not before. Maybe it's her diet – maybe she's eating too much rice. What about eggs – do you think they'll help her?'

Commentary: Here Hadija thinks aloud to me, weighing up the pros and cons of an immediate departure for the hospital, with the loss of food crops for the next year, as well as the problem of her sick sister-in-law, against the risks of delay. She also wonders why Amina has these symptoms, asking me for my opinion on the usefulness of eggs, a food traditionally eschewed in this area by pregnant women, but much advocated by the health workers in the village as a way of combating the chronic anaemia suffered by most women.

Scene 8: 23 June, midday

'I Don't Want Any More Children'

Amina is, as usual, lying down in the covered section of the courtyard. Bibi is cooking. Hadija has gone to the field with Saidia, who has come for the day, and two other women who have also agreed to help. This is reciprocal help, utilizing kinship ties, and will have to be repaid at some point in the future.

Saidia appears, very tired and hot, as it is an exceptionally warm day. I reflect that she has had a five-mile walk from her village, carrying the toddler, then spent the morning harvesting, and all of this while fasting. She tells Amina to give her any dirty clothes and she will do her washing for her. First, she sits down to breastfeed her toddler.

Saidia: 'I intend to wean her this month. (to the child:) Don't you feel ashamed, a big girl like you, still wanting the breast? (to me:) This is the last one. I don't want any more children.'

Pat: 'Will you use family planning then?'

Saidia: 'Yes, I'll go to the hospital.'

By this time, Saidia, aware of her sister's situation, has to risk leaving her own harvest in order to help her mother. Scarcely surprising that she announces that she herself does not want any more children – she has had six, of whom four are still alive, by her first husband, and two, both girls, by her present husband. In order to get contraception, she will have to travel 30 miles to the hospital in the district capital, Kilindoni, as it is unavailable at the village clinic.

We go together to the well where Saidia does her sister's laundry and we chat about the reasons for her divorce, and her experience of her new marriage.

Saidia: 'I don't feel angry or bitter about it any more, but at the time ... after all (when he divorced me) I had lived with him for seventeen years.'

Pat: 'Why do men want to marry more than one wife?'

Saidia: 'I don't know, I can't understand it. We women can't understand. But the law (*sheria* – Islamic law) says that they can. Perhaps it is so that if one is away or pregnant, the other will be there to do the work.'

She asks me about my children and their studies, and about marriage and divorce in England. She says she plans to leave by 3 p.m. in time to walk back home and cook supper. We return to the house to find the two boys pounding rice. I ask them if they have been harvesting that day – no, they hadn't been asked. With three adult women to help her, the boys are let off the hook and do not have to be pushed into harvesting.

Commentary: Women not infrequently told me that they did not want any more children, or that children were a lot of work. As one woman put it: 'You are so hassled – now one cries, then the other.' But women who are divorced and remarried are likely to have two sets of children. Divorce rates in the village are relatively high, and figures which I collected in the 1960s indicate that men and women over the age of 60 were likely to have had an average of two partners.

Saidia's first marriage had ended when her husband decided to take a second wife, which is permissible under Islamic law, although only a minority of men are polygamously married. Some men, when asked why they married more than one wife at a time, answered in terms of the practice enabling them to have more children. One man said, 'It's to get more children. They are a great asset. One might become a doctor or a teacher or a rich person. So they'll help you and also help the country.' His reply indicates that children are seen as an asset. But other replies from men suggest that the women themselves are an asset, particularly because one will usually be available if the other is unavailable because of pregnancy. Such men do not have to depend on other female kin to feed them when their wives return to their natal homes to give birth. Nonetheless, polygamy is not usually appreciated by women, and may, as in the case of Saidia's first marriage, precipitate a divorce.

Scene 9: 1 July

'We Both Have to Work'

Amina is by now in the hospital in Kilindoni, and her father and I have been to visit her. Hadija is staying nearby with relatives. Amina's blood pressure and oedema are down, but she still has her severe cough. I go by the house to catch the latest news and find Mwalim Ali at home. In the course of a long conversation, I ask him:

Pat: 'In your opinion, is it better to be a man or a woman?'
Mwalim Ali: 'Our state is the same – we both have to work.'
Pat: 'Who works harder?'
Mwalim Ali: 'Neither, we pay people to do it. We don't work very hard at the moment.'
Pat: 'What do you think are the problems of life here?'
Mwalim Ali: 'No really big problems. It's much better here than in the town. When you finish your agricultural work here, you can relax.'

Commentary: Mwalim Ali's statements are interesting in a number of respects. He certainly does not recognize that women work harder than men; indeed, he does not see either men or women as having to work very hard, since it was possible to hire the agricultural labour of recent immigrants from the mainland. The use of such labour had become increasingly common in the 1980s, but it is striking to note that the labour which was replaced was that of males, not females. Hence, even in a crisis situation like this one, where women's labour is plainly stretched to breaking point, additional help is not sought through paying extra workers. Rather, women obtain help, if at all, through their networks, on a reciprocal basis. They simply do not have the necessary cash to buy themselves out of agricultural labour in the way that men, who control most of the cash crops (coconuts), can do. His point about relaxation at the end of a day's work sounds rather hollow in the light of the burdens carried by most women during the harvest season, and particularly by his wife and older daughter during this difficult period. But women neither expect extra help from men, nor are they likely to get it.

Scene 10: 7 July, morning

'I Do Want One More Child – a Boy'

Mwalim Ali is preparing to go and visit his wife and daughter in Kilindoni again. He is taking with him another bag of rice, commenting, 'If you stay with people who live in town, these days of course, you have to take some food with you.' By now, Amina has been temporarily discharged from hospital and is staying with her mother in the relatives' house. Saidia had come the night before, bringing all her children with her for a stay of a few days, since her husband is away. She remarks that it is a pity that I have not met him, as he is unlikely to be back before I leave. She asks me to come and take some photos of her and the children before I go. She also tells me that she plans to leave the toddler with her husband's mother, as she has weaned her now. Our conversation continues:

Pat: 'What's been happening then?'

Saidia: 'Amina's husband has been to see her, so has his mother. I'll go myself on Monday.'

Pat: (thinking that as she's now weaning the toddler, she's more likely to get pregnant) 'Will you try and get some contraceptives while you're in Kilindoni?'

Saidia: 'No, I've decided against it. I do want one more child – a boy. I've only got two sons now, and none by my present husband.'

A few days later, on 21 July, Mwalim Ali came to tell me that Amina had given birth to twins but that one of them, a boy, had died, while the girl was still alive. Saidia came down again to help out until her mother and sister returned. On 23 July, Amina was discharged from hospital and needed a lift home. I sent a message for the driver of the vehicle which was coming to fetch me on my departure to bring her with him. Thus as I left the village, they arrived. There was time only for a quick greeting, and a photograph.

Commentary: Saidia rethought her plans to stop bearing children in the light of the fact that she had 'only' two sons. Given the high rate of infant mortality, that is too few to be certain that at least one will live to adulthood. Furthermore, she had not presented her second husband with a son, and although he had sons by his other wife, she was well aware that the security of her marriage would be enhanced by the arrival of a male child.

Following Amina's delivery, the two sisters, Amina and Saidia, had had remarkably similar childbearing experiences. Both had borne six children of whom four were still alive. Fully aware of the material costs of childbearing, both had expressed a reluctance to have more children. Nonetheless, at the time of my departure from the village, neither appeared likely to take action to prevent future pregnancies.

Parental Motives: A Child of One's Own

As the foregoing case study demonstrates, the consequences of a pregnancy extend far beyond that of the household of the woman herself. For that household, if the last part of her pregnancy coincides with a peak agricultural period, either planting or harvesting, the members are likely to have relatively little food for the following year, except what they can afford to buy. But other households may also be affected – that of the woman's mother at least, and also possibly that of other relatives. In the case of Amina, the household of her older sister, which gives a great deal of labour time, and that of her husband's mother, who ends up taking care of three small children, also feel the impact. Had Amina had an easier pregnancy, things would, of course, have been easier. Yet even under normal circumstances, a woman in the last few months of pregnancy cannot do as much agricultural work as she might otherwise do, thus her productivity is lessened. She turns for help to her mother's household and this in turn lessens its productivity. Fertility thus has a profound impact on productivity.

Women are perfectly aware of this situation and are ambivalent about having children. Many said they would like fewer, or to space them more widely. A number of women in the village put their names down at the clinic with the hope that contraception would soon be available there. But many also reported that they did not see eye to eye with their husbands on this matter. Men with whom I discussed this issue usually expressed enthusiasm for having children, although a number of women made the point that this was because the women did most of the work associated with their care.

So why do women go on having many children when they recognize their costs and when they are overburdened with both productive as well as reproductive work? It would be over-simplistic to assume that it is only because their husbands force them to do so. Women themselves want children – for the joy they bring and for the help they can give, both when small and when older. Furthermore, due to the high rate of infant mortality, it is necessary to bear extra children in order to allow for some losses.

Sexual preferences also play a role here. Men and women have different priorities. Men want boys and women prefer girls for themselves, although they also want boys for their husbands. So couples who have children of only one sex will seek to have more children in order to get some of the other sex. Furthermore, where women have not yet given birth to male children, they are likely to become pregnant again more quickly in order to have a boy. This in turn makes it more likely that a girl will be weaned early, thereby decreasing her well-being.

Why is there this sexual preference? Part of it may be explained in terms of labour. Each parent wants children of their own sex so that they can be assisted in their tasks. Women know that they can only command the labour of small boys; soon enough they will evince reluctance to help their mothers, whereas daughters are viewed as a constant source of support. Yet in fact, frequently, daughters themselves require the help of their mothers – when they are pregnant or giving birth, or in the case of their divorce when mothers are the most likely people to take the children of the broken marriage. Men see having boys as a symbol of prestige and virility, and they hope that sons will be successful and get well-paid jobs away from the village, an ambition which is in fact achieved only by a small minority. Even so, the chances of this happening are much greater with sons than with daughters. Both men and women want *mtoto mwenzangu* – a child which is 'like me' and therefore 'really mine'.

In bearing children, women have to weigh up the risks – of child mortality, of husband's displeasure, of their own workloads – and gains – such as future help from daughters – and strategize. Women's calculations are made in the context of restricted access to labour and other resources. In the process, women are, as Sen (1990) has recently pointed out, agents as well as victims. Sen distinguishes between well-being and agency. In terms of well-being, women in Mafia are worse off than men as measured by mortality, morbidity and control of fertility. But agency is different from well-being, and, as Sen notes, women may be agents in utilizing the very norms which constrain their lives as a way of strategizing. Papanek (1990) argues that such behaviour is explicable in terms of both the 'honour of voluntary deference' (to men's wishes) and 'compulsory emotions'. On Mafia Island, as elsewhere, such 'compulsory emotions' include the desire to create more human beings.

Epilogue

Three years later, I received the following letter from Kombo, the brother of Amina and Saidia in Dar es Salaam:

I have been here on Mafia since the 19th of August, and I will be leaving for Dar on the 27th. The reason for my coming here is the death of our sister Saidia. She died on the 12th of August and was buried on the 13th. Father, mother, the children and everyone are weeping bitterly. Sister Saidia died as a result of her pregnancy. She died before giving birth – it is said that the baby died first.

Notes

1. Fieldwork on this occasion was funded by the Nuffield Foundation.
2. I was not, in the short time available, able to collect detailed statistics on this, but I did ask people how many months' food they had grown the previous year, and for how many months they were dependent upon purchased food.
3. These figures are extremely crude and are not broken down by age, a procedure which is virtually impossible in an area where people do not know how old they are, and there are no records.
4. One woman with whom I discussed the issue said that she had heard that some Tanzanian groups practised postpartum abstinence for the period of breastfeeding. Her comment: 'I don't know how the women stand it. Thank goodness we don't have anything like that here.'
5. The graph on the card has four sections: red for danger (60% or less of desirable body weight, indicating marasmus or kwashiorkor), grey for underweight (60–80% of desirable body weight), green for normality (80% or above) and white (for above average). The cards are kept by the mothers.

References

Caplan, P., 'Perceptions of Gender Stratification', *Africa*, vol. 59, no. 2, 1989
—, *Choice and Constraint in a Swahili Community,* London, 1975
Mascarenhas, O. and M. Mbilinyi, *Women in Tanzania: An Analytical Bibliography*, Scandinavian Institute for African Studies, Uppsala, and Swedish International Development Agency, Stockholm, 1983
Papanek, H., 'To Each Less than She Needs; From Each More than She Can Do: Allocations, Entitlements and Value', in I. Tinker (ed.), *Persistent Inequalities*, Oxford, Oxford University Press, 1990
Sen, A., 'Gender and Cooperative Conflicts', in I. Tinker (ed.), *Persistent Inequalities*, Oxford, Oxford University Press, 1990

8

Mothers, Healers and Farmers in Congo

Marie-Claude Dupré

Introduction

When I started my fieldwork in 1966, structuralism was at its height. We were instructed to follow the 'scientific approach', the hallowed realm of the learned student. Any other approach was stigmatized as romantic, foolish, or politically activist. People's actions in the communities we studied were supposedly determined by unconscious laws of collective behaviour. Despite my eagerness to obtain a seat among my superiors, I encountered experiences leading me beyond remote 'objectivity' to the exploration of such diverse paths as healing rites, iron smelting, political history, Kidumu masks, and relations between structure and actual local systems throughout Teke. The Tsayi proved to be good teachers in comprehensive anthropology.

What gradually became apparent to me is that informal economies and feminine agriculture elude capture by statistics. These spheres are no longer considered to be fertile soil for the germination of western-type market economies. Many conveniently believe that they are local phenomena doomed to recede into insignificance as soon as 'development' gets underway.

This paper, citing examples from four Congo societies, the Tsayi and Kukuya Teke, the Bembe and Nzabi, rejects this line of thinking. In the savanna and forest areas of central Africa, female agriculturalists live in communities which control their matrimonial alliances, residence and divorce, give access to fields, provide help and health care and order daily life, social harmony, well-being and fecundity. These organizational structures condition the way the everyday toil of women is spurred and endured.

The foregoing describes village life in Congo, emphasizing local, informal activities that congeal into social systems in which women have central roles to play and can not be considered merely 'dominated' individuals. The forest people, the Tsayi Teke and Nzabi, live not far from the savanna people, the Bembe and the Kukuya Teke. All of them have acephalous, matrilineal social structures.

Separate migrations brought the four societies in close proximity to each other in the southern part of the Congo during the nineteenth century. Their contrasting ways of life support widely differing population densities. The Kukuya live on a plateau with cultivating patterns that ensured a relatively high population density of approximately 29 people per square kilometre at the time of my fieldwork. The Bembe exhibited even higher population densities up to 74/sq km with 15,000 already living in towns outside Bembe country. Early migrants to the forest, the Tsayi Teke established a rather prosperous society, assimilating local people and smelting iron for their southern and eastern neighbours. In 1909, they declared war on the French colonialists, refusing to pay taxes, and paid heavily for their action. A few years later, only about one-tenth of the population were still alive. In 1966, they numbered 13,000 with a very low population density of about 0.1/sq km. The Nzabi, forest-dwelling smelters, came later. They also lost many people in the tax wars and had a low population density of about 2/sq km at the time of my fieldwork.

In all four societies, women are farmers, healers and mothers. These three roles are braided together by cultural tradition to form patterns of fertility and family provisioning. Each society displays a distinctive pattern with different agricultural work experiences for women as will be explained in the following sub-sections of this article.

Healing Ways

It has often been noted that African women are mothers, that their main, if not sole, ambition is to have numerous children. Many western observers tend to think that pre-industrial societies have no prospect for their women, except motherhood. With the introduction of modern health care, it is opined that women have too many babies who then grow up! The continuation of high fertility practices is considered as an obstacle to economic take-off. Meanwhile, local knowledge and organization are virtually unknown. Development programmes consider the creation of community clinics as the only way to deal with local diversity. A development bias, listing hospitals and community clinics as important milestones to improved health, can be irrelevant.

In Congo societies, women traditionally had their part to play in a social system that was based on gender opposition. Men were in charge of political well-being. Female resentment could be voiced. Matrimonial codes were meant to give wives fair treatment and a reasonable standard of living. Male political supremacy, in all four matrilineal societies under review, was assured because the male head of the family was in charge of the malevolent side of the pervading extra-human powers. Many illnesses or deaths were reported to be necessary. Men had to 'feed' these obscure ambivalent powers. Misfortune had a bright side. It helped provide bonds uniting human beings to their non-human background. This holistic, all-pervasive system is described for the Kukuya (Bonnafé 1978). It is not surprising to find that development strategies which do not take account of the existing health systems do not succeed.

The Bembe, a prosperous market-oriented farming people had, and still have, specialized medicine women to take care of infertility, pregnancies, nursing infants and young children. When I lived in Mouyondzi, in 1973, I witnessed a renewal of the Mukisi spirits rituals. Women were being possessed by the water spirit, seized by it and, after a small number of ceremonies, they were turned into mother-and-child health specialists. Sacred paraphernalia existed as part of, rather than in place of, a functioning health system. Mukisi women existed for a long time in savanna societies of southern Congo. In the late 1960s, the Bembe decided to turn their backs on old times and get rid of sorcery. Every family was invited to take to Malanda Victor, a healer established not far from Brazzaville, the artefacts used in magical operations and swear they would never pick up their obscure traditions (G. Dupré 1985). And yet, as women complained soon after, misfortune did not disappear. Illness and death were rife throughout Bembe country. Mukisi water spirits, being the most benevolent ones, had to be invited back. Men agreed. It was a big affair. Artefacts had to be gathered again, memories and knowledge had to be reformulated. Groups of specialists met week after week during the dry season when farming chores were less imperative.

I witnessed the ceremonies, saw women shake and shiver, dance round the fire, then tramp burning coals. I felt the soil quiver under me and listened to the head of the family proclaiming he would relinquish part of his power and hand it over to Mukisi women that night. During the following days, I inquired about the origins of the spirit and recorded wonderful tales of strange people who sprang up from rivers, got caught in fishing nets with complete medical kits and female figures who vanished into waterfalls. I took a short herbalist course, made lists of herbs, roots, twigs, leaves, seeds, barks, and tried to match them with various symptoms of illnesses.

Through these activities, I discovered that such turmoil had precedents in Bembe country. The etiology of misfortune, though linked with ritual and fraught with magical procedures, was at times revisited and new theories, tied to new recipes, were experienced. In 1973, water spirits gained ascendance, and concoctions of roots and barks, ground on small millstones, were in disrepute. Dry spirits were declared too familiar with the malevolent side of magical manipulations. Their priests had to be initiated anew and enrolled into the groups tied to the water spirit. In the long run, lineages who possessed a medicine woman were put down, or gained a higher place in clan hierarchies. Old and bitter conflicts were brought to light and put to an end. Male heads of lineages reconsidered their place and women were invited to use their affinities with the world of spirits for the sake of general welfare.

The people who gesticulated near a big fire, flourishing hens, catskins and bottles of palm wine were modifying their health organization along new lines. According to the Bembe and most Congo societies, illness betrays deteriorating social relations. People fall ill when things do not go right in the 'family' which is roughly defined in clan and lineage organization. Misfortune, then, can be worked upon. What is usually termed 'domination', 'social inequalities' and 'hierarchies', are tools handled by senior men to provide the necessary conditions which bar the entry of disease. Each individual cure is part of a preventive strategy.

I was rather pleased with my reading of Mukisi ceremonies (M.C. Dupré 1981-82) and was showing off in a Paris workshop in 1988, when a colleague recalled the recent access of Bembe women to 'traditional' male trading activities. She asked whether the enhancement of healing activities was a male means of pushing women back into the female sphere. When women are busy with healing and general welfare, they will stop bothering about getting their peanuts and maize to town markets. I asked the opinion of a Bembe man who was attending the workshop. He readily answered that things were actually worse. 'Our women', he said, 'have become entirely free. They tend the fields as they used to, but now they also buy Mercedes lorries and pay men to drive their crops to Brazzaville. We have been turned into mere stallions', he moaned. 'We are only resorted to, to beget children.'

Fertility of the Womb and of the Soil

A female person only becomes a fully-fledged human being after she has given birth. Through pregnancy, delivery and child raising, a woman gains her place in the society; she is socially accepted. Child rearing requires cooperation, not restricted to a father and mother, but of a much larger group of relations. Some people say a woman must be on good terms with herself in order to give life. The Yaka of Zaire explained their theory to Devisch (1984) who watched their healing rites and described them in terms of praxeology and gnoseology. A woman has to know her place in society, inside the restricted circle of her parents; and she also has to experience what it is to be a female human in her ecological environment (1984).

The savanna Bembe adhere to different 'demographic laws' when compared to the Nzabi living in the forest. Nzabi polygyny is less frequent and involves fewer women, rarely three at the same time. The birth rate is lower. Amongst the Bembe, co-wives are more numerous and large families are frequent. The savanna Kukuya Teke occupy a middle position. They have a high incidence of polygyny but their birth rate is moderate. These three groups living in geographical proximity to one another, nonetheless, exemplify a striking range of fertility and patterns of motherhood. In all three societies, however, still births and baby deaths are considered to be forms of infertility.

Table 1: Demographic Patterns within Three Congo Societies

Year	1972	1965	1966
Environment	Savanna	Savanna	Forest
% of Population under 15 years	43.8	40.0	24.8
Polygyny Rate	1.75	1.85	1.40
% of Men Married between:			
20-24 Years	43.0	9.0	13.3
25-29 Years	84.2	53.0	74.3
Reproduction Rate	1.68 (1.23 within territory)	1.36	1.18
Average No. of Children Born Alive to Women over 45	46% have >8	4.6	69% have >2
Average Birth Interval (months)	30	53	28 under 30 years, longer thereafter

The above figures are based on the work of: Guillot (1967; 1970; and 1973), a geographer who did fieldwork with the Nzabi and Kukuya; G. Dupré (1982; and 1985), an anthropologist who lived with the Nzabi and the Bembe; and Bonnafé (1978; 1987; and 1988), an anthropologist who observed the Kukuya for nearly twenty years; and my own fieldwork of the Tsayi Teke in 1966-72 (M.C. Dupré 1990). Though information quoted is not strictly comparable, the figures nonetheless prompt questions regarding the distinctive patterns of each society.

Why do Nzabi women rear so few children when Bembe wives have numerous progeny? The incentives to become a mother appear to be the same. Widows get new husbands. Spinsters do not exist. Worry over infertility is pervasive everywhere. Male domination is a feature of all three societies.

Social matters which can bear on fertility are numerous (Fetter 1990). For this Congo region, they include: expensive or cheap bridewealth, a free or restrained sexual life, young (13) or oldish (16) brides and grooms (18 to 35), effectiveness of health rules, steadiness of marital unions, agricultural techniques and ecological surroundings. Agriculture, however, has been cited as the most important variable (G. Dupré 1982; and 1985).

In the forest, men have to cut fields for their wives out of the woodland. Apart from a few political leaders, and despite a general habit of collective work, few men have enough energy to fell forest for numerous wives. Polygynous men are older, i.e. those who can ask for help from their young relatives without being obliged to reciprocate the favour on their helpers' fields. Fertility of the fields is insured after some 30 to 40 years of natural vegetation regeneration. Fields are tended with one all-purpose tool (M.C. Dupré 1993a). Large parts of the land are devoted to hunting. For these reasons, the forest cannot support a dense population. Suitably, both polygyny and birth rates are low (Guillot 1970; G. Dupré, 1982; M.C. Dupré 1993b).

By contrast, in Bembe and Kukuya savanna areas, women do most of the agricultural work. They are able to hoe grass fields by themselves. Kukuya and Bembe practise a traditional form of cultivation whereby grass and roots are placed in a mound and set on fire a few days before the beginning of the rains. The mounds burn slowly and ashes yield important fertility to the soil (Guillot 1973; G. Dupré 1985). Bembe women work much more than Nzabi forest-dwelling women and have many more children.

Do fertility rates somehow adjust to the fertility of soils, without Malthus' dire predictions asserting themselves? No doubt, part of the balance can be explained by the fact that young Bembe of both sexes migrate to towns. A natural reproduction rate of 1.23 within Bembe country is significantly less than that of the Kukuya (at 1.36), but more than the Nzabi (at 1.18). The Nzabi are also in the habit of migrating to towns, but in smaller numbers composed mainly of men. The exceptional fertility of Bembe women coincides with a recent and exceptional expansion of Bembe people outwards into a wider geographical territory. Town relatives help newcomers, but they also keep in touch with their rural relations, continue to pay their subscription to village help societies, return for medical cures, raise money for modern projects such as the building of a secondary school, etc. Some are called home to become heads of families and have been known to warn that, due to their ignorance, they can not deal with delicate matters as it was done before. Since the 1970s, Bembe women have become businesswomen. As businesswomen, they still beget children but pay poorer women to tend their fields and rely on older daughters to raise their offspring. Domination is now from rich to poor, irrespective of sexual identity.

Sexual Freedom and Restraint

An important difference between forest and savanna societies seems to be the degree of sexual freedom experienced by women. Forest women are freer and have more space to move about. This can again be related to modes of livelihood. Nzabi women farm but their plant-gathering and hunting of small game are also important. Less tied to agricultural work parties than Bembe and Kukuya women are, Nzabi women often work alone on fields surrounded by the forest. While farming, they often take their clothes off in order to save them from unnecessary wear and tear. Visitors are obliged to start singing or speaking loudly when they approach a field, to avoid an embarrassing encounter.

Nzabi men, while not being very polygynous, are involved in a succession of matrimonial alliances. The first wife is 'given' to a young man by his father and the bridewealth, paid by the father, is not very expensive. In the second marriage, the woman has to be snatched away from another man. The new husband has to pay twice the value of the bridewealth for his new wife. He is then considered to have reached adulthood. A man can marry a third wife provided he is wealthy enough to pay another double bridewealth. It may prove cheaper, and a better strategy, to 'buy' a young girl. Elderly men, who marry late, know that their young wives will eventually elope. Thus elderly men can just wait for the inevitable to happen and get compensated with the payback of the bridewealth plus maintenance expenses incurred in the interim! Young wives have been nicknamed 'savings banks'.

Savanna and forest societies alike prohibit outdoor sexual relations. A proper bed inside a house, is the only safe place. Offenders contract fearful diseases whose origins are easy to trace for any diviner. But Nzabi young men decided a straw mat was a good equivalent to a bed, and it is easy for a woman to take one along with her, since she may need a rest when she is away all day long in the forest. Such adulterous behaviour is not strictly against the rules since one is obliged to marry at least twice. Some women even receive encouragement from their mothers-in-law. The older woman may carry the mat herself, and/or pretend she is going to work in the same field as her daughter-in-law.

Demographically, this social 'instability' appears responsible for the small number of children women have. Guillot (1967; 1970) noted a short interval between pregnancies before the age of 30, i.e. before the manoeuvres leading to the second union. An affair may last for some months (G. Dupré 1982). When the woman resumes her marital status, she gives birth to fewer children thereafter.

Nzabi society lacks the feminine healing rites, dedicated to feeble infants or exhausted women, that their Tsayi Teke forest neighbours have (M.C. Dupré 1978). Tsayi left the savanna for the forest some centuries ago and never forgot their origin. Their Mukisi rites were borrowed sometime in the nineteenth century from savanna Mukisi healing procedures, and mixed with ancient healing rites dedicated to Nkita spirits. Despite residence in the forest, Tsayi women are said to be both faithful and good partners in sexual play. Ecological pressure is not the only influence on demography.

So too, kinship rules and prescriptive alliances do not singularly determine fertility. But they do influence everyday life. Nzabi men must marry a matrilateral cousin called '*mutekheda*', granddaughter (of the mother's brother). Over 90 per cent of marriages conform to the prescription. And they do so very easily. When G. Dupré drew a genealogical tree, his informant was able to point to several *mutekheda* in different places. He added that only *mutekheda* belonging to other lineages of the same clan could be married, and this increased the number of would-be spouses. He concluded, with a large grin, that, though he could not marry all his *mutekheda*, he could have sexual relations with nearly all, and not be blamed for it. We then went on a four-day walking tour and listened to his very free conversation and jokes addressed to the many *mutekheda* he met.

By comparison, Bembe men of the savanna 'choose' in about 50 per cent of all cases to marry a patrilateral cousin, the daughter of their father's sister. Intermarriage involves far fewer women from distant villages. Patrilateral alliance, as C. Levi-Strauss remarked, builds shorter exchange circuits. It goes on, in Bembe country, with village endogamy. It often happens that wives working on adjacent fields were born in their husbands' villages. They are not isolated individuals brought together by lineage strategies and prescriptive marriage. Farming parties do not include only co-wives, mothers and daughters-in-law, or mothers and daughters from the age of 5. It is difficult to find a time, place and the secrecy to meet with a lover. Savanna women are virtuous. Adultery is a serious matter. At the turn of the century, it could result in the execution of the lovers.

Though adultery also induces lawsuits and fines in the Nzabi forest society, it is not considered a crime. I remember a sweet smoky twilight suddenly torn to pieces with howls and furious words. A wife had seen all her savings, a 5 Franc coin, pinched by the husband who had given it to his lover. The culprit was leisurely strolling towards the men's house and tossed a few words her way which raised merry laughter from the male party. 'Why are you so mean? My friend is a woman, just as you are. She is not a dog. She was good to me and deserved a gift.'

Who Decides? Who Profits? Who Shares?

Work and fertility are not difficult to measure. Demographers can list living children, note the age of the first and last pregnancies, chart divorces and ponder the influence of western religions. Ergonomists can count working hours, weigh hoes and farming knives, add up the time spent in carrying jugs of water with that devoted to knead cassava roots. But figures and charts will always miss the target of meaning, because they ignore the holistic social environment.

In Congo societies of the savanna or the forest, women spend more hours than men working. But what is work? Raising children, getting food for all, roots or meat, shelter, water, healing, ensuring the identity and perpetuation of the society (social reproduction in Marxist terminology), enforcing laws and modifying them to suit new needs, keeping genealogical charts and magical devices in good order? Is work mere toil? Certainly it becomes so when the worker, notably the female farmer, becomes isolated and has to assume responsibilities that were formerly shared or performed by others.

Work is a relative concept. Women work more than men and it appears that they work more than in previous times. According to G. Dupré, in 1967, Nzabi forest-dwelling women worked to give men enough free time to be able to control their work and their sexual life. This is a dark view corresponding to the situation existing at the time. Game was becoming rare, even in the forest. Trading activities were waning along with all crafts, iron smelting and weaving. No wonder women, who still had to provide the food, worked longer than men and resented men's idleness.

The savanna contrast is illuminating. Bembe women worked much harder in the fields. They had to resort to local fast foods. Their favourite dish was boiled sweet cassava. By comparison, the Nzabi stuck to bitter cassava loaves which required much longer preparation. The entire Bembe society, at the time of anthropological observation, seemed to run on the principle of profit. People were endeavouring to make profit in any possible way including: trading, raising pigs, hens or cows, growing oranges, bananas, cassava, maize, peanuts, potatoes, onions, switching to one staple or another according to rains, pests or prices.

Bembe women were proud of their ability to work hard. They were organized. When a low level of technology prevails, as was the case in these Congo societies, the only multiplicating power (bio-force) is social organization, namely the incentive to work and cooperative effort (Bonnafé 1987; 1988). Bembe women had both. The incentive to work has many roots. Relative autonomy, personal profit, control of the money earned, became increasingly important for all Congo women, but were not realities everywhere. Kukuya savanna women, for example, gradually lost their incentives to work between 1965 and 1986, as the local economy declined because of lack of markets for the main local crop, tobacco.

In the Nzabi and Teke forest societies, male leaders desperately clung to their past forms of authority. Bembe men, though individually rather tough on their wives, established rules that could enhance women's 'freedom'. Women had freedom to work harder than everywhere else, but also freedom to choose their places to farm, ability to obtain land from their mothers, permission to sell their own crops and sometimes to keep a small part of the money for themselves. Significantly, the first big traders were divorcees or widows. There was scope to create female networks for travelling, recruiting workers, and organizing healing groups. The social rules had always been careful to ensure spouses for young men. The bridewealth was low. Boys married early at 18, girls late at 16. When the bridewealth became inflated, as it did in most Congo societies, Bembe heads of families decided to cut the high amounts down to 10,000 F. The Nzabi, on the other hand, went on paying more and more, teetering to over 150,000F. Bachelors grew more numerous. The situation was still worse amongst the savanna Kukuya where men had to pay some 300,000F. They married late, at about 30 years of age.

Different observers living in the savanna-based Kukuya society some years apart published different results. In the mid-1960s, Guillot (1967) admired the female working parties, the tidiness of the fields, the fertilized mounds, general order, prosperity and social steadiness. Twenty years later Bonnafé came to the opposite conclusion. Female parties lacked leadership. Women lived too far away from their families and lacked autonomy in the choice of their fields. As wives, they were obliged to do a great amount of farming work for their husbands with little or no return. He saw men selling women's cash crops, beans, tobacco, potatoes without sharing the money. Women fed their families with maize and cassava and were always short of money for a little meat, oil for the lamp, and medicines for the children (Bonnafé 1987; and 1988). Some years later, a young agronomist even described the Kukuya close to famine (Duhem 1987). Bonnafé (1987) watched ritual ceremonies dedicated to the etiology of misfortune come to nothing. Their cognitive system, the dynamics of political hierarchy, traditions dealing with the relations and invisible powers, all were vanishing.

In Tsayi Teke forest country, I saw a young father driven to despair after the death of his child and the departure of his wife. Misfortune, here, was attributed to the head of the family who punished his attempt to support new political forces which were trying to revive the old society. The mother went away because she wanted to have children and to raise them. In all Teke parts, and in most Congo societies, except Bembe, young men had to give their salaries to elders, just to stay alive. The old laws were not amended. Formerly, in Teke societies, young people could not keep any material possession. They worked and were cared for, and eventually were offered a wife and bridewealth. They obeyed elders that were generous only when they were rich. Bridewealth was paid by their fathers and uncles to the bride's fathers and uncles. Surplus arising from young men's work was used to enforce their obedience. Welfare was meted out to obedient people, male and female alike. Teke societies experienced periods of prosperity, when food was abundant and leaders were magnificent in the eighteenth and nineteenth centuries. But female work has nowadays become a tedious, solitary and exhausting affair.

Anthropological Blindness or Statistical Domination?

Important items such as health care, fertility and agricultural work are targets for development. Because we consider them as separate fields of activity in the west, we transfer this perception of discrete phenomena to rural Africa, ignoring that they are interlocked and socially embedded in people's lives. Our global view is that of market laws extending over the world, of a generalized 'scientific' attitude towards demographic or health matters, of an optimal way of distributing work hours.

Male oppression is a mild joke when compared to statistical tyranny. 'Scientific' oversight starts at home, in the western world. General unfair trading conditions are promoted by virtuous economic 'laws'. Laws that have successfully rooted western development upon ignorance and rejection of domestic female economies and local knowledge systems. We are now faced, in most African countries, with social facts that we are not capable of taking into account. Development is tied to a market economy which puts the American midwestern machine-ploughed thousand-acre farm side-by-side with the African small plot hoed by a woman who walked to it carrying her baby and her tools.

The first step leading to modern development and a better standard of living for women in the west was the lessening of domestic chores. Hot and cold tap water, heating, easy washing, miles and miles of pipes, wires and sewers culminating in tons of sophisticated machines using fuzzy logic, industrial food processing and fast food, have alleviated the modern housewives' everyday lives. How much did male, overpaid, overfed and over-clean western agents promoting development in the Third World contribute to the betterment of material conditions of African rural women? Is the incessant observation that African women work extremely hard all day long congruent with the near absence of programmes devoted to the alteration of their down-to-earth, hard-working conditions?

Is the issue African women's domination by their men? It can be argued, but not by feminists, that the world economy does not give a man many chances to assert himself, apart from the possibility of living off women. Limiting the focus solely to women's domination leads to the subsequent foolish hope: let them get 'free' and things will be better. Many rural African women are already helplessly 'free'. They have become the only economic agent in what is still called a 'family' in statistical tabulations. The husband's economic contribution is missing; yet women's work goes on unnoticed by national statistics. The informal economy, as well as feminine agriculture, are not local phenomena doomed to recede as soon as development gets started. If we could accept them as antagonistic modes of production, rooted in an enduring and necessary opposition to the market-centred economy, we could then accept them as a perennial way of life. I am not arguing pessimistically, that domination is an inescapable condition, be it underdeveloped, female, informal, or local. Rather, I am trying to convey how assorted local and global laws, informal and market economies, long-term development goals and short-term material needs, male and female pleasures, men and women's work, all get woven together into rural women's daily lives in Sub-Saharan Africa.

We try to ignore embeddedness because it gets in the way of so-called rational planning for development. Embeddedness is a tangle of hierarchies, networks and relationships that even anthropology is sometimes reluctant to fully observe. Feminist theory has picked up one important contrast, the inequality between men and women. But taken alone this contrast can distort or hide many other oppositions. What we see are women working, getting food and water for their husbands and children. But observation and measurement of these activities does not reveal why Kukuya women work less than Bembe, but they are more tired. Nzabi work even less, but they resent their life more.

A holistic view accommodates embeddedness. It attempts to understand various levels of social organization, perceiving contrasts and oppositions as dynamic forces which belie the nature of a society and its place in the world economy, as well as providing a base for change – a change that is not directed at ensuring the domination of the world market, but rather pays attention to local facts as permanent forces to be used, or rescued, to bring about fair trading conditions and better living conditions. It offers a world where black and white statistics take on the colours and contours of everyday life and in so doing reveals lives worth living.

References

Bonnafé, P., *Nzo Lipfu, Le Lignage de la Mort. La Sorcellerie, Idéologie de la Lutte Sociale sur le Plateau Kukuya*, Nanterre, Recherches Oubanguiennes 5, 1978
—, *Histoire Sociale d'un Peuple Congolais, Livre I: La Terre et le Ciel*, Paris, ORSTOM, 1987

—, *Histoire Sociale d'un Peuple Congolais, Livre II: Posséder et Gouverner*, Paris, ORSTOM, 1988

Devisch, R., *Se Recréer Femme. Manipulation Sémantique d'une Situation d'Infécondité chez les Yaka du Zaïre*, Berlin, Dietrich Reimer Verlag, 1984

Duhem, C., 'Essai d'Interprétation d'une Disette : L'Evolution du Système de Production Agricole du Plateau Kukuya au Congo', Communication présentée à 'Dynamique des Systèmes Agraires', Paris-Grignon, INA, November 1987

Dupré, G., *Un Ordre et sa Destruction. Economie, Politique et Histoire chez les Nzabi de la République Populaire du Congo*, Paris, ORSTOM, 1982

—, *Les Naissances d'une Société. Espace et Historicité chez les Beembé du Congo*, ORSTOM, Paris, 1985

—, sous la direction de *Savoirs Paysans et Développement*, Paris, Karthala-ORSTOM, 1991

Dupré, MC., 'Comment être Femme. Un Aspect du Rituel Mukisi chez les Téké de la République du Congo', *Archives de Sciences Sociales des Religions*, vol. 46, no. 1, 1978, pp. 57–84

—, 'Histoire et Rituels; L'Observation du Siku en Pays Beembé (République Populaire du Congo)', *Cahiers ORSTOM, Sciences Humaines*, vol. XVIII, no. 2, 1981-82, pp. 179–94

—, 'Une Catastrophe Démographique au Moyen-Congo; La Guerre de l'Impôt chez les Téké Tsaayi, 1913-1920', *History in Africa*, Madison, vol.17, 1990, pp. 59–76

—, 'Les Structures Sociales sont-elles Nécessairement Inconscientes?', *Revue Canadienne des Études Africaines*, vol. 26, 1992, pp. 393–411

—, 'From Field to Kitchen: Women's Tools in the Forest of Central Africa', Paper presented at the 'Transformation, Technology and Gender in African Metallurgy' Workshop, Centre for Cross-Cultural Research on Women, University of Oxford, May 1993a

—, 'L'Outil Agricole des Essartages Forestiers. Les Couteaux de Culture au Gabon et au Congo', Association F. Gonseth, *Cahiers de l'Institut de la Methode*, no. 2, Biel, Switzerland, 1993b

Fetter, B. (ed.), *Demography from Scanty Evidence. Central Africa in the Colonial Era*, Boulder, Lyne Rienener Publishers, 1990

Guillot, B., 'Le Pays Bandzabi au Nord de Mayoko et les Déplacements Récents des Populations Provoqués par l'Axe', COMILOG, *Cahiers ORSTOM, Sciences Humaines*, vol. IV, nos. 3–4, 1967

—, 'Le Village de Passia, Essai sur le Système Agraire Nzabi', *Cahiers ORSTOM, Sciences Humaines*, vol.VII, no. 1, 1970, pp. 47–90

—, 'La Terre Enkou (Congo)', *Atlas des Structures Agraires au Sud du Sahara* 8, Paris La Haye, Mouton, 1973

9

What Women Can Do: AIDS Crisis Management in Uganda

Christine Obbo

Introduction

Although my main research focus has always been social change and gender relations or more generally development, it was not until I became involved in HIV/AIDS research that both my insider view as an African and my outsider view as an anthropologist were challenged. I have always worked with women who actively sought change in the status quo (Obbo 1982; 1990). Some succeeded, others did not, but it was understood that there was a price for confronting the social controls. My research on HIV/AIDS was a new experience. In this case, *all* women, not just the pacesetters, were confronting a *natural* catastrophe. Everyone had to react to life-threatening conditions imposed on them and manage the resulting crisis situation individually and collectively (Obbo 1992; and 1993).

In 1989, I worked with women who described themselves as having lived at the war front both physically and psychologically for two decades. I observed how they had reinvented many coping mechanisms to help themselves and their communities survive (Barnett, Blaikie and Obbo 1990). These were the women of Rakai district, Uganda. From the mid-1970s, Rakai was the locus of a lucrative, but dangerous smuggling trade, and served as the war path between Ugandan and Tanzanian troops in 1979. Since the mid-1980s, it has been one of the most devastated areas in Uganda in terms of HIV/AIDS infection rates. In 1990 alone, there were 15,000 clinical cases of AIDS reported in hospitals throughout Uganda, roughly 18 per cent of these were from Masaka hospital which services Rakai district.[1]

I was surprised by how these crises of political instability, war, a shrinking economy and the AIDS epidemic, brought into sharp focus

165

the unfinished business of 'Women and Development', that had been the centre of much debate and documentation during the previous two decades (Bryceson 1985; Monson and Kalb 1985). AIDS highlights the jeopardy that women face in connection with fertility, mothering and sexuality as normal members of their societies (Panos 1990; Berer 1993).

This paper discusses women's productive and reproductive roles within the context of the HIV/AIDS epidemic. Using 1989 case material from Rakai district, how women combine work and motherhood, and how they 'manage' their sexuality and fertility in the context of AIDS are examined. With particular attention to women as either suffering victims, care givers or bereaved, I consider the changes women have made to their work lives and the personal and community coping mechanisms which have been adopted in households afflicted by AIDS, i.e. with a sick person or dead member of the family. I then move on to review some attitudes of African women and western professionals regarding sexual practices in rural Africa generally, before drawing some conclusions about the impact of AIDS on rural women throughout Sub-Saharan Africa.

Women Farmers Caught in the Line of Fire

It needs to be emphasized that the civil and political unrest, war, and disruption to the national economy experienced in Uganda during the 1970s and 1980s, resulted in population movements as people sought safety alternatively in rural and urban areas. Many, out of desperation or speculative opportunity, engaged in the underground economy of smuggling and illegal trading. Women who were traders in commodities and women who provided services, such as cooked food or beer, often found that in addition to paying 'road tolls' or 'operating fees' in cash like men, they were also expected to pay with sex at the insistence of male 'gatekeepers' of the black-market. Soldiers, bandits and traders, often armed, not only goaded women into sex work near their areas of operation, but also used women to store their goods, and to provide sexual comfort on a non-commercial basis. The earliest cases of AIDS deaths occurred among traders and soldiers, soon followed by the deaths of their wives and girlfriends.

This fiery cauldron of political, economic, and gender conflict was inflicted on the rural economy of Rakai district, undermining normal daily life. Women in Rakai hitherto had been mainly occupied with hoe agricultural production. From the time they woke up to the time they went to bed, their lives were dominated by agrarian concerns. Mothers continually socialized their daughters not to be lazy farmers, while harbouring the ambition that their children would attend school and eventually obtain a non-agricultural job. This ambition entailed sacrifice on the part of mothers since they could not rely on their children's labour. Children were either sent to school, and helped significantly only on Saturdays, or they were fostered to homes of better-off relatives or friends who lived near 'good' schools, often situated in urban and peri-urban areas.

Prior to the upheavals, at least 25 per cent of farming households in Rakai were well-off and this affluence was experienced by women as well as men (Obbo and Southall 1990). Women of this economic group could reduce the amount of garden work they did and become supervisors of labour and managers of agricultural or dairy enterprises. This freed their husbands to be weekend farmers, pursuing careers as traders, teachers or even members of parliament. The women relied on the labour of poor relatives or foster children or, in other instances, on the hired labour of poor people. They had domestic help as well to assist with childcare, food processing and homestead keeping.

In poor households, unless children cried insistently, or were often ill, women did not regard mothering as a job. Childcare was an integral part of production and 'leisure time' (Obbo 1990). When women sat down to nurse, wash, massage and play a little with their children, while concurrently shelling beans and nuts (and pounding them), cleaning vegetables or grains or peeling bananas, cassava or potatoes, it was regarded by men and women as leisure time. Sunday was usually a 'free' day, when they wore their Sunday best, visited friends or engaged in hair dressing or basket and mat weaving. To have this day off, women doubled their efforts on Saturday, ensuring that the usual large Sunday meals did not tie them to the kitchen.

While the daily experiences of the rural women of Rakai differed according to economic circumstances, in matters of sexuality and reproduction the women shared many common features. The roles of wife and mother were viewed in much the same light, whatever the class standing of the woman.

The current AIDS epidemic has put a heavy load on women generally. At the time of my fieldwork, it was noticeable how thin many women were. Cultivating, caring for children and nursing a sick husband is strenuous. Many young people who contracted AIDS returned to their mothers for nursing. There is a common saying that the poorest peasant is one without a wife. Now there is a new saying that an AIDS patient without a sister or mother is doomed. This is in recognition of women's indispensable roles in production and nursing.

The AIDS epidemic occurred just as the IMF's structural adjustment and cost-recovery programmes were being implemented. The cost of caring for AIDS patients is being borne disproportionately by women. Nowadays, policies reinforce the assumptions and stereotypes of women as nurturers. The current vogue of community or family-based health care obscures the reality that women are becoming overburdened with providing these services. Women have coped by re-instituting traditional community networking mechanisms that had fallen into disuse during the affluent 1960s and early 1970s. In fact, many had been reduced to mere proverbs.

Reinventing Collective Action: *Munno Mukabbi*

The development of state kingdoms and later the colonial state reduced women's solidarity networking and made them so-called 'dependents' of their husbands. One area in which the loss of solidarity was manifested was in cooperative labour. For example, visitors to a household, staying over a period of time, occasionally helped with pressing chores such as weeding, planting and harvesting, but they were not obliged to do so and many did not. In areas with individualized systems of land tenure and cash crop production, people paid for labour. In areas with no privatized land, collective labour was no longer rewarded in kind by feasting with one's neighbours, except if one was very wealthy. Instead, participants in communal labour expected the host to pay them in cows or goats. There is, however, a gender distinction in the level of material reward. In 1992 in Nebbi district, seven men tilled a field for one hour and received a goat for their efforts. In the same home, women hoed a field with deep-rooted noxious weeds for several days and received half a kilo of salt. This reflects the differential control of resources between men and women.

Munno Mukabbi is an all-purpose coping mechanism revived to deal with extreme personal and community difficulties. It is no secret that women played a major role in its revival, as they had to deal with the financial expenses, increased agricultural labour demands and physical and psychological toll exerted on households affected by AIDS. Funerals are very expensive in Uganda for both rich and poor people. *Munno Mukabbi* fund-raising was reinvented in the 1970s because of the many deaths resulting from political unrest. Traditionally, contributions to funeral expenses were voluntary. The revival involved collection of a fixed fee from each household in the 'mourning community', which often consisted of two or more villages. The money is used to buy the funeral shroud, food for the mourners, a coffin, and sometimes gravediggers have to be paid. Initially, it was women who engaged in fund-raising because they had few sources of income, but men thought it was a good idea. Villagers raise funds, just like urban poor people, because they do not have jobs that give them the financial means for funeral expenses and, in cases of a family member dying in the town or some other distant place, transport assistance for body repatriation to villages is needed.

Funerals, in the age of AIDS, have been found to be diverting time away from production. Again, women led the way, insisting on one day of mourning instead of three. This caused a lot of debate in the communities and, in the end, women's common sense approach prevailed: 'We must respectfully put the dead to rest but we have a responsibility towards the living. Everyday is a funeral day. Funerals are stopping us from planting, weeding and harvesting. Surely we do not want to starve as well as die of AIDS.'

The time-saving argument, as well as the availability of funds to cover funeral expenses, led to two new practices. First, mourners abstained from agricultural work, i.e. hoeing, for only one day, the day of the funeral when they joined other community mourners. Second, whether expressed by the deceased while still alive or not, the second funeral to install the heir and divide up the inheritance began to follow immediately after the first funeral, instead of the traditional practice of waiting six months or a year. These were radical changes. People could no longer be ostracized as witches for breaking the three-day non-agricultural work taboo. Furthermore, people were too busy with the ubiquitous AIDS deaths and funerals to worry about saving money and convening second funerals.

Munno Mukabbi evolved from being just an impromptu community effort to assist the bereaved to one which helped with nursing the sick and lent support to widows and orphans. Women soon realized the physical and psychological duress of prolonged AIDS nursing and informally organized takeover days during which a group of two or three women, usually but not necessarily close friends or neighbours, helped the woman in an afflicted household to take a break and rest. The woman would either just sit and converse with neighbours who would listen and offer supportive stories of encouragement or comic relief, or she would go to the shops or market or even visit distant relatives and friends while her neighbours tended the AIDS patient. The relieved woman would return home to find that her house had been given a spring cleaning, the banana grove had been spruced up, food had been cooked and the children had received good supervision. The patients too seemed to benefit from this attention. This is one way AIDS-afflicted families were saved from the isolation that results when women are overwhelmed with work and nursing an illness that does not go away. The women who had offered the assistance said that they would like someone to be there for them should they be burdened with AIDS nursing.

Munno Mukabbi was also used as a coping mechanism when the economic responsibility for orphans exceeded the extended family's capabilities. As the AIDS death toll rose, it was quickly apparent that the women caretakers, often widows or elderly grandparents, had access to fewer resources and less income compared to men. Moreover, the prolonged nursing had usually drained the family's resources. Women with political connections solicited funds from banks and set up farms to help the women caretakers generate incomes to feed and school their children. Although these farms were centrally controlled by the owners of the farms, they were known as *Munno Makabbi*. It is necessary to note that women who wanted to help others, unless well-connected, had to grovel to please men who often denied them loans but granted loans to men with proposals for less pressing matters such as weed control or chicken raising schemes.

Remedial measures to address the problem of orphans revealed the strength of women's support networks. Grandmothers in their sixties or more were returning to long hours of hoeing so as to raise food for their grandchildren. Divorced women were fostering their ex-husband's orphaned children, and barren women, who had always fostered their brothers' and sisters' children, were taking on even more children. Still, their heroic efforts were not enough to solve the orphan problem. The sheer number of orphans exceeded the extended family's nurturing capacity. Under normal circumstances, brothers and married sisters of both parents were expected to act as guardians to orphans. Many orphans were initially cared for by relatives or unattached relatives who were persuaded to live in the natal home of the children. A critical stage was reached when a sufficient number of relatives or friends could not be found to look after the orphans. Children began to be left on their own to raise themselves. Some fared better than others by incorporating themselves in neighbourhood activities or begging.

Middle-aged widows and single independent women in the neighbourhood started providing the 'roving orphans' with lunches and ensuring that they returned home to sleep. Soon women on the government's local Resistance Council committees, organized along the lines of *Munno Mukabbi* to assist the women, in some cases assisted them to take the very young children into their own homes. This collective action later was officially constituted as a part of a national Uganda Women's Effort to Save Orphans (UWESO). The women involved explained their actions with an aphorism: 'AIDS has become every parent's uniform, none will escape wearing it.'

Women's Life-giving and Death-defying Actions

In this section, the risks connected with women's health are examined. Here, the concern is with women's actions in response to pain, illness and symptoms. Their attitudes with regard to reproductive health and sexually transmitted diseases are briefly outlined, as a way of explaining the context in which women have had to face the personal risk of contracting AIDS.

Pregnancy is taken as a normal state that is entailed in being a woman. Pregnancy shows that one is a complete woman who is sexually attractive and fertile. Because of the AIDS epidemic, conversation among young women often centres on whether they are pregnant. During my fieldwork in Rakai, there was a misconception that the women who are infected could not become pregnant. It was, therefore, difficult to persuade HIV-positive women to avoid getting pregnant. In the five village radius in which I was working in 1989, the appearance of the first AIDS baby born to a 'healthy' secretary at a local school caused a lot of rethinking. Both men and women claimed that they had no business having children who would suffer so much. There were declarations of abstinence from sex until a cure for HIV is found. Three months later, it was business as usual. Celibacy is a short-term option for men. Many women wish for extended celibacy, but others feel that the 40 per cent chance of a baby being born without HIV from a woman possibly harbouring HIV infection is a risk worth taking, given that they are never certain they are AIDS carriers until the symptoms begin.

Reproductive health has always been taken seriously by women. Pregnant women constantly drink and bathe in medicines that protect the baby's health and make delivery easier. Mothers worry when their daughters' first menstruation is delayed or when their menstruation intervals seem irregular. Herbs from home gardens or the wilderness, from street herbalists, or from divine herbalists are usually administered as juice. Women who have problems in conceiving or who suffer frequent miscarriages invest a lot of time and money to visit diviners, usually travelling a distance of five miles or more away from the village. In the area of my research, there was a diviner herbalist whose clients included rural as well as urban women, and Sunday seemed to be the day when she did most of her business.

Pregnant women continue to do normal agricultural work until the eleventh hour. I was frequently surprised to hear that a woman I had seen the day before picking coffee or pruning banana trees had delivered during the night. Women worked, but at a pace that preserved their energies. For example, they took opportunities to do 'restful' work that involved sitting down. And, since it is impossible to avoid heavy work completely, it is customary for women to either have a sister come and assist, or for them to go and stay with their mothers in the last weeks of pregnancy and some weeks after childbirth.

Childbirth is likened to death, and new mothers are visited and given presents to congratulate them for escaping the throes of death. Women are given special delicacies, such as liver, to help their recuperation. Women who give birth at their husband's homes, or are briefly hospitalized for the delivery usually go straight back to work. Often, after a short elapse of time, they have to be treated for anaemia at clinics or diviners because they have neglected getting sufficient rest or eating nutritious foods. I realized the wisdom of taking time away from the work place to recuperate. Under such circumstances, I have heard African women assert that hoeing 'breaks the back'.

When women eventually take to bed, they are usually very ill. Women postpone taking care of their pains by continuing work because they 'have to do it now or else the planting or weeding or harvesting will not be done'. Thus, women bear backaches, headaches and stomach pains, including vaginal pains, with fortitude. This stoicism was partly based on women's perception of themselves as responsible producers. Some women fussed a lot about their illness and pregnancy, but even they had to face the dilemma of showing the fruits of their labour at the end of the agricultural season or in the way they fed their families.

When a woman or her children become ill, medical treatment is sought immediately if the woman has money, if not, she sometimes waits almost to crisis point before telling her husband that their child needs medical care. She tries home remedies, putting off a visit to the clinic in the hope that she will not have to ask her husband for money for medical treatment and drugs. When all family members are ill, priority for immediate treatment is accorded to the children and the husband. Women practise self-treatment, underplaying the extent of their pains. When employed, men usually have access to treatment at their work place and can easily attend the clinic during working hours. Their wives rarely have access to these services either because they are not provided, or because the distances to be travelled with children are too far to walk, or the transport services are too costly. It is widely believed that, in better-off homes, women keep themselves and their children healthy because money makes medical services more readily accessible. Interestingly, when men are asked who in the family cares for the sick, the men claim that they do because they pay for the medicines. The opportunity costs of women's nursing services are totally discounted. It is merely something which 'women do'. This division of health care responsibilities has far-reaching implications for women's and children's health.

Specifically, in relation to sexually transmitted diseases (STD), women's postponement of treatment not infrequently leads to miscarriages or sterility. When a woman experiences a syphilitic rash, she consults a trusted friend or relative who might suggest a herbal treatment. Unlike a man, the woman does not rush to the hospital. I am not sure to what extent the women associate rashes with syphilis, but they know that it is something that they contract sexually from men. Again, gonorrhoea is treated with herbs to remedy the infection and to reduce the excessive vaginal discharge to normality. A woman may complain about a husband infecting her but never confront him with the issue or demand that he seek treatment. Men are driven to seek STD treatment because of great pain. Women cope with STD as just another one of 'women's burdens'. STDs have become an established co-factor in HIV transmission, with women who have latent ulcers and scars being the most vulnerable.

The fact that people do not tell each other when they have sexually transmitted diseases says a lot about the nature of sexual relations between men and women. It seems that the non-verbal negotiation of sex can be read loud and clear in some respects but in others leads to an ominous silence.

Attitudes towards AIDS and Sexuality in Africa

The AIDS epidemic caught social scientists unprepared to answer basic questions about sexuality. The World Health Organization's 'Knowledge, Attitudes, and Practice' (KAP) questionnaire, which was administered in Africa during the late 1980s to solicit information on sexual customs, hardly addressed the key issues in African sexuality. Some naively believed the findings could be used to predict which societies might adopt or resist condoms.

Ethnocentric tendencies were often revealed when dealing with the KAP question regarding the frequency of sex. One European doctor in Uganda was quoted by a fellow expatriate as having said in 1989: 'Two times a night will produce the equivalent of one teacup of semen, no wonder infection rates are what they are!' A British epidemiologist, now considered an expert on Africa, when asked what he meant by there being too much sex in Africa replied: 'I consider sex five times a month more than adequate.'[2] With such attitudes amongst medical professionals, it is hardly surprising that the western press latched on to the theme of negative exoticism, sensationalizing African women's sexual practices.

The HIV/AIDS control advocates missed constructive opportunities for designing strategies aimed at AIDS prevention that used prevailing beliefs and practices regarding sexuality. They failed to listen to what people had to say because HIV transmission was regarded primarily as a public health issue and a disease of loose sexual morals. Just to illustrate the need to understand the practitioners' perspectives on sexuality, I present below extracts from conversations I had in 1990 with women in five African countries. Altogether 200 women in small focussed discussion groups of 12–15 were involved. The questions that were discussed are followed by the women's answers in inverted commas:

- Why do some groups insist on two rounds of sex? Is not once enough?: 'Men are always in a hurry – so they get their satisfaction (orgasm), but women too need satisfaction. So one for him and one for her!'
- Why use herbs to dry out the vagina?: 'This tightens the muscles so the vagina and penis fit together and in case of men in a hurry, the woman still gets satisfaction. It is difficult for a woman to get satisfaction with a slosh vagina.' (According to a doctor who worked in Africa and the USA, some western women in the 1960s and 1970s were opting for Caesarean births to keep their vaginal muscles unstretched.)
- But some of the stones and herbs are coarse, don't you think that they increase the chances of a woman getting HIV?: 'We will have to use others.' 'There are herbs that just warm up the woman and make her ready.' 'One does not need all that, we just squat by the fire and smoke ourselves with incense – it is particularly pleasurable after sex!'

- What pleasure does a woman derive from having elongated labia minora? Isn't that purely for the satisfaction of men?: 'Perhaps, but they fill up the vagina and this increases the tug on other areas that give pleasure.' 'Women without this have a difficult time getting satisfaction.'
- Apart from the widespread fears expressed by various women that a condom might get lodged in their wombs and cause them to be operated on or die, what are the other reasons why women would object to condoms?: 'We will tell you. People like natural sex and condoms interfere!' 'I do not understand what you mean!' 'You know men want to deposit their semen in women, and women want to feel its warmth in them.'
- So what are women going to do about the conflict of these intrinsic beliefs and preferences and the danger posed by HIV infections?: 'We need a drug or something that we can control the use of ourselves for protection.'
- Would women wear a condom?: 'If it is to save life.'
- What about your feelings towards natural sex?: 'We women are not like maize caterpillars that do not listen to advice to get out before the maize is roasted or cooked. We want to survive.'
- But are women prepared to assert their rights, dictate and negotiate when to have sex with men, whether or not to have children, whether or not to marry?: '[Laughter]... These are hard times. It is better to have a husband then to have none.'

Men's Rights, Women's Duties

African women find themselves in a 'quadruple jeopardy' as they play their roles as sexual partners, as mothers, and as members of a family, and members of society. The rapid spread of HIV in heterosexual communities is largely due to women's powerlessness when it comes to demanding fidelity or refusing sexual interaction.

In Africa, motherhood is a must and infertility and being unmarried are despised. However, urban migration, education and independent sources of income have freed single or barren women from pity and possible witchcraft accusations within their communities. Homes of such women are always full of nephews, nieces and other foster children whose parents send them ostensibly to help their female relations, but really for the children to benefit from undivided economic support.

Women say that they lack control over their sexuality because those who assert their rights not to sleep with a husband infected with a STD can be divorced. Marital sex is a man's right and a woman's duty. This is often true in matrilineal societies as well where it is commonly believed that women have more relative social and economic autonomy (personal communication with Asante and Lunda women, 1990).

Pre-marriage counselling generally tells the African bride-to-be never to refuse sex with their husband except during menstruation. In some societies, pre-marriage counselling for men encourages them to ensure that women are sexually satisfied, i.e. not too much or too little sex. But they are not told that sex is an area that women might have a say in.

Although few polygamous men would ever claim that they acquire additional wives because they want more sex, it is often assumed that a woman who refuses sex with her husband is driving him to polygamy, be it of a formal nature, in terms of new wives, or informally by having mistresses and girlfriends. Dutiful women, often married to promiscuous men, are always at risk since a husband's STD or AIDS infection is only discovered when symptoms develop. African societies in general tolerate multiple sexual partners for men, but exert moral and social sanctions on women. Women's infidelities, sometimes by looks and touch rather than sex, or appearances of sexual autonomy are branded as prostitution.

It is quite common to find childless women, widows and divorced women, living by strict puritanical sexual codes. There are also independent women in the above categories who disregard public opinion on the exercise of sexual freedom. While sex workers do exist in African communities, particularly in towns, the AIDS literature tends to overemphasize the role of African women's promiscuity and its link to the general economic crises in African countries. Some women may have turned to prostitution, but the majority of African women continue to survive by growing food, processing it, feeding it to their families or selling it. On the other hand, the plight of women who have been faithful and dutiful in servicing their husband's sexual needs, and have found themselves infected with STDs and/or HIV are not mentioned in the literature to the same extent. Even less attention has been paid to the masses of women caretakers, quietly tending their sick and burying their dead.

Conclusion

In many parts of Africa, the AIDS epidemic has hit rural women in the midst of, or just recovering from, low intensity wars. To compound the situation, the HIV/AIDS epidemic has coincided with the implementation of structural adjustment programmes. Women and children bear the brunt of reductions in education and health cuts. Women are reluctant to upset their marriages because raising children and working the farm alone is very difficult. In other words, the labour of able-bodied men is indispensable in a period of material adversity. Nonetheless, the fact that HIV is transmitted in Africa primarily by heterosexual intercourse, and that young and middle-aged adults are a prime target, has brought about a generational and gender effect in AIDS crisis management. Widowed or elderly women have had to step up their roles as producers, providers and nurses.

The AIDS tragedy in rural Africa dramatizes the social contradictions embedded in women's equity concerns. Both the sexual demands and the role expectations placed on women have imposed a high disease risk and an onerous burden on them as caretakers, nursing the sick and fostering orphaned children. Their cherished life-giving role as mothers has taken on a new dimension, that of life-prolonging. They have no time for idle discussion about the gender division of labour, social rights or economic opportunities in their societies. Women are doing what they can; what they consider they must do under the prevailing circumstances.

Notes

1. Kampala, the capital city, accounted for 27 per cent of the total number of AIDS cases, but Kampala has a population density of 2423/ sq km, whereas Rakai has only 71 people per sq km.
2. Remarks during exchanges at the Conference on Anthropological Studies relevant to the Sexual Transmission of HIV organized by the International Union for the Scientific Study of Population, Sonderborg, Denmark, 19–22 November, 1990.

References

Barnett, T., P. Blaikie and C. Obbo, 'Community Coping Mechanisms in the Face of Exceptional Demographic Change', Overseas Development Administration of Great Britain, Contract No. R4491, 1990

Berer, M., 'The Epidemiology of HIV/AIDS in Women', in M. Berer (ed.), *Women and HIV/AIDS*, London, Pandora, 1993, pp. 38–57

Bryceson, D., 'Women's Proletarianisation and the Family Wage in Tanzania', in H. Afshar (ed.), *Women, Work and Ideology in the Third World*, London, Tavistock, 1985, pp. 128–52

Monson, J. and M. Kalb (eds), *Women as Food Producers in Developing Countries*, UCLA African Studies Center, African Studies Association, OEF International, 1985

Moock, J. (ed.), *Understanding Africa's Rural Households and Farming Systems*, Boulder, Westview Press, 1986

Obbo, C., *African Women: Their Struggle for Economic Independence*, London, Zed Press, 1982

—, 'The Role of Women in Development: Achievements, Constraints, and Prospects', Report of Third Government Consultation of World Conference on Agrarian Reform and Rural Development in Africa, Rome, FAO, WCARRD/GC/III/B, October 1989

—, 'East African Women, Work, and the Articulation of Dominance', in I. Tinker (ed.), *Persistent Inequalities*, New York, Oxford University Press, 1990

—, 'Kampala Health Needs, Demands and Resources', Save the Children Fund, Kampala, 1992

—, 'HIV Transmission: Men are the Solution', *Population and Environment: A Journal of Interdisciplinary Studies*, vol. 14, no. 3, January 1993

Obbo, C. and A.W. Southall, 'Social Dimensions of Structural Adjustment', Country Assessment Paper for Uganda commissioned by the World Bank, Washington, D.C., 1990

Panos Institute, *Triple Jeopardy: Women and AIDS*, London, 1990

IV

'DEVELOPING WOMEN': ROLE OF OUTSIDE AGENCIES IN ADDRESSING WOMEN'S NEEDS

10

Must Women Work Together? Development Agency Assumptions versus Changing Relations of Production in Southern Malawi Households*

Jean Davison

Introduction

International development agencies eager to enhance the development of rural women in Africa, have tried various means to improve the material quality of women's lives. Rural development and income-generating activities requiring women's cooperative production have been part of development agencies' tool kit over the last decade. In some places these efforts have taken hold, as in Kenya and Zimbabwe, but in other areas such as Malawi, they have been less than successful for a variety of reasons that include lack of sufficient profit from an activity for the number of women involved, mismanagement of funds and lack of leadership. However, equally important to the success or failure of an activity is the sensitivity of donor agencies to socio-cultural factors that shape local relations of production. This chapter singles out for discussion a key contributing factor in the failure of externally-inspired income-generating projects in southern Malawi – the assumption that women prefer cooperative production to individual production.

This chapter examines major changes in household productive relations that have intensified women's agricultural workload while undermining their economic autonomy in matrilineal, peasant communities in southern Malawi. The viability of donor-funded projects in Malawi that depend on cooperative production are considered in view of existing rural labour patterns.

The first section of this chapter considers 'cooperative' forms of labour and questions their universal applicability to rural Africa. The next section takes up key historical factors that have altered household productive relations in southern Malawi. The third section examines the preference given, historically and currently, to individual family production over collaborative production in agriculture. The conclusion outlines the implications of women's avoidance of cooperative work for donor agencies' efforts to encourage women's development.

Problems in Conceptualizing 'Cooperative' Labour

The assumption of a generic African production mode based on co-operative labour does not hold for much of central-southern Africa where matrilineal societies in various phases of change predominate. In such societies, a woman has direct control over land through her membership in a matrilineal descent group. In theory marriage is uxorilocal, the husband leaves his natal home and joins his wife in her village, although whether uxorilocality is practised depends on the husband's status and land availability. If more land is available in the husband's matrilineal village, a couple may choose to live in the husband's village rather than the wife's. When they live in the wife's village, the general rule is that they work the land she has inherited from her matrilineage, usually through her mother or grandmother. The husband also may be given a plot by the wife's matrilineage which the couple works together, only drawing on the labour of matrilineal relatives during the harvest season.

The tendency to gloss cooperative production for most of Africa without taking into consideration cultural and regional variations of the kind outlined above has implications for rural development projects, whether they are community self-help projects designed to provide services such as water and sanitation, or income-generating activities. Most often the implementation of such projects depends heavily on the collaborative labour of women. The assumption that rural production is based on collaborative labour stems partly from the weight of empirical evidence derived from patrilineal, virilocal societies that often, but not always, make use of collaborative work modes.

Collaborative production refers to a group of individuals who agree, either by invitation or by volunteering, with or without remuneration, to work together for a specific time period in order to accomplish a particular task. Collaborative production does not imply that the outcome of production will be shared, in any way, among the producers. The products may or may not be shared. The work groups, or work parties, found in many African societies fall into this last category, as do productive relations organized along kinship lines (Kaberry 1952; Hoben 1973).

Collaborative production is readily applied to the community or the household level of production. For example, the *ngwatio* among the Agikuyu of Kenya, involves women's rotation in hoeing and weeding one another's fields. The women, usually from the same age set, come from nearby, patrilineally related households, and collaborate in accomplishing a specific task within a time limit with the expectation that they will receive remuneration in the form of food and drink at the end of the day. There also is the expectation that the woman whose field is being worked makes a reciprocal labour contribution (Lambert 1956; Davison 1989).

Maale male cultivators of southeastern Ethiopia have a similar arrangement (Donham 1985). The Shona of Zimbabwe also have a form of collaborative labour, *majangano*, which draws on labour beyond the family unit (Holleman 1951). The *ilima* collaborative labour arrangement of the patrilineal Mponda in the Transkei demonstrates that not all collaborative labour is reciprocal, particularly in the short term (Kuchertz 1985). Consequently, periodic collaborative production among the Mponda is orchestrated by a male head of household or his wife to meet his own individual labour needs. The labour provided is contributed according to ties of friendship and kinship.

In northeastern Zambia, among the matrilineal, uxorilocal Bemba, a work party closer to that described for matrilineal groups in Malawi exists. The *ukutumya* is a work party arranged between single, often matrilineally related households, an arrangement that often obscures consumption patterns, which are more apt to be communal (Stromgaard 1985). Although a husband or wife may organize *ukutumya* for millet cultivation, it does not mean that they are expected to distribute a portion of the harvest to those who have contributed their labour, even though they may share a meal with them. Unlike the *ilima* of the Mponda, however, *ukutumya* is based on reciprocal kinship obligations.

Although similar types of work parties to those found among the Bemba were found historically in Malawi among the matrilineal Chewa in the central Region and among the matrilineal, uxorilocal Yao and Mang'anja of the southern Region, few such arrangements are found today (Phiri 1984). The next section outlines some of the changes that have occurred in household relations of production in the highlands and valley areas of southern Malawi which have contributed to the demise of collaborative labour in agricultural production and increased dependency on individualized household production.

Gender Relations of Production in the *Banja* Household

The way that gender is socially structured varies over time historically and through cultural space. No two societies structure gender relations in quite the same way, and even within national boundaries differences exist. For example, in some parts of Malawi, marriage patterns dictate that a husband moves to his wife's village upon marriage (*uxorilocality*) while in other areas a wife moves to her husband's village (*virilocality*). Theoretically, uxorilocal patterns of marriage are associated with matrilineal systems of descent and land inheritance where clan affiliation and land are inherited through the mother's lineage or *mbumba*. However, interchange with groups practising virilocality and the impact of westernization have affected such patterns over time so that in some locations, particularly in the central Region, a husband living in a group that historically has practised uxorilocal marriage may earn the right to bring his wife to his father's village by transferring bridewealth to her parents. Equally important, demographic changes identified with increasing land scarcity tend to modify customary practices dictating where a person resides upon marriage (Phiri 1983; Trivedy 1987).

Turning to household productive relations, gender as an analytical concept identifies ways that labour is organized for agricultural production and for other tasks that sustain and reproduce family labour. Historically, in pre-colonial southern Malawi, the basic production/ reproduction unit among the matrilineal Mang'anja, Yao and Lomwe was the *banja* household headed by the wife and her husband and included the wife's children and in some cases her elderly female relatives such as her mother (Mitchell 1952; Rangeley 1964; Pachai 1972; Schoffeleers 1980).

The matrilineal *banja* household centres on the woman who has primary rights in land through her *mbumba* lineage and who, together with her husband if he is present, shares responsibility for household decisions. Over time, the transforming of gender relations in the wider society, at all levels, has contributed to modifications in gender relations in the *banja* household. The next sub-section traces some of the linkages between macro- and micro-level changes.

Precedents Set in the Mid-Nineteenth Century

The mid-nineteen century, which marks the beginning of the British intrusion into the territory they called 'Nyasaland', acts as a historical benchmark for documenting major changes that have affected gender relations of production in southern Malawi. Early explorers' accounts and missionary records provide the data. In his study of the lower Tchiri (Shire) valley, Mandala (1990) describes how the intersection of three historical developments – the East African slave trade with its attendant slave raiding in which women, as well as men, were captured and sold to Portuguese landholders as agricultural labourers; the drought of 1862-63; and the influence of the militant, patrilineal Kololo – undermined both the socio-political power and the economic stability of Mang'anja women. Village leaders, who were just as likely to be headwomen as headmen, found the relative stability that they had earlier enjoyed eroded by slave raiding. Shadowing this traumatic upheaval in the mid-nineteenth century was an environmental crisis; a severe drought that made agricultural production in the villages negligible. That village leaders could not 'produce rain' further weakened their authority.

Travelling on the heels of the drought was the consolidation of Kololo elites, who had first accompanied Livingstone as guides on his exploration of the Shire river. They were able to take over the weakened Mang'anja villages, particularly in the northern part of the lower Shire valley. In the process, where the patrilineal Kololo found a village headwoman holding authority, she was dismissed and a sympathetic male head was found to take her place (Mandala 1990). As a result, by the time British missionaries gained a hold in the lower Shire valley in the 1880s, other forces within southern Africa already were in place that contributed to the erosion of women's authority and socio-economic power.

In the Shire Highlands, a similar erosion of Mang'anja women's socio-economic power to that which occurred under Kololo hegemony in the lower Shire valley was beginning in the 1870s. It was exacerbated by early missionary efforts. In Mang'anja society, the custom was for a man to marry into his wife's home village where they jointly cultivated land belonging to her lineage. Church of England missionaries, particularly Bishop John McKenzie, directly undermined Mang'anja land tenure and marriage customs by allocating mission land to Mang'anja men, rather than women, on their marriage. 'Despite all the Bishop's homilies about equality and fidelity in marriage', White (1987) observes, 'what he had done in the eyes of the Mang'anja was to lend support to the pattern already evolving (at the mission) by which the most important rights and powers were vested in men, to whom women became subordinate'. We do not learn what Mang'anja women's response was to this usurpation of their customary rights, except that when deprived of their control over land, they began to steal peas from the gardens of the local chiefs sympathetic to the missionaries (White 1987).

By the 1890s, in the Shire Highlands not only were the missionaries challenging Mang'anja gender relations of production, but British settlers, with an eye to cash crop production, had found a way to further destabilize gender relations. With a recipe for land alienation wrought by Sir Harry Johnston, the British began gobbling up land. The excuse for territorial conquest on the part of the British was to put to productive use land that had been ostensibly idle. The key crops were to be cotton and coffee. However, the linchpin to production was labour and labour was scarce.

The hut tax was proposed as a solution to the labour shortage because it would necessitate earning money to pay it. Although this device forced the Yao and Mang'anja to pay the British in cash, it did not provide the 'captured labour force' the planters had hoped for. The alternative was hiring migrant labour from the north, which provided only an illusory solution. Finally a partial answer came when immigrants escaping punitive labour codes in Portuguese Mozambique began to 'beg land' from Yao chiefs. Others settled farther north where they were allowed to become tenants on estate land in exchange for *thangata* labour (White 1987). The precedent set by such a labour arrangement had far-reaching implications for gender relations of production in the Shire Highlands.

In its original indigenous form, *thangata* amounted to communal labour provided to a village chief which was rewarded by large amounts of food and beer. However, under the estate system of production it was perverted into a dependency relationship that left male *thangata* labourers on the estates with less land, less pay and more work (Kandawire 1979). In the meantime, the women to whom they were married, accustomed to matrilineal, uxorilocal arrangements, carried on in the Yao and Lomwe villages without the benefit, for much of the year, of their adult male family members. The result was that women in these *banja* households were shouldered with the bulk of the agricultural workload.

By the end of the nineteenth century, then, the incursion of English and Scottish missionaries with their attendant patriarchal ideas about women and property, and the related commoditization of agriculture and labour through the advocacy of British settlers worked in tandem to significantly alter gender relations of production in the Shire Highlands.

Women's Production in the Early Twentieth Century

The capitalization of labour was not uniform in the early twentieth century. The situation in the lower Shire valley was less disruptive of gender relations in agricultural production. Peasants were able to inter-crop cotton, the cash crop best suited to the region, with food crops such as maize and millet. From the income generated from cotton sales they were able to raise cash to pay the insidious 'hut tax' underwriting the Nyasaland colonial administration. Thus, *thangata* as it was applied by British estate holders in the Shire Highlands never succeeded in the lower Shire valley as a means of capturing indigenous labour because the peasant producers of cotton had other means of paying the tax than exchanging their labour (Mandala 1990). In fact, evidence suggests that during the cotton era, women benefited equally with men as their role in production was ensured and they received a fair share of the proceeds, either in cash or in kind. As a result, they experienced relative economic autonomy (Schoffeleers 1984).

The husband/wife team met their new demands for labour with the introduction of cotton by intensifying their control over their children through *chikamwini* bride-service arrangements which controlled the labour of betrothed male youths, through the control of what their children grew in *chilere* youth gardens, and through *nomi* youth associations (Mandala 1990). The latter included both girls and boys, who after fulfilling their labour obligations in their parents' gardens, joined together to offer their labour to smallholder peasants. Consequently, gender relations of production in smallholder production of cotton were similar to what had existed previously at the household level. What was intensified was the use of youth labour on a cash or kind basis (Schoffeleers 1984).

In the larger patrilineal Sena households, *zunde*, which were often polygynous, cotton was usually not inter-cropped but cultivated separately and came under direct control of the husband, while wives continued to cultivate subsistence food crops. Consequently, in these households the association of cash crops with males and food crops with females, a phenomenon which led to the marginalization of women in the development process in much of Africa, was more prevalent than in the monogamous *banja* households (Boserup 1970).

Nonetheless, it was estimated that only 10 per cent of *banja* households in the lower Shire during the 1940s were polygynous, while 90 per cent remained monogamous (Duly 1964). A similar pattern was reported for the Lomwe where polygyny was permitted, but rarely practised (Roberts 1964). Farther north in Machinga district, a study of matrilineal, uxorilocal Yao households revealed an identical situation. Very few households, other than those of headmen, were polygynous and 'as a rule husband and wife cultivate(d) a garden together' (Mitchell 1952).

However, inter-ethnic marriages were on the rise throughout the southern region by the mid-twentieth century. Where people came from ethnic groups that practised the same matrilineal inheritance and uxorilocal marriage patterns, such as the Mang'anja, Yao and Lomwe, a pattern generally continued that stressed these features (Mitchell 1952; Hirschmann and Vaughan 1984; White 1987). On the other hand, in areas such as the lower Shire district, where the patrilineal, virilocal Sena lived alongside the matrilineal Mang'anja, two patterns emerged. Where Sena men married Mang'anja women, the marriage led to matri- or uxorilocal residence and no bridewealth was transferred. The children of the marriage belonged to the matrilineal *mbumba*. However, if a Mang'anja man married a Sena woman, he was required to transfer bridewealth and was allowed to take his bride to his village (Duly 1964). Thus inter-ethnic marriages were leading, in some cases, to new residence patterns, but decisions concerning production in the large majority of households continued to be made by the husband and wife together.

Duly, translating one of his male informant's observations of gender relations into English in the 1940s, states that: 'A man and his wife should agree on everything regarding the division of work and crops. The agreement binds the family together. If they fail to agree, the family will break up' (Duly 1964). Whether the informant actually used these gender-relational terms is debatable. Most likely, Duly provided an English male perspective in the choice of the phrase 'a man and his wife' to describe the relationship rather than 'a woman and her husband,' which says something about the way gender is written into history.

Impact of Male Labour Migration on Banja Households

The involvement of men in exchange-value labour beginning in the 1890s and accelerating in the twentieth century set a trend. Increasingly, men found themselves engaged in wage-labour migration, first to meet the demands of the colonial administration for tax payments and later as a means of raising cash to pay for commodities that formerly had been bartered. Another factor was growing land scarcity. Adult males became involved in wage-labour migration not only inside Nyasaland, but in southern Rhodesia, now Zimbabwe, and South Africa too.

Since the 1930s, southern Malawian households have become increasingly dependent on market exchange to meet basic consumption needs. The introduction by British traders of new items such as matches and paraffin, cooking oil and sugar, not to mention European clothing and other goods, created new demands. In order to produce a cash income, male labourers were forced to leave their households in search of wage employment.

A related factor that pushed men to emigrate was increasing land scarcity. As the population grew in the twentieth century and people were faced with less arable land on which to grow basic food crops such as maize, *banja* households were forced to purchase maize and other staple foods seasonally to supplement what they were able to produce. With less available land for cultivation, men began emigrating to secure wage labour.

The rise in male emigration, whether internal or external, placed an increased burden on *de facto* female heads of households, that is, those women whose husbands were (and currently are) absent for six or more months of the year and who were, for all practical purposes, managing their households alone. Although the lower Shire experienced the sharpest rise in male labour migration, nonetheless by the late 1950s, 20 to 25 per cent of Nyasaland's adult male population emigrated outside for wage employment (Kettlewell 1965). With the growth of the estate sector in Malawi between 1966 and 1977, men in the southern Region tended to shift away from smallholder production to take up wage jobs in the new national capital at Lilongwe or on tobacco estates, so that by 1977, 69 per cent of those working on their own holdings in the southern Region were women (Kydd and Christiansen 1982). This is a pattern that has persisted.

A study in the mid-1980s found that male emigration accounted for 60 per cent of female-headed households (FHHs) (Chipande 1987). In a later study of 210 households in the southern part of Zomba district, 35 per cent of households sampled were headed by women, of which 60 per cent were *de facto* FHHs where the husband had either migrated to South Africa to take up wage work or he was employed away from the village in Malawi and was absent over half the year (Peters and Herrera 1989). Chipande (1987) argues that 'fragile marriages', which Trivedy (1987) attributes to the matrilineal system of land inheritance and uxorilocal pattern of marriage, contribute to male emigration. The lack of security in land for out-marrying males, as well as increasing land scarcity, means that men are less willing to make a labour investment to *banja* production, preferring wage-labour as a more secure means of generating income and maintaining control over its distribution.

Hirschmann and Vaughan's (1984) study of 70 women farmers in Zomba district in the early 1980s revealed that 45 per cent of the women had no husband or their husband was absent for much of the year. Similarly, in my labour allocation survey of 120 female maize producers in Zomba district carried out during 1992, I found that 45 per cent of the women interviewed headed their own households, with 20 per cent of the 45 per cent being *de facto* FHHs.

Women's Preference for *Banja* Production in Zomba District

In cases where the husband lives with the woman and jointly manages the household, the woman usually depends on her own labour for tasks related to maize production from land preparation, planting and weeding, to storage and seed selection. Women prefer individual *banja* production even where they cannot count on a husband for labour.

Women's preference for *banja* agricultural production has historical roots. Although descriptions of pre-colonial productive relations are sketchy at best, it appears from the accounts of early explorers, that the only form of collaborative production among women related to food procurement was the collection of *nyika* (water lily) bulbs in the lower Shire (Mandala 1990).

Even with non-agricultural production of items such as salt, managed by women, there appears to have been little collaboration. Although the Mang'anja in the lower Shire went to collect salt at the same time of the year, the distillation process was an individual *banja* operation as '... there was nothing in the labor process itself that necessitated inter-household cooperation' (Mandala 1990).

This pattern was observed in the Lake Chirwa area and the central Region at Kasungu where women went to produce salt with the help of mature children rather than groups of women working collectively together (Phiri 1984).

In the 1940s, Mang'anja husbands and wives shared cultivation tasks with their children of both sexes and women stored the grain, a commodity over which they had complete control (Duly 1964). Yao women tended to work their gardens solely with their children (Mitchell 1952). Women in the southern Region, then, continued to produce their crops autonomously on a *banja* basis, with or without husbands, throughout the colonial period.

This preference for *banja* production on the part of women gained post-independence legitimacy when President Banda pointed out the centrality of individual family production in Malawi's rural areas during speeches given in March and September of 1975. 'In so far as I know Africa,' he observed, 'if they (Africans) have any economic system at all, it is not capitalism, it is not communism, it is not socialism, it is definitely not statism, but individualism. Here (in Malawi) a man and his wife want first to have a hut of their own, a garden of their own' (cited in Pryor 1990).

Not insignificantly, the tenacity with which southern Malawian women have clung to *banja* production, despite development agencies' efforts to involve them in collaborative agricultural production for income generation, may signal a last defence against the historical erosion of women's economic and political power in matrilineal societies. It also may signal their resistance to the ultimate annihilation of women's relative autonomy, in terms of being able to support themselves and their families, within the context of a national economy increasingly dependent upon monetized goods and services.

Studies of women farmers in Zomba district by Hirschmann and Vaughan (1983; 1984) in the early 1980s and by me a decade later, point to the reasons why women in southern Malawi prefer *banja* production to collaborative production with other women. The following sub-sections examine these reasons.

Labour Allocation in Smallholder Production in Zomba District

The majority of women farmers in Zomba district are smallholder producers of maize. Zomba district is the fifth most densely populated district in Malawi with currently just over 171 persons per square kilometre, up from the 121 persons per square kilometre when Hirschmann and Vaughan did their study (Malawi Government 1987; 1991). Of the total population, 90 per cent lives in the rural areas. During the inter-censal period (1977-87), the population in the rural areas grew by 17 per cent (Davison and Kanyuka 1990). Growing land scarcity and increasingly depleted soil conditions characterize the ecological constraints that face women farmers. On average, farmers in the region have less than a hectare of land on which to grow maize, as well as other crops such as groundnuts, beans, rice and vegetables grown for food and to sell in local markets.

Peasant farmers in Zomba with less than half a hectare grow primarily local maize for consumption and may sell seasonal surpluses. Hybrid maize is grown by farmers with sufficient land to plant both local and hybrid varieties and sufficient income to purchase the required fertilizer. In analysing women's preference for *banja* production, reference to the allocation of labour in maize production refers mainly to the cultivation of local maize but does not exclude hybrid maize for the few households that are able to grow it concurrently with local maize. Tools used for cultivation are short handled hoes and *ibanga* (machetes).

Residing in their maternal villages where they were married uxorilocally, the majority of women producing maize rely primarily on their own labour and that of their husbands and children. Hired labour provides a secondary source of labour, particularly in jointly-managed households. Women depend very little on collaborative labour, either within the matrilineage or outside of it.

For 35 per cent of the 70 women interviewed by Hirschmann and Vaughan (1984), the woman prepared the land for maize cultivation without assistance from others while in about 28 per cent of the cases, a woman worked with her husband. However, because the division of labour is not disaggregated by household type (jointly headed or female headed), it is difficult to know what percentage of the women preparing land themselves, without assistance, were from female-headed households. In my later interviews with 120 women farmers, over a quarter of them prepared the land themselves and 20 per cent prepared it with the assistance of their husbands. However, of the women who prepared the land themselves, without assistance, nearly three-quarters were women who headed their own households. Women's work in maize production, then, falls particularly heavily on female-headed households.

In jointly-headed households, tasks performed solely by husbands accounted for only 1 per cent in Hirschmann and Vaughan's study and 1.2 per cent in my study. For tasks performed jointly by wife and husband, the percentage was slightly higher for the earlier study (24 per cent) than for the later study (21 per cent). On average, a husband's aggregate labour in maize production appears not to be appreciably different in the two samples. What is different is the proportion of labour contributed by children. In Hirschmann and Vaughan's survey, only 15 per cent of the aggregate tasks in maize production were performed by children, whereas in the later study nearly 24 per cent of the tasks were performed by children. Although the samples are different, it may well be that the need for children's labour has increased over the decade. It is interesting to note that in the 1992 study, the smaller percentage of husbands helping their wives is offset by the increased use of child labour.

Only a small percentage of the women in Hirschmann and Vaughan's study were assisted by their sisters and/or by their mothers during harvesting. And only 2 to 3 per cent drew on sisters' labour for storage, seed selection and fertilizer application. Although sisters' assistance accounted for almost 5 per cent of total labour allocation for maize production in the 1992 study, female-headed households were more apt than jointly-headed households to draw on sisters' labour in all tasks except harvesting. For this one task, the number of jointly-headed households drawing on sisters' labour was nearly twice that of the FHHs. Thus for all tasks in maize production except harvesting, the women producers in this study depended only minimally upon the collaborative labour of other women.

In the process of carrying out a time allocation study in two Yao villages north of Zomba in 1991, Kaufulu (1992) found that only occasionally do sisters work together, usually during the peak weeding season, and during harvesting. Most often women work alone with their children or hire labour, usually young men, from outside their village. A woman in her fifties gave as a reason for the increased use of hired labour, the availability of cash income, arguing that women prefer to pay for labour rather than depending on matrilineal relatives, who in turn might make demands on their labour. The female chief of one village remembered that families used to assist one another during the harvest season in exchange for locally brewed beer. But now this custom has disappeared.

Interviews with two women in their seventies confirmed that women had rarely worked with female relatives and that they depended most on the labour of their husbands in the past and now on their children. In informal observations of women working in their fields over a two-year period, I found only three instances where women were working collaboratively with other women in their gardens.

Tensions between sisters and other female relatives in a matrilineage may stem from competition over land. Peters (1992 personal communication) in a follow-up study to her 1987 survey in Zomba district, relates that with increasing land scarcity in the district, she found that relations between sisters in one village who control adjacent plots of land are strained. The source of the tension is over who will inherit which piece of land from the grandmother. As land fertility dwindles due to soil depletion and insufficient moisture, competition for control of the most fertile portions of a finite communal parcel becomes an issue.

The daughter of a woman farmer in a Yao village related that her older married sisters had been given most of her mother's land. Her father had been forced to go to the chief of a neighbouring village to ask for a parcel of land close to her mother's for the two younger, unmarried daughters. As less land is available, younger women may be forced to migrate elsewhere or seek employment in towns.

Women's Labour and the Matrilineal Question

Ready access to land and family labour have in the past given women producers in southern Malawi a sense of relative autonomy. Yet increasingly, these women find that they are without the labour of their husbands and even their children's labour becomes a precarious source once they begin to participate in formal schooling. Hired labour on a seasonal or temporary basis, as suggested by the women in Kaufulu's (1992) study, becomes the alternative.

In Hirschmann and Vaughan's study, women farmers depended upon hired labour for only 10 per cent of the aggregate labour needed for maize production, whereas in my study the percentage was 13 per cent. It is difficult to reach any conclusions about the use of hired labour over the decade because the samples differ, even though they were taken in similar rural villages. Nonetheless, the use of hired labour is noteworthy.

Why are women turning to hired labour? Partly it is because they do not want to place themselves in the position of depending upon matrilineal 'sisters', as was suggested earlier. And partly it may be the effect of crop commoditization and the need to produce cash income. One woman interviewed by Kaufulu (1992) attributed the preference for hired labour to the competitive spirit that exists among women who now produce crops for cash as well as for subsistence. The women do not want to contribute to one another's profit. They prefer to maximize their own profit (Kaufulu 1992).

It is important to stress that the largest proportion of tasks in maize production is carried out by women themselves. What little leisure time these women have in a 16-hour day that begins at 4.30 a.m. and ends at 8.30 p.m., they want to preserve for themselves. They are disinclined to engage in activities that require an additional labour contribution over which they have limited control of the output. Nor do they have a cultural tradition that encourages collaborative production among women except in certain instances such as harvesting. A certain ambiguity exists between the preference in matrilineal societies for production which tends to be by a conjugal household, as it is in southern Malawi, and distribution processes involving social relations that are often, but not always, cooperative and communal (Stromgaard 1985). Women's preference for *banja* production does not preclude their collaboration in distribution, particularly where food for direct consumption rather than sale is concerned. There is ample evidence of women drawing on their matrilineal relatives during times of food shortage as I observed during the recent 1992 drought and as Vaughan (1987) documented. Nonetheless, in terms of food production, as distinct from distribution and consumption, women prefer *banja* production.

Implications for Rural Women's Development

Where women in matrilineal villages have access to sufficient household labour, they are less disposed to become involved in gender-specific collaborative forms of production. This particularly applies to women whose family's economic subsistence largely depends upon their food production. Family labour, namely children and to a lesser degree, husbands, are the mainstay of a woman's productive capacity.

In the matrilineal context, at least for those women with enough land to be self-supporting, individual production allows a woman to maintain a sense of autonomy. Because a woman usually has direct access to and control over land through her matrilineage she feels a particular responsibility to use it wisely and to protect it for future generations. Her first priority, then, is to optimize production for her family's benefit. The tenacity with which women in these matrilineal, largely uxorilocal communities cling to individual *banja* family production rather than participating in gender-specific cooperative forms of production derives from historical antecedents and current priorities concerned with the need to optimize production at the household level.

The fact that women in some African societies have a preference for individual family production over collaborative forms of production has not been adequately taken into consideration by development agencies anxious to advance the cause of rural women's development. In most African societies that are patrilineal and virilocal, women who out-marry often find it necessary to form alliances with other women in a community to maximize their productive capacity on land which they control only indirectly through their husbands.

Women in matrilineal societies tend to have more relative control over land and labour, which gives them a comparative advantage over their sisters in patrilineal societies. It also means that because they are relatively independent they think twice before participating in collaborative forms of production with other women in their village with whom they may have conflicting claims to land or whose commodity crops may compete with theirs in the local market.

In a large Ministry of Agriculture survey of over 1000 smallholder households, which included both jointly-headed and female-headed households, Culler et al. (1990) found that 59 per cent had at some time been involved in an income-generating activity project, but only 25 per cent were involved in 1990. Of the projects, 62 per cent were for crop production. When asked which type they most preferred – individual, family or group income-generating activities – 50 per cent of women in the FHHs preferred individually operated types, 44 per cent of the jointly-headed households preferred those which were family operated and only a small minority in either category preferred the group variety. These results confirm that group 'cooperative' labour has a low priority for smallholder women producers even when income is being generated.

Beginning a decade ago, the Malawian government with donor assistance initiated a host of income-generating activities for rural women, from restaurants and bakeries to fish processing operations. Very few of these projects have succeeded. Although failure can be attributed to many factors, certainly a key reason for women's lack of commitment has been that the projects have emphasized cooperative production in a social context that does not encourage cooperative group production. Only in the less populated, patrilineal north have a few of these projects succeeded. In other cases, the women end up disbanding after a year, often citing mistrust of the leaders managing the cooperative as the reason. In truth, this may be only a partial reason, the real underlying reason appears to be that women are not interested in cooperative production because they prefer individualized production over which they can maintain direct control, including control of the profits.

In summary, why do Malawian women, in many cases, shy away from group projects? Firstly, in cases where women are largely responsible for household production and where they have matrilineal ties to land, they are apt to be less inclined to participate in collaborative income-generating activities that take them away from their land, and which may earn income over which they have little control. Secondly, because their first priority is to family production and most of their time is allocated to this effort, they are likely to have less time to devote to women's projects, particularly if they are women with young children. Since women have a 16-hour day, out of which only two hours in the afternoon are not spent working, a project which robs them of their leisure time is not likely to be greeted with enthusiasm unless it also includes a component that reduces women's overall workload through labour-saving devices. Finally, in view of the historical emphasis on individual *banja* production and the increased cultivation of crops that will generate income, it appears that these women prefer working individually with their families, maximizing their own production and profits.

If development agencies are concerned with advancing women's development in the impoverished rural areas of southern Malawi, they must take into consideration the socio-cultural factors that shape relations of production between women and men, and between women themselves. One way of assessing these factors is to follow a participatory model that includes women at the local level in the development of a project that best suits their needs using strategies that are culturally appropriate to the specific community. By involving women in planning their own development projects, be they individual or cooperative, the projects have a better chance of sustainability.

In conclusion, this case study of women in Malawian matrilineal societies raises questions about the assumptions that development policy planners make about women and gender relations of production in Africa. Donor-funded projects designed to enhance the quality of rural women's lives must be tailored to the social contexts in which they are situated. Just as recipes intended for one elevation may not work at another elevation, a project designed for one group of women may not work with another group.

Notes

* This is an expanded version of articles that were published in the *Journal of Contemporary African Studies*, vol. 11, no. 1, 1992 and the *Journal of Southern African Studies*, vol. 19, no. 3, 1993.

References

Boserup, E., *Woman's Role in Economic Development*, New York, St. Martin's Press, 1970

Chipande, G., 'Innovation Adoption Among Female-headed Households: The Case of Malawi', *Development and Change*, vol. 18, 1987

Culler, C., H. Patterson and I.C. Matenje, *A Survey of Women in Agriculture in Malawi*, Ministry of Agriculture, Lilongwe, 1990

Davison, J., 'Women's Agricultural Production and Land: The Context', in J. Davison (ed.), *Agriculture, Women and Land: The African Experience*, Boulder, Westview Press, 1988

——, *Voices From Mutira: Lives of Rural Gikuyu Women*, Boulder and London, Lynn Rienner Publishers, 1989

Davison, J. and M. Kanyuka, *An Ethnographic Study of Factors Affecting Girls' Participation in Education in Southern Malawi*, Lilongwe, USAID/Malawi Ministry of Education, 1990

Donham, D.L., *Work and Power in Maale, Ethiopia*, Ann Arbor, UMI Research Press, 1985

Duly, A.R.W., 'The Lower Shire District, Notes on Land Tenure and Individual Rights', *The Nyasaland Journal*, vol. 2, 1964

Hirschmann, D. and M. Vaughan, 'Food Production and Income Generation in a Matrilineal Society: Rural Women in Zomba, Malawi', *Journal of Southern African Studies*, vol. 10, no. 1, 1983

——, *Women Farmers of Malawi: Food Production in Zomba District*, Berkeley, University of California Press, 1984

Hoben, A., *Land Tenure among the Amhara of Ethiopia*, Chicago, Chicago University Press, 1973

Holleman, J.K., 'Some Shona Tribes of Southern Rhodesia', in E. Colson and M. Gluckman (eds), *Seven Tribes of British Central Africa*, Manchester, Manchester University Press, 1951

Kaberry, P., *Women of the Grassfields*, London, HMSO, Colonial Research Publication No. 14, 1952

Kandawire, J.A.K., *Thangata: Forced Labour or Reciprocal Assistance?*, Blantyre, The Hetherwick Press, 1979

Kaufulu, F., *A Comparison of Women's Use-Value and Exchange-Value Time in Three Communities in Zomba District*, unpublished M.A. thesis, Zomba, 1992

Kettlewell, R.W., *Agricultural Change in Nyasaland: 1945–1965*, Stanford, Food Research Institute, 1965

Kuchertz, H., 'Organizing Labour Forces in Mpondoland: A New Perspective on Work-Parties', *Africa*, vol. 55, no. 1, 1985

Kydd, J. and R. Christiansen, 'Structural Change in Malawi since Independence: Consequences of a Development Strategy Based on Large-Scale Agriculture', *World Development*, vol. 10, no. 5, 1982

Lambert, H.E., *Kikuyu Social and Political Institutions*, London, Oxford University Press, 1956

Mandala, E.C., *Work and Control in a Peasant Economy*, Madison, University of Wisconsin Press, 1990

Mitchell, J.C., 'Preliminary Notes on Land Tenure and Agriculture among the Machinga Yao', *The Nyasaland Journal*, vol. 5, no. 2, 1952

Pachai, B., *The Early History of Malawi*, London, Longman, 1972

Peters, P. and G. Herrera, *Cash Cropping, Food Scarcity and Nutrition*, Cambridge (Ma.), Harvard Institute of International Development, 1989

Phiri, K.M., 'Some Changes in the Matrilineal Family System among the Chewa of Malawi since the Nineteenth Century', *Journal of African History*, vol. 24, 1983

—, 'Production and Exchange in Pre-Colonial Malawi', in *Malawi: An Alternative Pattern of Development*, University of Edinburgh, Centre of African Studies, 1984

Pryor, F.L., *The Political Economy of Poverty, Equity and Growth*, Oxford, Oxford University Press, 1990

Rangeley, W.H.J., 'The Ayao', *The Nyasaland Journal*, vol. 16, no. 1, 1964

Roberts, S., 'A Comparison of the Family Law and Custom of Two Matrilineal Systems in Nyasaland', *The Nyasaland Journal*, vol. 17, 1964

Schoffeleers, M., *The Lower Shire Valley of Malawi: Its Ecology, Population Distribution, Ethnic Divisions, and Systems of Marriage*, Limbe, Montford Press, 1968

—, 'Trade, Warfare and Social Inequality: The Case of the Lower Shire Valley of Malawi, 1590–1620 A.D.', *The Society of Malawi Journal*, vol. 33, no. 2, 1980

—, 'Economic Change and Religious Polarization in an African Rural District', in *Malawi: An Alternative Pattern of Development*, University of Edinburgh, Centre of African Studies, 1984

Stromgaard, P., 'A Subsistence Society under Pressure: The Bemba of Northern Zambia', *Africa*, vol. 55, 1985

Trivedy, R., *Investigating Poverty: Action Research in Southern Malawi*, Blantyre, Oxfam, UK, 1987

Vaughan, M., *Story of an African Famine*, Cambridge, Cambridge University Press, 1987

White, L., *Magomero: Portrait of an African Village*, Cambridge, Cambridge University Press, 1987

11

Wishful Thinking: Theory and Practice of Western Donor Efforts to Raise Women's Status in Rural Africa*

Deborah Fahy Bryceson

Introduction

In the space of two and a half decades, documentation on African rural women's work lives has moved from a state of dearth to plethora. Awareness of women's arduous workday and the importance of women agriculturalists to national economies are now commonplace amongst African policy-makers and western donor agencies. Throughout the dramatic upheaval in African development policy of recent years, as state and market forces realign, donor agencies have consistently espoused a concern to improve the material conditions and status of rural women at the household level. Nonetheless, economic and social forces intensifying rural women's working day throughout Sub-Saharan Africa overwhelm donors' scattered projects directed at alleviating women's workload. This paper considers shortcomings of western donor agency intervention and recommends alternative measures for easing rural women's workload. Western attitudes to African women's working day are schematically reviewed before examining existing types of interventions and suggesting other possible forms of donor action. The central question posed is how external donor agencies can extend beyond localized project efforts to help provide the material foundation for widespread change in women's working day of a self-determining nature. A 'homestead economics' approach is suggested as a catalyst for change.

Western Perceptions of African Rural Women's Work

Ester Boserup's (1970) work entitled *Women's Role in Economic Development* was a watershed in western perceptions of African rural women's work. Sifting research findings world-wide, she related patterns of the sexual division of labour and population density to different agricultural modes of production. Her argument confirmed what most colonial administrators had taken for granted: female labour is the linchpin to African hoe agriculture. This knowledge, however, had new implications.

In rural areas, government taxation had moved from simple poll and hut tax collection to exactions on agricultural production. Post-colonial governments and donor agencies had embarked on ambitious programmes to *'develop'* agriculture, *'modernizing'* it and raising its productivity. Hoe production was considered inefficient. Boserup's title summed it all up. Women had a role to play in economic development. As Sub-Saharan Africa's mainstay producers, they were a valuable productive asset.

Boserup's book also attracted western feminists but for different reasons. More than anywhere else, African women cultivators approached the feminist ideal of autonomous female producers. So began the tireless enterprise of feminist researchers, documenting the gender division of labour in rural societies throughout the continent. Highlighting female labour contributions in detailed labour allocation studies, these researchers have generated a veritable mountain of ethnographic data.

In general, the research findings (for example, Hafkin and Bay (eds) 1976; Bay (ed.) 1982; Robertson and Berger (eds) 1986; Stichter and Parpart (eds) 1988; and Davison (ed.) 1988) suggest that whatever autonomy African women have is conditioned by their ascribed role and relationship to others in the community. Studies repeatedly document the corrosive force of the market and the state on rural communities and women's place in those communities (Bukh 1979; Afonja 1986; Sender and Smith 1990). Given men's headstart in dealings with the state and as participants in labour and commodity markets, women's access to productive resources mediated by the state and market are systematically disadvantaged. Women's commitment to food crop production for household consumption becomes a liability, while men are free to capitalize on cash crop production opportunities. State provisioning of improved inputs and agricultural extension is beamed at men who produce the taxable crops, as opposed to the subsistence crops. Female heads of households without male spouses are usually doubly disadvantaged (Bukh 1979; Kossoudji and Mueller 1983). They frequently lack even indirect access to *modernized* agriculture and its associated cash income. Alongside these tendencies, women's labour day has intensified in response to population pressure and, in some cases, environmental degradation. Fallow periods are reduced leading to the need for fertility-enhancing measures which, in the case of women, tend to be labour rather than capital-intensive (Airey and Barwell 1991). As population pressure builds up, distances to firewood and water sources as well as agricultural fields increase, necessitating long daily journeys for women laden with heavy loads (Bryceson and Howe 1993).

Western donor agencies' response to recent research findings has been conditioned by uncertainty. The existing literature on rural women in Sub-Saharan Africa is primarily in the form of field studies by social scientists, especially anthropologists. Despite the clear finding that gender inequities permeate African agrarian societies, the sheer weight of case study detail has been an obstacle preventing the collation and generalization of findings at national and regional levels, which would facilitate relevant policy formulation for rural women. Furthermore, external agencies have an ambiguous role vis-à-vis the African rural population. Donor agencies are there to '*develop*' rather than to '*civilize*' the resident population. The colonial *civilizing* mission was bent on direct cultural transfer. In stark contrast, western donor agencies currently espouse a willingness to accept local customs and mores.

However, donor agencies' handling of women's development issues is an obvious example of the impossibility of external funding agencies' cultural neutrality. Because the role of women has been so hotly contested in their own societies, external agencies are under pressure to promote a normative notion of what activities women in recipient countries should be pursuing to gain gender equality. This has led to an entrenched pattern of western donor initiatives directed at rural women.

Redundancy of Housewives

Barbara Rogers' (1980) book *The Domestication of Women*, published ten years after Boserup's contribution, built on the work of Boserup and feminist scholars, formulating a cogent argument which challenged donor agencies' and development planners' assumptions about rural women's 'natural place' in non-industrialized countries. Tracing western misconceptions back to the colonial period, Rogers charged that Third World women, traditionally used to being productive agents in their own right, had, through external intervention, been relegated to the domestic sphere, encouraged to conform to western middle-class notions of a housewife's familial role. She went on to suggest that the decline of staple food production experienced in many countries could be related to donors' failure to provide incentives to women producers.

Rogers' book signalled a turning point. Western donor agencies were establishing much more serious and better funded women's programmes. Some donor agencies, notably USAID, had taken an early lead in requiring all their project proposals to include a consideration of the project's impact on women, whatever the nature of the project (Tinker 1990). During the 1980s, emphasis was on rural women's capabilities as autonomous producers. Efforts to 'domesticate' women through a home economics approach were repudiated. Instead, women were to 'go public' seeking economic activities outside of the home.

Projecting the Right Role

Reaching rural women directly was a major concern of donor agencies. Field study evidence suggested that rural women were increasingly encircled by male-dominated markets and the state. Male bias in national and regional policy formulation led donor agencies to distrust the male bureaucracy with the implementation of women's programmes. Grassroots projects were the obvious way of circumventing this constraint and coincided with western feminist preferences for non-hierarchical structures. Projects tended to be vested in local non-governmental organizations and based on the principle that after initial training by an external agent, the women participants would take control. Women-only projects were the norm, justified in terms of the desire to avoid male interference in decision-making and disagreements between women and men over the project's resource allocation. This formula for women's projects evolved quite naturally.[1] Controversy, however, raged in donor quarters and amongst feminist academics about the projects' ultimate objectives, i. e. whether they were essentially offering economic improvement or political empowerment. It was over this issue that the orientation of donor agency women's programmes divided.

Moser (1989) traces the changing aims of western donors. The family welfare approach was an orientation drawing from the colonial model which viewed women primarily as mothers through which child welfare could be addressed. In the 1970s this approach came under heavy attack and was increasingly supplanted by the 'Women in Development' (WID) approach. WID's original goal was to gain equity for women vis-à-vis men. It forked into: 1) 'Women and Development' (WAD) which toned down gender considerations and focussed on class by taking an anti-poverty stance; and 2) the WID mainstream with its emphasis on efficiency, specifically the need to increase women's work productivity. Disillusionment with the shortcomings of these approaches gave rise to 'Gender and Development' (GAD) which stresses the empowerment of women as a way of achieving equity with men. Rathgeber (1990) identifies WID with modernization theory, WAD with underdevelopment theory and GAD with socialist feminism, arguing that GAD offers a more holistic approach to women and their social relations to men, taking account of women's reproductive activities as well as their productive work *both inside and outside the household.*

While the aims and philosophical underpinnings of women's projects have steadily evolved, the actual form of donor support and external intervention has not evidenced as much change. There are three main types of donor projects, namely: 1) income-generating projects; 2) the introduction of labour-saving technology; and 3) efforts to improve women's local resource access.

Income-generating projects have dominated. The belief that women can begin to gain equality with men by earning cash 'outside the household' has been implicit or explicit in most approaches and project designs. Projects directed at introducing labour-saving technology have arisen largely out of the realization that women often do not have time for income-generating activities in addition to their normal workload. Efforts to improve women's local resource access, another and the newest form of women's projects, are also hinged to a growing appreciation of the range of constraints on women's productive labour. The following sub-section reviews the practical shortcomings of each of these three types of donor projects in turn.

Off-target Projects

Due to their prevalence, income-generating projects have received substantial critical scrutiny (Buvinic 1986; Bruce and Dwyer (eds) 1988). Women's heavy workday is the main obstacle to the successful adoption of income-generating projects in rural areas.[2] Women with the spare time to participate in such projects tend to be older or wealthier women who, it could be argued, are the least needy of cash amongst the female population (Bryceson and Kirimbai 1980). The limited time and erratic participation of younger women, i.e. mothers with heavy childcare and household provisioning responsibilities, usually yields insufficient individual benefits to warrant their project involvement.

Income-generating projects tend to offer a relatively restricted horizon for participants. Normally traditional female skills, such as sewing and cooking, are called upon rather than developing less gender-defined skills. Projects are commonly launched before sufficient market research has been undertaken. In extremely competitive or non-existent market situations, women participants have difficulty selling their labour-intensive products. In other cases, disillusionment is related to participants' dissatisfaction with their project leaders' financial management. Often leaders fail to appreciate the importance of timely distribution of project proceeds to motivate participants (Bryceson 1990). If and when participants get reasonable earnings from a project, there is no certainty that women's increased income will change gender relations in the household. Detailed case study evidence provides no proof of a positive correlation between female earnings and a more balanced sexual division of labour within the household (McCormack et al. 1986; Turrittin 1988).

As regards the second project type, the introduction and spread of labour-saving devices has made a deep impact on women in many areas (ILO/Norway 1984). Most notable is the introduction of grinding mills. Women are recorded willing to headload their maize several kilometres to and from mills in order to avoid having to pound it by hand with the traditional mortar and pestle. Mbilinyi quotes one rural Tanzanian woman saying: 'Pounding? That's colonization. I'd rather go without some of my food to pay for the milling' (Mbilinyi 1987). Hand mills that women could use in their homes scored a big success already in the 1950s in the Cameroons (O'Kelly 1978). The provision of village water supplies is also a large step forward, saving women from walking long distances carrying extremely heavy loads (Curtis 1986).

McCall (1987) observes that most of the labour-saving devices and schemes so far introduced have concentrated on macro-scale technology delivery rather than introducing technology into the home. He speculates that state and donor agencies may prefer this scale due to ease of installation, maintenance and ultimate control. In the already cited example of hand mills which were utilized in the home, Chilver (1992) notes that they were eventually displaced by large mechanized mills that were considered to be more modern. Cooking stoves, which are disseminated to households, are exceptional in this regard. Nonetheless, their main target user has been urban rather than rural women, due to fuel crisis concerns in towns (Cecelski 1987).

While women, as firewood and water collectors, take responsibility for most of household load carrying, nonetheless men are far more likely to gain access to intermediate forms of transport capable of reducing human effort in travel and load carrying (Bryceson and Howe 1993). In a village setting, ownership of scarce intermediate transport technology like bicycles symbolize status and are usually monopolized by men. In some cases, productive utilization of bicycles by men or their female relations is foregone, since such usage would jeopardize the working order or appearance of the cycle from the perspective of the prestige-conscious male owner. Most often, however, ownership is a business proposition. Load carrying and passenger transport are services that are sold rather than put at the disposal of household subsistence provisioning. Men's easier acquisition of intermediate transport technology is primarily related to their greater purchasing power. 'Appropriate' intermediate technology from the perspective of village women is usually 'too expensive' rather than 'low-cost'.

The main criticism of the labour-saving project approach is the narrow range of devices being disseminated. Women's work could be facilitated by numerous tools and organizational improvements (Carr 1984; Bryceson 1985).[3] The range of devices presently being promoted only begins to address the reality of women's high physical mobility amidst continual multi-tasking and childcare responsibilities. A much more comprehensive array of devices is required. For example, various time-saving and light-weight kitchen utensils using local materials are needed to reduce the time women spend preparing food. Multi-purpose tools could be designed to save female energy on agricultural tasks and load carrying. Technological innovations to alleviate the difficulties posed by both the cumbersome size and weight of the multi-item loads women carry are a precondition for the introduction of many other labour-saving innovations.

Projects pursuing improvements in women's resource access are most recent and have not congealed into a set pattern, having first emerged in the context of South Asian local struggles over forestry and land usage. As population densities increase and reach critical levels in many rural areas of Africa, and as communal systems of land tenure give way under international pressure for African governments to sanction a market in land, women's extensive usufruct land rights are unlikely to be replaced at anywhere near parity levels. It is apparent that women's rights will have to be defended at regional and national levels, as well as the local level. The South Asian model of localized struggle between large landowners and poor farmers is not strictly applicable in the Sub-Saharan African context. In many cases, the power broker is a multi-tiered government rather than a rich, private monopolist. Action aimed at improving women's resource access in the rural African context will often have to confront national laws which overlook women or, in the case of more sensitive laws, make rural women aware of their rights.

Despite the diversity of approaches found in the three types of projects under review, two features remain common to all. The objective of project intervention is to raise women's status vis-à-vis men. Secondly, the projects are geographically localized and of limited duration. Their direct effect is usually restricted to relatively small numbers of women, whereas their indirect effect is difficult to measure. Limited in time and space, their impact tends to be ephemeral. Specific projects may register marked success in their project area, but disappear virtually without trace at the completion of the formal project, having achieved little or no influence in a broader geographical sense. In theory, the projects are high-minded and status-conscious about women, while in practice they are small and in need of status-raising themselves.

Female Endurance Assumptions: Women in Structural Adjustment Programmes

Under the crisis conditions of the late 1980s and the 1990s, donor project orientation generally has increasingly given way to balance of payments support and sectoral finance to maintain crumbling infrastructure. In return, African governments have been forced to scale down state-led initiatives and give precedence to the market. Despite pronouncements to the contrary, women's projects have been vulnerable to budgetary cut-backs favouring infrastructural maintenance over social service development, the categorization that most women's projects continue to be lumbered with.

A countervailing tendency has however appeared amidst the economic crisis. The first hints of sectoral attention surfaced when the World Bank, USAID and Ford Foundation introduced programmes in 1988 that went beyond a project framework in an attempt to favourably influence policy formulation and sectoral development in relation to women.[4]

Nonetheless, on the whole, evidence points to rural women faring poorly under structural adjustment programmes (Ardayfio 1986). The collapse of government finance has led to drastic retraction of essential public services. Serious cracks in the provisioning of health facilities, schools, rural water supplies, etc. have increased the work burden on rural women (Wagao 1988; Leach 1990). Furthermore, the heightened emphasis in structural adjustment programmes on production for the market poses a dilemma (Bryceson 1992). How can women participate in increased commodity production in addition to their activities in food production, household maintenance and childcare? If they do not succeed in squeezing time out of their working day to increase participation in commodity production, they run the risk of being further marginalized from cash and access to local resources relative to the men. In circular fashion, we arrive back at our starting point: women's over-booked working day is the major stumbling block to their involvement in what donors perceive as 'status-enhancing' productive activities.

Western Impact for Better or Worse

Recent debates in a deconstructionist vein have questioned such fundamental concepts as *development* (Ferguson 1990). The term 'development' is infused with western cultural values and donor agencies whose *raison d'être* is development, can not take the word for granted in the context of Africa. This section critiques some of the assumptions and aims of western donor agency intervention in relation to African rural women. Elements of an alternative analytical framework are proposed to facilitate interventions better designed to comprehensively address rural women's labour constraints while trying to remain sensitive to rural women's occupational and lifestyle preferences.

Miscasting Women in a Household Setting

While Roger's anti-domestication argument has successfully exposed the fallacy of the 'homemaking' image for African women, western perceptions of women's working life in rural areas remain slanted. Despite intentions to the contrary, Barbara Rogers and other feminist theorists have perpetuated western bias through their frequent reference to rural women's activities *in* and *outside* the household. Through this simple phrase, a welter of theoretical assumptions are implied regarding the function of the market and state as public institutions on the one hand, and the household as a private institution on the other.

In western industrial societies, work within the household was traditionally restricted to 'housekeeping' and childcare, reflective of the household's function as a unit of consumption and reproduction. *Productive* work took place outside the home, both physically and organizationally. Such production was mediated by the market.

In the rural African context, this dichotomy is distorting. Domestic residences are units of production, as well as units of consumption and reproduction. Work, especially women's work, tends to be for subsistence, but also encompasses agricultural production destined for the market. In the course of their working day, women are not confined to the house. They provide the basic needs of household members for food, water and fuel which takes them far beyond the geographical perimeter of the house, into the village and surrounding countryside. Furthermore, unlike their female counterparts in western countries, their work is a classic example of vertical integration. A domestic residence's food, water and fuel supply are: 1) directly produced at its natural source in the field; 2) physically delivered to the living quarters; and 3) processed, undergoing value added production, i.e. 'transformation work'; before being 4) distributed to residential occupants for consumption.

This vertical productive process is not adequately captured by 'home economics'. Home economics, formerly termed 'domestic science', is a western approach to women's household management. Conditioned by the European and North American experience of women's domestic activities, it is largely limited to the third and fourth spheres outlined above.

Ironically, the acceptance of Rogers' argument and the dismissal of a home economics perspective has led to very little systematic attention to the details of African rural women's domestic work burden. It is vital that due attention be placed on streamlining, if not eliminating, the arduous tasks that rural women perform in all spheres listed above. By focussing on women's 'productive' work in agriculture and for the market, primarily the first sphere, without giving sufficient attention to the severe labour constraints they face in the second and third spheres, western donor agencies have, in pendulum fashion, over-reacted. Neither the colonial emphasis on women as housewives, nor the present emphasis on women as market-oriented producers provides a balanced perspective for formulating effective interventions to ease rural women's daily workload and materially improve their lives.

An Alternative Approach: Homestead Economics

Weighing up the evidence from current rural women's projects, it is not difficult to argue that there is need for a new approach towards rural women which acknowledges that their workday, not only spans, but *integrates* agricultural fieldwork, transformation work and childcare in logistically complex arrangements. The term 'housework' is not applicable here. *Homestead work* is more appropriate since it encompasses work in the domestic unit and on family agricultural holdings. The term homestead has been used to describe rural residential/ work units in various parts of the continent.[5] *Homestead economics* can be defined as the study of the allocation of rural women's labour as a scarce resource. In this section, the terminology and approach of homestead economics is outlined.

Homestead work consists of women's daily livelihood management. From the perspective of women themselves, such work is aimed at meeting basic needs and improving the standard of living of homestead members. While the latter objective is usually considered to be achieved through cash-earning opportunities such as increasing marketed agricultural production or participating in income-generating projects, the homestead's standard of living can also be improved through increased work efficiency which gives women more time to devote to homestead goods and service provisioning. Alternatively, the freed time could be spent as leisure, thereby raising women's standard of living.

Homestead economics, as a field of study, would entail the dissection of the *detailed mechanics* of women's work, questioning what, when, where, how, and why women's tasks are performed. The existing literature tends to be overly focussed on a handful of technical solutions, namely grinding mills and improved cooking stoves, and usually does so from the perspective of limited project defined objectives, rather than considering women's working day in its entirety. There are a wide range of agrarian and non-agrarian modes of livelihood represented in Sub-Saharan Africa. It can not be assumed that women's labour day constraints are the same everywhere and that solutions are universally applicable.[6] Women's own perspective must be used as a starting point. This necessitates household and village level studies employing a participatory research methodology to probe women's views regarding their work objectives and problems (Bryceson, Manicom and Kassum 1981; Anderson 1984; Information Centre for Low External Input and Sustainable Agriculture (ILEIA) 1989; Chambers 1992).

Besides attitudinal study, various combinations of multi-disciplinary teams of social scientists, agronomists, engineers, technologists and ergonomists, working in conjunction with local women in different agro-economic zones are needed to systematically review the time, effort and spatial dynamics of women's work. These findings would reveal labour bottlenecks and provide the basis for advancing testable ideas regarding technical and socio-economic improvements. Improvements could include a wide range of measures tailored to the availability of local resources, the agricultural calendar, average household size and composition, etc. Emphasis should be placed on better management of the temporal and spatial dimensions of women's work which would help streamline multi-tasking activities and the demands of childcare. Family planning which takes account of household labour needs should be included. Most importantly, a homestead economics approach would aim to generate a far larger array of different functional types of appropriate technology tailored to the work demands of women in specific circumstances.

The question of dissemination and popularization of the studies' findings arises. The participatory research approach, if successful, would ensure that the findings are part of a self-discovery on the part of the women themselves. Organizational improvements would emerge through interaction between the external researchers and the local women. However, the indigenization of better homestead management and the dissemination and sustainability of more appropriate technology usage both in the locality studied and over a wider geographical perimeter in similar agro-ecological zones is a matter requiring special attention. Training courses, the publication of practical handbooks for literate women and the activation of women's groups are recommended but are not enough. Many women, who are not directly involved in the research, will not have the time, interest or literacy to be reached in this way. Thus, a new forward-looking strategy has to be developed to overcome the usual obstacles encountered in reaching women.

Generational Change: Mind over Matter

It is odd that while the influence of western feminism has spilled into foreign donor programmes in Sub-Saharan Africa, bringing about a much needed focus on rural women, much of the accumulated experience and success in raising feminist consciousness in the west has not been distilled and used to sensitively inform donor project design in Africa. During the 1960s, the groundswell for change in the west consisted primarily of *youthful* women who challenged the view that they were destined to be first and foremost wives and mothers. The feminist movement's continuing momentum has been fuelled by women's expectations of career options in addition to or in place of marriage and motherhood. And significantly, this process of change has taken place within the context of widespread availability of material conveniences such as piped water, electricity, gas, and domestic appliances, as well as advances in birth control technology.

Given the very real differences in rural African women's material environment, their role expectations are profoundly different from western women of the 1990s. Most rural African societies are strongly pro-natalist. Children are valued for economic and social reasons (Bryceson and Vuorela 1985; Caplan in Chapter 7). A woman's role as mother largely defines her identity in the rural society. Birth rates are high.[7] Infertility is viewed by the society at large and by infertile women themselves as a personal failure and is often grounds for divorce. Through giving birth, women achieve social acceptance and security. Group approval and solidarity is central to a woman's life in rural Africa where fluctuations of climate and health create a high risk environment.

A rural woman's daily workload is primarily directed at meeting the basic needs of children and other homestead members. Women rely on work support from their children. Without an array of domestic appliances and public utilities to lighten their work burden, children's labour input is of considerable utility (Kamuzora 1986). Increasingly, however, children are attending school which reduces their labour contribution to the homestead and places more pressure on women's labour. It is in this context that women's need for the innovations that homestead economics could generate is particularly acute. Nonetheless, it is women of childbearing age with families to provision who have the least amount of time to respond to donor-initiated women's projects aimed at lessening their labour constraint.

There is, however, a way out of this seemingly intractable situation. Not all of the female population have 'over-booked' work schedules. Teenage girls, who in many African countries are school-leavers with up to seven years primary education, tend to have less time commitments. Without children of their own, they are homestead 'helpers' rather than central provisioners (Mbilinyi 1969). Since virtually all rural women marry, these girls' status can best be summed up as *nubile*, absorbed temporarily into the homestead workforce while waiting for betrothal. In some areas, marriage comes very soon with girls wedded in their early and mid-teens and starting to bear children quickly thereafter.

Outline of a Girls' Homestead Training and Income-generating Programme

A national homestead economics training programme focussed on teen-aged girls who are not within the formal education system has several advantages. It may prolong their age of marriage, and thereby help to slow down population growth. But more significantly, it harnesses the talents and energies of the one category of women who are least affected by a labour constraint and who are at an impressionable age, a time when lifetime attitudes are formed.

The form and content of the programme would necessarily have to vary from country to country, depending on institutional capacity and levels of female literacy. Furthermore, within any one country, the programme would have to be adapted to individual localities, taking account of social customs, agrarian and non-agrarian modes of livelihood and resource availability. The programme could be envisaged as having two main components: 1) training in 'non-traditional' skills related to homestead management and maintenance; and 2) promoting the formation of female youth groups for mutual support and income-generating activities. The short-term objective of such a programme would be to disseminate the research findings and innovations arising from preceding local research on the homestead economics of women's working day. The more long-term objective is to provide a future generation of rural women with ways and means of avoiding much of the drudgerous labour that their mothers have endured. In so doing, it is hoped that they will gain more social choices and economic opportunities.

The homestead economics training could cover a number of non-traditional skills including:

- building skills to improve and maintain living quarters and other functional buildings;
- engineering skills for improving and maintaining village infrastructure such as paths, water supply installations, etc.;
- as knapsacks and animal panniers;[8]
- carpentry for making wood products including improved kitchen utensils, wheelbarrows and other load-carrying devices;
- forestry for the planting and maintenance of woodlots;

- agronomy, including agricultural planning to maximize labour time inputs and land usage;
- convenience food preparation that reduces labour time and can easily be taken and eaten away from the compound to save walking to and from the fields;
- time management to streamline the physical effort expended on agricultural activities and transformation work;
- accountancy and business skills to facilitate the running of income-generating activities as well as enabling female participants to assert influence on household budgeting in their future adult life; and
- family life education to assist them to withstand the pressures on them as young, nubile women, as well as preparing them for their future reproductive lives as wives and mothers. This could include: education to prevent the incidence of pre-marital pregnancy and sexually transmitted diseases including AIDS; the advantages of family planning and limitations on family size; and enhancement of their image as women with decision-making power and control over their own fertility.

The formation of young women's groups for mutual support and income-generating activities would complement the training programme. The concept of youth economic groups is not new. In Tanzania, for example, youth economic groups (YEGs) have been promoted by government and donor agency efforts for over a decade. On the basis of restricted starting capital, YEGs have nonetheless been successful in mobilizing the labour of youths in both urban and rural settings. However, the labour mobilized has been overwhelmingly male. Girls' participation has been hampered by a number of factors primarily connected with their nubile status. Parents have had reservations about their daughters involvement in groups containing boys and girls. Because most girls marry young and, in patrilineal areas, move to their husbands' home locality, their commitment to participation in the group is of limited duration. Finally, girls, more than boys, are expected to hand over their earnings to their fathers which has a disincentive effect on their involvement (Bryceson 1992).

YEGs designed specifically for girls could overcome most of these drawbacks. Initially, efforts would be needed to get parents to sanction their daughters' involvement and to reduce pressure on girls to marry early. This would help lay a foundation for girls to use YEGs as a medium for increasing their social roles beyond that of wife and mother. The groups would offer girls an opportunity to earn and manage their own cash which could in turn: 1) make it possible for them to buy the consumer durables such as bicycles and radios that their brothers purchase with their earnings; 2) give them a start in building up a capital endowment; and 3) enhance their economic expectations of life.

Finally, homestead training in non-traditional skills could enhance girls' future adult lives in both domestic and market settings. Recent research comparing African men's and women's entry into informal sector occupations reveals that women's inferior access to apprenticeship training is a major limitation in their skill acquisition compared with men (Dijkman and van Dijk 1993).[9]

Sliding into Gender Stereotyping?

The first reservation that no doubt springs to many readers' minds is that a homestead economics programme, dealing with women's spheres of work and targeting improvement measures on girls, is promoting rather than eliminating gender stereotyping. Some might try to equate homestead economics training in Sub-Saharan Africa with domestic science training for girls in western industrialized countries. But are they the same? Domestic science was discredited by western feminists because it was a subject that only girls were required to take and it was premised on a sexual division of labour which relegated women to being primarily housewives and mothers (Allan 1990). Often girls studied it in place of science and mathematics. It was directed at training girls to be good housekeepers, thereby raising the standard of living of their families rather than being directed at personal fulfilment of the girls themselves.

Homestead economics also deals with 'women's work' and is focussed on girls, but its objectives differ. Acknowledging the existing sexual division of labour, it is premised on giving young women who have already left school the training and technology to change the status quo. Its fundamental aim is to extend young women's opportunities in their future adult life rather than to narrow them. It attempts to reduce rural women's workload systematically through the application of technology and organizational improvements that women themselves can control.

It can be argued that western feminists and donor agency concern has been in line with these principles from the outset. Nonetheless, efforts to attain these goals have been distorted by current western perceptions. Feminist influence in donor agencies' operational policies has led to the incorporation of equity goals but several steps in the realization of these goals have been skipped.

It is difficult to identify what is most fundamental to women's work careers 'outside the home' in western countries when considering the influence of: domestic technology which minimizes housework; limitations on the number of children they bear; state infrastructural support like crèches; paid maternity leave etc. and their husbands' willingness to share the burden of housework. Arguably, all have been necessary developments in enhancing women's status and continue to need improvement to facilitate women's careers. So too, in rural Sub-Saharan Africa, an amalgam of improved domestic technology, reductions in fertility, state infrastructural support vis-à-vis women's production and reproduction, and the productive input of men in homestead work are needed. Concentration on any one in isolation from the others makes gains in equity extremely difficult to achieve. Any agency involved in rural women's development should be aware of linkages between these factors and make efforts to contribute to their balanced interaction.

Synchronization is possible and indeed vital in another respect. Donor agencies' development efforts should be established on the basis of women's existing identities, motivations, and priorities. Once rural women's perspectives are incorporated into programme designs and continuously monitored, the programmes are far more likely to be relevant and effective.

Conclusion

Throughout this century, women in African farming systems have been subject to mounting labour demands. This paper has argued that the nature of their work, a vertical production process including raw material extraction, value added production and distribution to the point of consumption, has not been adequately addressed by donor agencies' piece-meal project intervention. In the main, western donors have set extremely ambitious targets of raising the status of women in the household and community using western criteria of judgement. The underlying premise has been that money is power in the hands of rural women. Income-generating projects have dominated. Projects directed at labour constraints and gender imbalances in resource allocation have arisen largely to support the goal of women's increased work 'outside the home'.

In general, the approach adopted by western donors has not been well-grounded in existing material conditions. Donors' views about potential changes in the gender division of labour and power balance between the sexes has been presumptuous. Women's projects have focussed on women generally without taking sufficient account of variation in women's productive roles by age. It is often older women, past childbearing age, who are the most able to respond to income-generating projects. Their participation, however, is the least likely to generate multiplier effects.

A homestead economics programme is a strategic way of overcoming these drawbacks. First, women's labour constraints rather than income generation is given precedence. Multi-disciplinary teams of technologists and social scientists in collaboration with women of childbearing age would seek time and labour-saving solutions to work bottlenecks through the systematic study of the spatial pattern and complex multi-tasking activities of women's working day. Second, teenage girls, outside of the formal education system, would be specially targeted for training and income-generating activities, with emphasis on creating new economic and social expectations. It is argued that changes in young women's attitudes and skills could have a far-reaching effect. Alleviating women's daily workload through technical innovation and better organization establishes a material foundation for women to challenge gender imbalance. The combination of technical improvement in women's working day and different life expectations on the part of youth, could provide an enduring basis for change.

Notes

* An abbreviated version of this paper appeared in *Development Policy Review*, vol. 12, no. 1, March 1994.
1. Buvinic sanguinely argues that this approach conformed with donor agencies' needs. Projects based on voluntary labour were cheaper and easier to implement than other types of interventions. Reliance on NGOs offered an easy entry point at a time when most governments in developing countries were not convinced of the legitimacy of gender issues. Overall, '[t]he project orientation favored by donor agencies to expand poor women's economic opportunities was more compatible with

the limited financial resources allocated to women's issues; with the restricted clout of and access to policy makers that practitioners had in recipient countries; and with the need to build up a concrete record by the end of the Women's Decade that was easier accomplished through discrete interventions' (Buvinic 1989).

2. This is a well-known problem outside of Africa as well (e.g. see Mayoux 1993).

3. For example, the Intermediate Technology Development Group's (UK) publications catalogue provides a wealth of technical and organizational ideas for application to women's work lives.

4. The World Bank's Safe Motherhood Initiative and the USAID's Micro-enterprise Lending for the Poor Program (Buvinic 1989).

5. E.g. see Ekejiuba's article (Chapter 3) on rural Nigeria in this volume for a discussion of the inadequacy of the household category to denote the primary socio-economic unit in rural Nigeria as well as Russell (1993) for a stringent attack on the use of the term 'household' to denote the *umuti* rural homestead in Swaziland.

6. Anderson (1984) draws attention to the need to refrain from assumptions of wide applicability of domestic innovations in the absence of an appreciation of the needs of women in a specific work setting.

7. According to World Bank statistics, in 1991, the total fertility rate for low and middle income countries of Sub-Saharan Africa was 6.4 compared with 5.3 for North Africa and the Middle East, 4.2 for South Asia, 3.1 for Latin America and the Caribbean and 2.7 for East Asia and the Pacific (World Bank 1993: Table 27).

8. This is not intended to suggest that sewing is a 'female task', but rather that women can be directly involved in measures to alleviate the heavy transport burden that they face in rural Sub-Saharan Africa as argued in Bryceson and Howe (1993).

9. In a study of the Ouagadougou informal sector, women's employment tended to be concentrated in activities which were an extension of female domestic duties. Seventy per cent of men and only 28 per cent of the women interviewed had had apprenticeship training. The gap was similar for on-the-job training: 83 per cent men and 40 per cent women (Dijkman and van Dijk 1993).

References

Afonja, S., 'Land Control: A Critical Factor in Yoruba Gender Stratification', in C. Robertson and I. Berger (eds), *Women and Class in Africa*, New York, Africana Publishing Co., 1986, pp. 78–91

Airey, T. and I. Barwell, 'Village-Level Transport and Travel Survey's and Related Case Studies', I.T.Transport Ltd. Consultancy commissioned for the Sub-Saharan Transport Programme by the ILO/World Bank, 1991

Allan, D., *Wasting Girls' Time*, London, Virago, 1990

Anderson, M.B., 'Technology Transfer: Implications for Women', in C. Overholt, M.B. Anderson, K. Cloud and J.E. Austin (eds), *Gender Roles in Development Projects: A Case Book*, West Hartford (Conn.), Kumarian Press, 1984

Ardayfio, E., *Rural Energy Crisis in Ghana: Its Implications for Women's Work and Household Survival*, Geneva, ILO, WEP Working Paper 39, 1986

Bay, E.G. (ed.), *Women and Work in Africa*, Boulder, Westview Press, 1982

Boserup, E., *Women's Role in Economic Development*, London, George Allen and Unwin, 1970

Bruce, J. and D. Dwyer (eds), *A Home Divided: Women and Income in the Third World,* Stanford, Stanford University Press, 1988

Bryceson, D.F., *Women and Technology in Developing Countries: Technological Changes and Women's Capabilities and Bargaining Positions*, United Nations International Research and Training Institute for the Advancement of Women (INSTRAW), Santo Domingo, 1985

—, 'Women, Rural Labour Processes and Structural Change: Review of Literature from the ILO's Programme on Rural Women', Consultancy Report commissioned by the ILO, Geneva, 1990

—, 'Women Producers: Market Response vs. Household Responsibilities', Agricultural Diversification and Intensification Study, Working Paper No. 8, Oxford, Food Studies Group/Sokoine University of Agriculture, March 1992

Bryceson, D.F. and J.Howe, 'Rural Household Transport in Africa: Reducing the Burden on Women?', *World Development*, vol. 21, no. 11, 1993, pp. 1715–28

Bryceson, D.F. and M. Kirimbai, 'Subsistence or Beyond? Money Earning Activities of Women in Rural Tanzania', University of Dar es Salaam, BRALUP Research Report No. 45/UWT (Tanzanian National Women's Organization), 1980

Bryceson, D.F. and U. Vuorela, 'Outside the Domestic Labor Debate: Towards a Theory of Modes of Human Reproduction', *Review of Radical Political Economics*, no. 17, 1985, pp. 4–27

Bryceson, D.F., L. Manicom and Y. Kassum, 'The Methodology of the Participatory Research Approach', in F. Dubell, T. Erasmie and J. de Vries (eds), *Research for the People*, Sweden, Linkoping University, 1981

Bukh, J., *The Village Woman in Ghana,* Uppsala, Scandinavian Institute of African Studies, 1979

Buvinic, M., 'Projects for Women in the Third World: Explaining their Misbehavior', *World Development,* vol. 14, no. 5, 1986, pp. 653–64

—, 'Investing in Poor Women: The Psychology of Donor Support', *World Development,* vol. 17, no. 7, 1989, pp. 1045–57

Carr, M., *Blacksmith, Baker, Roof-sheet Maker: Employment for Rural Women in Developing Countries,* Nottingham, IT Publications, 1984

Cecelski, E., 'Energy and Rural Women's Work: Crisis Response and Policy Alternatives', *International Labour Review,* vol. 126, no. 1, January 1987

Chambers, R., 'Participatory Rural Appraisal', paper presented at the BRAC Workshop sponsored by NOVIB, The Hague, September 1992

Chilver, E.M., 'Women Cultivators, Cows and Cash Crops in Cameroon', in S. Ardener (ed.), *Persons and Powers of Women in Diverse Cultures,* Oxford, Berg Publishers, 1992

Curtis, V., *Women and the Transport of Water,* London, Intermediate Technology Publications, 1986

Davison, J. (ed.), *Agriculture, Women and Land: The African Experience,* Boulder and London, Westview Press, 1988

Dijkman, H. and M.P. van Dijk, 'Female Entrepreneurs in the Informal Sector of Ougadougou', *Development Policy Review,* vol. 11, 1993, pp. 273–88

Ferguson, J., *The Anti-Politics Machine: Development, Depoliticization and Bureaucratic Power in Lesotho,* Cambridge, Cambridge University Press, 1990

Guyer, J.I., 'Intra-household Processes and Farming System Research: Perspectives from Anthropology', in J.L. Moock (ed.), *Understanding Africa's Rural Households and Farming Systems Research,* California, Westview Press, 1986

Hafkin, N. and E.G.Bay (eds), *Women in Africa: Studies in Socio-Economic Change,* Stanford, Stanford University Press, 1976

ILEIA (Information Centre for Low External Input and Sustainable Agriculture), *Participatory Technology Development in Sustainable Agriculture,* Leusden, April 1989

ILO (International Labour Office)/Government of Norway, *Technological Change, Basic Needs and the Condition of Rural Women,* Geneva, ILO/World Employment Programme, 1984

Kamuzora, C.L., 'Population Growth and the Development Problems of Africa: Origins and Implied Solutions', *Utafiti,* vol. 8, no. 1, 1986, pp. 1–12

Kossoudji, S. and E. Mueller, 'The Economic and Demographic Status of Female Headed Households in Rural Botswana', *Economic Development and Cultural Change,* July 1983

Leach, V., *Women and Children in Tanzania,* Tanzania/UNICEF, Dar es Salaam, 1990

Mayoux, L., 'Integration is Not Enough: Gender Inequality and Empowerment in Nicaraguan Agriculture Co-operatives', *Development Policy Review*, vol. 11, 1993, pp. 67–89

Mbilinyi, M., 'Co-operative Organisation in Isange Village', in B. Koda, M. Mbilinyi, A. Muro, A. Nkebukwa Kokubelwa, A. Nkhoma, Z. Tumbo-Masabo and U. Vuorela (eds), *Women's Initiatives in the United Republic of Tanzania*, Geneva, ILO, 1987

—, *The Education of Girls in Tanzania: A Study of Attitudes of Tanzanian Girls and their Fathers towards Education*, Institute of Education, University College, Dar es Salaam, 1969

McCall, M., 'Labour Saving Devices and Renewable Energies for Women', in B.C. Groen and C.R. Huizenga (eds), *Have Planners Understood Poor People's Energy Development Problem? Socio-Economic Aspects of Energy Technology*, Technology and Development Group, University of Twente, Enschede, 1987

McCormack, J., M. Walsh and C. Nelson, *Women's Group Enterprises: A Study of the Structure of Opportunity on the Kenya Coast*, Boston, World Education Inc., 1986

Moser, C., 'Gender Planning in the Third World: Meeting Practical and Strategic Gender Needs', *World Development*, vol. 17, no. 11, 1989, pp. 1799–825

O'Kelly, E., *Rural Women: Their Integration in Development Programmes and How Simple Intermediate Technologies Can Help Them*, London, 1978

Rathgeber, E.M., 'WID, WAD, GAD: Trends in Research and Practice', *Journal of Developing Areas*, vol. 24, July 1990, pp. 489–502

Robertson, C. and I. Berger (eds), *Women and Class in Africa*, New York, Africana Publishing Co., 1986

Rogers, B., *The Domestification of Women: Discrimination in Developing Societies*, London, Tavistock Publications, 1980

Russell, M., 'Are Households Universal? On Misunderstanding Domestic Groups in Swaziland', *Development and Change*, vol. 24, 1993, pp. 755–85

Sender, J. and S. Smith, *Poverty, Class and Gender in Rural Africa: A Tanzanian Case Study*, London, Routledge, 1990

Stichter, S.B. and J.L. Parpart (eds), *Patriarchy and Class: African Women in the Home and the Workforce*, Boulder and London, Westview Press, 1988

Tinker, I., 'The Making of a Field: Advocates, Practitioners, and Scholars', in I. Tinker (ed.), *Persistent Inequalities*, New York, Oxford University Press, 1990

Turrittin, J., 'Men, Women and Market Trade in Rural Mali, West Africa', *Canadian Journal of African Studies*, vol. 22, no. 3, 1988, pp. 583–604

Wagao, J.H., *Analysis of the Economic Situation of Urban and Rural Women in Tanzania*, UNICEF, Dar es Salaam, 1988

World Bank, *World Bank Development Report 1993*, New York, Oxford University Press, 1993

V

LISTENING TO WOMEN: EFFORTS TO RECORD FEMALE PERSPECTIVES

12

Documenting Women's Views through Participatory Research: Diaries of Daily Activities in Rural Zambia

Else Skjønsberg

Until recently, under the influence of positivism, scientific research in the social sciences aimed at discovering facts or relationships and tended to avoid the exploration of people's attitudes and opinions. Researchers' direct participation in local issues, as well as key informants' involvement in the research itself, was antithetical to the notion of scientific research.

During the 1980s, these research dictates were loosened. Students of rural life and feminist research challenged the idea that science is best achieved by distancing oneself from the world.[1] An important underlying principle of participatory research was awareness that the social setting in which researchers operate heavily influences the way they think about the phenomena they observe.

It was in this context that I went to Zambia hoping to solicit the active participation of villagers in mapping and analysing rural life. I wanted to be certain that it was their everyday life that would prevail rather than my views and biases as a foreign social scientist. My goal was to go into a dialogue with people of a different culture, a different economy and ecology, a different language, and maybe even at times a different logic than my own. I was tired of having Third World village living moulded into the straitjacket of western sociological and anthropological thought. I had already contributed to that myself in a sample survey in Uganda and a village study in Sri Lanka and found the results most unsatisfactory. I felt the need to shed the jargon of social science in order to be able to listen to the voices of some fellow men and women from the South. It was from this perspective that a detailed time allocation study based on participatory research seemed the most suitable medium. It afforded the community in question an opportunity not only to participate but even to decide on what data to include and how to address and interpret issues which arose.

This chapter describes the methodology I employed to study the daily activities of sixteen households in the small, semi-subsistence village of Kefa in eastern Zambia.[2] The first section provides some background on everyday life in the village. Various objectives and organizational features of the study are discussed in the next section, followed by a review of the time allocation data collection methods and findings. The gathering of additional qualitative data on why people do what they do is described, before the advantages of participatory research are reconsidered.

The Rural Scene

Kefa village is situated in the eastern Province of Zambia. Its 250 inhabitants live from subsistence agriculture with maize and groundnuts as their staple food. As no one can do entirely without cash, most villagers sell some of their agricultural surplus, including the occasional goat or duck or go outside the village in search of some paid work in the slack agricultural season. When the time allocation study was made, by the end of the 1970s, the annual average income was only $200. The women earned much less; it was the few rich cattle owners in the village that helped increase the village average.

The demographic setting of the village was remarkable, though it is shared by thousands of villages all over Africa. Almost every third household was woman-headed, while 15 per cent were polygamous, often with husbands commuting between the village and their outside working place. Traditionally, the village followed matrilineal rules of descent; however, there was an increasing shift towards patrilineage with respect to inheritance. Most households owned some small livestock which were mostly looked after by the women, while a few had cattle under male care. Agricultural land was abundant and comparatively fertile, but the technology limited the area cultivated. A few villagers – namely the cattle owners – could afford to hire tractor services for ploughing and transportation, but the majority, and that is mostly women, had to rely on their own woman power.

As in so many African rural areas, in Kefa village the women were indeed wielding the hoe. They also transported most of the harvested crops back home, using 'headpower'. Women were also the water carriers and water was collected from a water hole half a mile away from the village. The water source would dry up by the end of the dry season. Then drinking water had to be brought from a half mile away. In fact, the Kefa villagers were of the opinion that women were born with necks for carrying, contrary to the men.

The very skewed gender distribution was also particular, though shared with many other villages. Two out of every three adults between 23 and 50 years were women. Their contemporary menfolk were working elsewhere. Several of the men who lived in the village were incapacitated for various reasons. Some had tuberculosis, others suffered from ulcers, some were disabled, while others were simply defined as drunkards. Most of the fully fit adult men had gone away from the village in search of paid labour, because inside the village only a few individuals, that is the local basket weaver, doctor and female fish monger, had some regular cash income. About half the Kefa population was under 15 years of age. The younger ones were under the care of their mothers and grandmothers. Amongst those over 56 years old, men and women each constituted 50 per cent of the population. In effect, the village women still provided male retirees with their old age social security and care.

Research Ambitions and Accommodations

My research had two main objectives. One was to procure a detailed account of village affairs, that is how people used their time and labour in order to meet their needs and wants. The other was to make their everyday behaviour understandable to an outsider, not in terms of how it matches dominant social science theories and models, but simply by getting the villagers' own view on why they organized life the way they did, and how this tallied with local priorities and constraints, ambitions and fears. Participatory research seemed the best way to achieve these objectives.

The involvement of local assistants was key to the participatory approach and was necessary for language reasons anyway, since I did not speak Nyanja. But it was my choice to make use of helpmates selected in the local community, notwithstanding the fact that they had limited schooling. I could have chosen to use university students well-versed in sociological theory. Instead, five local assistants with between 7 to 11 years of schooling were hired and came to play an important role as data gatherers, informants and 'middlemen' and 'middlewomen' conveying local perspectives. The costs were less than those of hiring an expatriate for a month.

Three months were used for the initial training. By then the team recorded time usage professionally and notebooks were kept in good order. The two men in the team worked in shifts observing male villagers from early morning to evening and the women observed female villagers. The team leader supervised the operation, helped out in the case of absence of a team member due to illness or other business and observed and recorded non-scheduled and special events, as indeed did the rest of the team.

Gender differences made work more difficult for the female team members than the male. The women observed worked harder and longer hours than the men and consequently kept the female recorders more busy. And once work was over, our female team members had to carry water and get their maize to the mill for grinding just like other village women, while the men could sit down with other men, join in their conversation or retire to their mud huts and jot down bits of conversation or other salient events of the day. As a result, the qualitative data reflecting women's lives is less complete than those pertaining to the men of the village. And the recorded activities are more biased. One day one of the female recorders wrote the following in her notebook: 'I could not record all Tisalire's activities. She was too busy doing so many things. Her main activity was pounding maize, but she also breast-fed her last born, chatted with her neighbour Timeke, smoked a cigarette that she had got as a free gift from Square Banda, and ate the groundnuts that Timeke shared with her.'

Diaries of Daily Activities

Observations of human activities provide a unique insight into daily living, as what people do is often different from what they say they do, and even what they think they do. With time as a measuring rod, work patterns, social habits and the use of labour, money, produce and tools may be studied in great detail. On the basis of uniform or diverse behavioural patterns, hypotheses concerning individual and collective priorities and constraints may be formed and tested. And what is more, time usage can serve as a point of departure for detailed discussions on local priorities and preferences, problems and potentials.

To collect data on time use one may either ask people what they do and for how long, or simply watch and take systematic notes on activities and their duration. We did both. From a methodological point of view, time allocation studies are most rewarding. They offer a fairly objective account of behaviour, as long as one makes generalizations with care. The opportunity to continue observations is long enough to make the observed persons accustomed to being followed around. Equally important, they are easily carried out and can consequently be implemented with high validity and replicability by any motivated literate person. In fact, most target groups can be actively involved in gathering information about their own community in a systematic and reliable way. In collecting such data, those involved are provided with the opportunity to familiarize themselves with their own community, its resources, problems and potentials in a new way. They thereby enhance their understanding of their own environment and the means available to change or improve it. Systematic observations coupled to repeated discussions will facilitate the observer's ability also to identify, quantify and analyse key aspects of their own lives. In other words, time allocation studies provide a starting point for consciousness-raising.

Our time allocation observations in Kefa village extended over 15 months, five to six days per week. Each of the 16 household heads randomly sampled was observed on average three days each month for between 12 and 15 hours a day, and virtually every activity lasting for more than a minute or two was meticulously noted down. The result is an account of more than 6,000 hours of village activities. The time allocation study details gender divisions of labour in the field and at home, highlights the labour intensive nature of most local activities and indicates prevailing social demands on time and labour. It quantifies the dominant role of food processing in village women's lives and the gender division of labour in agriculture and various other economic fields. It suggests how social obligations in connection to birth, illness and funerals criss-cross everyday village life, placing definite demands on family time and labour. It also shows how men and women work under different expectations and obligations, and how community norms are often transgressed simply to make life in the family run more smoothly.

Like every method, time allocation studies have shortcomings. Being detailed and thorough, they are time consuming to do. In the Kefa study, the data collection could have been condensed, but this might have been at the expense of recording considerable seasonal changes that dictate not only economic life, but social life as well. Research aiming to address general issues must, therefore, cover the entire agricultural cycle. Time studies are essentially unsuited to the study of social structures *per se*, as opposed to the behaviour found within such structures. Furthermore, time studies may be hopeless when it comes to capturing rare events. However, supplemented by other methods (whether these include interviews, studies of secondary data, special enquiries or whatever), time studies like the one carried out in Kefa, are unique in terms of the close human relationship that develops from the proximity and intimacy created by longitudinal observations.

In view of its many benefits, it seems surprising that time allocation studies primarily have been used in industrial research to speed up production and enhance profitability. As time observations are part of the human dialogue everywhere, it seems strange that data so near at hand is not systematically collected. The data gathering as well as the findings may serve to bridge cultural and social spaces and create common ground for discussions and generalizations simply because time constitutes a medium shared by all.

Visualizing Women's Lives

The study of time use confirmed what less detailed data from Africa has long ago revealed, that women bear the main burden of maintaining village life. However, we found that most women's time is not spent on food production, but on food processing. The average women spent two hours daily on agricultural activities, as compared to two and a half hours for the men. Every day throughout the year, women's food processing activities took about twice that time, i.e. 4 hours and thirty minutes. If food processing was simplified, millions of African woman hours could be liberated for more productive work or some much-needed leisure. The men too did some cooking, thirty minutes daily, but mainly to roast meat which they subsequently ate themselves. We also observed fathers persuading their very young children to share food with them, and men sharing their beer with their toddlers. Seasonal variations as regards time used on food processing were modest, while individual variations were considerable.

In agriculture, gender differences were less marked than the individual differences, but of course the seasonal variations were very considerable. One-third of the time spent in agriculture was directed to maize production, by far the most important crop in the area. We found that it was the young men and the older women who wielded the hoe most intensively. This raises the issue of whether young female peasants of today will farm less than their elder sisters and their mothers in the future? In other words, is there a generational shift amongst women away from agricultural labour? Or is the observed difference attributable to the fact that older women rarely have male labour to help them and consequently have to work harder to make ends meet? The issue could boil down to the question of whether the young couples of today will experience the same degree of male out-migration as they grow older, leaving the main agricultural burden on the women.

The time women spent on looking after children was surprisingly low, on average only eleven minutes, and the men only spent a couple of minutes daily. The biases are many. Half of the women in our sample had only older children who could look after themselves and their younger siblings. Cooking food for the children was not recorded as time spent on children, but on food processing. Breastfeeding was not included as a separate activity as most women breastfed intermittently and often while doing other things, including what was defined as *relaxing* or *resting*. Childcare was consequently mainly defined as washing, dressing and admonishing children.

The time study confirms the seasonal character of village events. Funerals, and social gatherings dominate certain times of the year. People have a tendency to die in the rainy season and drink beer more frequently in the dry and cold season, when the granaries have been replenished. Again individual differences are considerable, but they do not obviate gender differences. Men were recorded to spend almost one hour a day on beer, women slightly more than ten minutes. While most daily activities are modified according to season, both men and women spend approximately the same time eating, three-quarters of an hour daily, with little variation throughout the year.

In the planting, weeding and harvesting season it is evident that women, as well as men, are very busy, working from early morning until nightfall, but women work much more intensively than the men. They know that if the agricultural activities are not carried out in time, the net result may be empty granaries and hunger at the end of the season. Headman Kefa often underlined that he and his followers settled in Kefa village to escape from *njala* (hunger). The fear of not being able to replenish the family granaries at the end of the harvest season is real for most farmers on the African continent, and more so for women whose obligation it is to feed their families. Men and women's unequal work burden is considerable. According to our findings, the men relaxed and socialized for six and a half hours every day, while women had less than half that time for relaxation.

Research as Cooperation: Less Direction, More Dimensions

When research aims to understand rather than predict and control social life, the relationship between researcher and target group or local community becomes a key factor. To subjectify former research *objects* means to establish a dialogue between partners. This may seem a radical break with traditional research relations which is also a power relation. The control over the research process is usually exclusively and solely in the hands of the researcher, who organizes and directs data gathering and interpretation according to preset designs or exploratory ambitions.

Cooperative research entails creating a setting where the so-called research *objects* participate in deciding issues as well as approaches. What the researcher risks is loss of control over the research process and even the project as such, and particularly the outcome. The gain, on the other hand, is the opportunity to get a deeper and more intimate understanding of the social conditions and relations under study. It is possible that a new focus will emerge which is more interesting and to the point than originally designed. The risk is also that the research *objects* refuse to cooperate. In the Kefa study, on a couple of occasions, a villager tried to stop the whole project. However, the support for our undertaking was far stronger than the misgivings. Protestations led to improved designs and greater satisfaction of the villagers. As time passed, the project became a joint venture with genuine village involvement. There was general pride in the project as expressed by one of the villagers: ' ... if our survey shall be worthwhile, it must be done well'.

As the time allocation study progressed, the team members were encouraged to jot down events, discussions or just anything they reflected upon while recording daily activities, or while they lived alongside their fellow villagers, sharing in their work and leisure. Anybody who had anything they wanted included in our study was encouraged to contact the recording team, and the team itself sharpened its senses as to what was happening in different sections and at different levels in the village. This resulted in a large amount of qualitative data which helped to bring the documentation of Kefa village to life, transforming its inhabitants from statistical entities to individuals of flesh and blood. This is how we learned how Mwada Simba managed her marriage with a man many years her junior: 'I confide in you privately that Mr. Phiri is too young in many ways, so I feed him with knowledge. I do so without insulting him. Because I am really old I have more experience in life than he, and so I decide many things. But I always obey his orders' (Skjønsberg 1989).

Through active and self-determined participation of villagers and the recording team, the detailed qualitative data introduced us to many issues that a closer scrutiny revealed were different from what they initially may have seemed to the outside observer. It also provided insight into villagers' strategies, like that of Mwada Simba cited above, and demonstrated how conflicts could be transferred from one sphere to another seemingly more acceptable sphere. For example, Tisekenji Phiri refused to cook for her husband, when in fact she really was endeavouring to refuse him sex because she was pregnant and did not feel like making love.

Whatever issue or problem, a close relationship between researchers and researched provides ample opportunity for discussions and analysis. A participatory approach allows space for 'peasants' to become individuals, each with their specific characters and strategies on how to plant, what crops to grow, or whether or not to get married. Tisauke Phiri, 34, the mother of several children shared this reflection with us:

> I have plenty of beans but my mind is on cash crops – on the cotton I am growing and the sunflowers. I have educated all my children by my own effort. I divorced my first husband because he never helped me, and the money to do so I earned from my groundnuts. Mr. Phiri is just as lazy as my first husband, but I am reluctant to divorce him. I do not want my children to remain without a father. (Skjønsberg 1989)

She is not the only Kefa villager who ultimately places her trust in herself. One of the male farmers had this view: 'I have this special fertilizer that I call planting fertilizer ... This system I started long ago and I tell you in truth, this is a way of cultivating from which I find much profit. The fact is that whatever other people tell me, I shall never use fertilizers in any other way.' Most people seem to rely on their own judgement and experience, something which helps explain why change agents, such as agricultural extension personnel, may have a hard time conveying their messages. But the gender factor is also here. Women are rarely visited by extension officers. Agnes Sakala thought she was too old to be useful to the extension agents and that this was why they never approached her: 'Maybe the government told them not to visit us because we have no strength to grow crops for the market?' (Skjønsberg 1989).

The qualitative data gives flavour to the Kefa study, but the time observations provide consistency which keeps the participatory research project together, methodologically, but also theoretically. Both approaches confirm over and over again the key role of women. Through the qualitative data, the strategic thinking of the women acquires a central place as we repeatedly follow their deliberations on how to maximize resources, or security, or please partners and family members. Women's central role is also manifested in their significance to the men. Young women were highly sought after as partners and spouses, or rebuked as trouble makers when expectations were not met. To quote Regina Shawa, one of the headman's five wives: 'Women hate other women who talk softly to their husbands. So when a man and a woman meet in the bush, and that is what they do when they want to love each other, or the woman needs the man's money, they take care so that nobody sees them. They don't want to trouble their friends' (Skjønsberg 1989). The older women largely dedicated their lives to looking after their family members of all ages and played a central role through their control of a major part of the food.

Participatory Research: Problems and Potentials

It was due to the proximity of the data gatherers to the villagers that discussions or more often short statements on a variety of issues could be jotted down in the notebooks virtually verbatim, next to the meticulously recorded time usage data. Individual statements that seemed of little interest at that moment could, as time went on, be read as components of some human drama that unfolded during the 15 months the recordings lasted. This is how we could follow the development from the very beginning of what turned into a witch hunt that almost tore the village apart, but was ultimately watered down by a politically astute village leader who nearly got incriminated himself. And this is how we came to understand the rights of women in connection with divorce, exemplified by Lire Banda whose husband, without her knowledge, sold the bricks they had made together to build a new house, and eventually moved to town.

People, including researchers, think and act within given social and cognitive structures which explicitly and implicitly provide them with interpretational rules which they use to order as well as organize their perceptions of the world. It is in light of such cognitive structures that data are evaluated as relevant or not. Participatory research is so challenging because it transcends the cognitive limitations of the researcher. The result is a meeting point between cultures, intellectual orientations and problem solving experiences where different and sometimes even contradictory experiences are placed on an equal footing.

Because researchers and the community studied usually represent very different points of departure, participatory research is constantly reformed by events and ideas, information and arguments. The net result is an open invitation to rethink scientific theory as well as methods. This strengthens both, as it becomes readily apparent that the issue is not only specific scientific findings, but the whole conceptualization of science as a delimited quest for knowledge.

Participatory research should, however, not be visualized as an alternative to existing social scientific research, but an important supplement. Its basic contribution is to widening our understanding of central scientific approaches, concepts and theories and exposing their middle class, male and western biases. Participatory research serves as a means of opening up the diversity of social life, defying preset designs which sort informants and information into categories of relevance and irrelevance. Perhaps one of the most striking characteristics of the Kefa village study was the diversity of life which it revealed. Even in a seemingly conformist small village, individual differences often emerged as more significant than gender differences.

A major gain when local people gather data and participate in research interpretation is that dominant ideological and social structures fade into the background. Less visible underlying intellectual and social processes have a chance of emerging. This can give strength to so-called 'silent majorities' like women vis-à-vis more powerful social groups. We cannot escape the fact that researchers are often classified in the latter category.

In the final analysis, participatory research contrasts sharply with the conventional scientific approach in which the community or social groups under investigation are treated as passive objects, or if they are invited to participate, do so to fulfil a preset research design. Participatory research provides a direct approach to elucidating rural women's forms of livelihood and alternative ways of cooperation and organization. In rural Africa, participatory research findings forcefully counter *a priori* assumptions about women's roles in hoe agricultural societies.

Notes

1. For example, in 1989, the Overseas Development Institute of Great Britain listed as many as 340 participatory research reports on farming alone (ODI 1989). Virtually all of them were published during the 1980s.
2. The completed study was published in Skjønsberg 1989.

Reference

Overseas Development Institute, *Farmer Participatory Research*, London, 1989
Skjønsberg, E., *Change in an African Village – Kefa Speaks*, West Hartford, Kumarian Press, Inc., 1989

13

Truth in Fantasy: Story-telling with and about Women in Msoga Village, Tanzania*

Ulla Vuorela

'*Once upon the time there was a woman who got married ...*'

This is the opening of a story told to me in the Tanzanian coastal village of Msoga, where I recorded over 100 stories between 1984 and 1985, while doing anthropological research on the position of women amongst the Kwere people. The story goes on: '... but her husband turned out to be a hyena, who devoured their first child and was going to eat her, too, unless her younger brother came and rescued her from her cannibalistic husband and in-laws'.

If the plot sequence and open-endedness of the stories were a surprise to me, it was because the stories clashed with the fairy-tale happy endings of my childhood. My first reaction when reading the stories that I recorded was to ask: why do the stories in Msoga start from the point where the European stories end, i.e. marriage? Why does the latter assume a happy ending and the other dastardly deeds, once the wedding takes place?

I started to examine the linkages between narratives and society. I became interested in studying the way in which subjectivity is constructed for women and men. Reflecting upon the stories has led me to increasingly think about the nature of the research encounter. The encounter between me and the people of Msoga village was not only one between people from different cultures, and between a 'researcher' and the 'researched', but also between different forms of knowledge and consciousness. This chapter is an outcome of my methodological excursion and the discoveries I made along the way. The chapter relates four stories, namely: 'The girl who married a hyena', 'The girl who married a baboon', 'The boy who married a devil' and 'The bird as a baby-sitter'. But before I describe the stories and read 'between their lines', it is necessary to discuss the activity of story-telling in its village context.

Story-telling: A Living Tradition

Story-telling is a vibrant tradition in Msoga village and an integral part of the annual alternation between work and recreation, production and reproduction. It is concentrated in a period of roughly four months, beginning with the harvest and concluding with planting for the new agricultural cycle. This is the period when most marriages are scheduled and a number of rituals celebrating the coming of age of youthful girls and boys take place. In Msoga, stories are told by both men and women, old and young, and a story-telling session may grow into a competition between good narrators that goes on all night. Story-tellers try to outsmart each other, getting inspiration from each other's stories. The story-telling may grow into an event, whereby one story is a comment, response or a continuation of another, and the sequence of stories becomes a larger story.

The persistence of the tradition suggests that stories contain meaningful messages. The stories told in the village make up a corpus that is known to practically everybody in the village. Over the years, people have heard the same stories time and again, albeit in different versions. In daily life, a song presented in a story may be used as an allusion to or a comment on an issue, without the story even being told. It seems not to be an accident what kind of stories are told at a particular time and place. The story-teller's selection during a session is often a commentary on current events. Furthermore, a well-known story can be given a new interpretation depending on the context.

It is characteristic of the stories in Msoga that clear-cut solutions to the problems presented are not necessarily provided in the end. What have been coined 'open-ended dilemma tales' in the study of African folklore are salient in the corpus of stories told in Msoga (Bascom 1972). The purpose of such open-ended stories is to invite the audience to debate about the meaning of the story. This is not only a characteristic of the genre, but also in accordance with the dynamics of the social organization in a matrilineal society, as explained later. Consequently, it can be emphasized that few of the stories can be interpreted in only one way. While some of the meanings may be universally shared in a genre as globally spread as tales, the interpretation of others requires knowledge of the specific society, the particular social context and even current village politics.

Most of the stories can be situated in the genre of magic tales. The story about the girl who married a hyena provides a typical example, illustrating the magical underworld that is unleashed when a girl chooses the wrong spouse. Below, an English translation of a Swahili text will be examined.

The Girl who Married a Hyena

'There was once a woman who got married. Some time after they had become man and wife, the woman moved with her husband to her parents-in-law. When the couple were preparing to leave, the younger brother of the woman started crying. He told her, "My sister, why don't we all go to your in-laws because otherwise you will be all alone there." She replied, "No, I can't take children along. You have to stay with your mother and I'm not going to take you along. I want to go alone."

The brother insisted, "My sister, why don't we go there together?", but the sister replied, "No, I want to go by myself."

But alas, that husband of hers was not human. He was a hyena who had come to catch her and take her to his place so that he could eat her!

So the brother stayed behind. After some time, he decided to make a basket that would take him to his sister. He sat down on the waste heap behind the house and started making a basket, thinking that it would help him go to his sister. It was already some time since the sister had gone. In the meantime, the sister had given birth to a child and was spending all her time with the child. The younger brother said to himself, "Wait and see, I must go and find out how things are with my sister." So he stepped into his basket and started singing,

"Fly up my basket, fly up my basket,"

"You sister of mine, you didn't let me come with you!"

So the brother travelled to his sister. On arrival, the in-laws received him happily as he landed on the waste heap behind their house, PU! He immediately requested to see his sister and asked her, "My sister, I hear you have a child. Where is the child?"

The sister replied, "Oh my brother, I don't know where the child is. It has disappeared."

The brother said, "Oh dear. But I have come to see you. Father and mother sent me."

"You are welcome my brother!"

So the brother was invited to some porridge by the mother-in-law. It was served in the mother-in-law's house where he was first given some water to wash his hands, so that he could roll the porridge in his hand and dip it in the soup. As he was eating, he was very surprised to see a little hand, a child's hand in the soup. He asked himself, "Oh my, is this some animal or a human being?" So he called his sister to come and see what he was eating and asked her, "Is this a human hand or some meat?" Then he said, "I am not going to eat this soup. You told me that your child disappeared, and lo! our friends must have eaten it! They slaughtered it and turned it into meat! This must mean that your friends have gone to the forest to look for firewood so that they can then eat you up when they come back. Listen, your husband is not a human being, but a hyena!"

The sister burst out crying and said, "My brother, how can we go back home to our mother without having them see us?"

The brother replied, "Oh my sister, don't worry, if your in-laws come, I will put you in my basket and we will fly off!"

Meanwhile, the in-laws who had gone for a hunt were bringing back a lot of meat. They were carrying their kill, giraffes and elephants on their shoulders. When they arrived, they told the sister to prepare some food. But she refused by saying that her stomach was quite full because of the amount of porridge she had eaten at noon. "What kind of cook is this now?" They asked, "Why don't you prepare us some food?"

"Oh, my stomach is full, I am not going to make any food."

So they told her, "But there will be a dance and music here tonight! Men will come and women and young girls will come and boys will come to dance and have fun here this evening."

So the brother told his sister, "Sister, listen! Do you hear what they are saying? Tonight there will be dancing and drum music! Prepare yourself, take all your clothes and put them in the basket. We must get ready and set off because all your friends will be coming and you know, they are all hyenas and they will come and eat you up." The sister said that she was ready to go and the brother said, "Very well my sister. Come into my basket and let us go!" So they sat in the basket and started singing,

"Fly up little basket fly up!"
"My sister who refused to take me along,"
"My friend is coming back home with me,"
"Mother we are coming back ..."

So they flew up and away. When they saw a big tree, they stopped and landed on its top to rest for a while. But the hyenas followed them and started singing at the base of the tree,

"Fall down tree, so we can get some meat for food,"

"Fall down tree, so we can get some meat for food,"

"Fall down tree ...."

And the tree fell down, but the brother and sister were singing their song

"Fly up my basket, fly up..."

So they flew up, and on and on, and when they approached the people's dwellings, the people down in the houses started talking, "Goodness, listen to the song up in the sky; there is a flying basket and it is singing!"

But they flew on until they came near the house of their mother. When they came nearer, their mother was sitting in front of the house and cleaning vegetables. She heard the song which was coming closer and closer, and she ran out while saying to the father, "Listen Baba Ndemigwa, listen to the song which is coming towards us!" Baba Ndemigwa came out and saw the singing basket.

Then the basket descended, PUU! The mother saw that her two children had returned. She asked them, "My children, are you all right?"

The daughter started crying, while the brother said, "Wait mother, let me tell you! Lo, our sister got married to a hyena! Those people were hyenas, not humans. After she moved there and had a child they slaughtered the child and made soup out of it. Now that very day when I was there they went to the forest to prepare for slaughtering my sister too, but it was just then that I happened to come. Mother, where we have escaped from, there are no people, only hyenas. Mother you can be grateful we got back here because we were going to be killed, both of us."

So the mother and the father started crying and they said, "Oh how good our children have come back. You did well to come back!"

This is where the story ended.'[1]

The discussion that followed the story-telling brought out the moral: 'If your father tells you, "My child, this man is not a man and I don't want him", don't agree to get married to him. If you do, you will be in trouble!' If we wanted to interpret this tale as a hero-story, it could be named 'Brother rescues his sister from danger', which would give the plot a happy ending, from the point of view of the brother and the parents. Yet, in the wider social context of the community, there is a different outcome. The rebellious girl gets duped by marrying a monster. She is rescued, but she has lost her first child and, by the end of the story, has an unsuccessful marriage behind her. Her life has been saved, but her return back to her parents symbolizes her acknowledgement of the error of her ways.

The Girl who Married a Baboon

Synopsis: 'There was once a spinster like so many girls these days are. Her father told her to get married, but the girl refused by saying that there was nobody around who would be fit for her. Finally she started worrying about getting too old and decided to marry. She went out on the road and saw an attractive looking young stranger and proposed to him. He agreed. The husband was given a plot for cultivation. He wanted to be given an even bigger plot, and when his in-laws offered help in cultivation, he did not accept any. But he was, in fact, being helped by various animals, baboons, hornbills and black ants. When the parents of the wife went to see the field, they praised their son-in-law for the amount of work he had done. He also received help from the animals during harvest time. The husband told his wife not to get angry if some food was taken away from the fields. However, when the wife discovered that a lot had been eaten from the field, she could not help reproaching the thieves. The husband told her that she should let them eat because they would not be able to finish it all. When the husband and the wife went to harvest together, they found the fields virtually empty. There was not a trace of any crop. The wife started abusing the workers, questioning what kind of people they were. The husband then changed into a baboon and told his friends to go and eat everything because his wife had insulted them badly. The helpers who all had grown tails in the meanwhile, sang as they devoured everything. When his in-laws heard the animals' singing they got worried. The baboons had devastated the fields and had even emptied the grain stores. The parents reproached their daughter and said that all of this happened because she had agreed to marry a baboon. The daughter then promised to marry her one-eyed cross-cousin. So they got married.'[2]

The obstinate woman who married a baboon also got into trouble. She delayed getting married and did not obey her elders. As a result, not only does she get into trouble, but her parents lose what they rightfully can expect from a son-in-law. The story with its strong didacticism could also be summarized as 'Heroine gets into a crisis but the situation eventually returns back to normal', or 'Heroine gets into a crisis because of her rebellious behaviour'. But as in the previous story, a return back to 'normal' is ambiguous. Yes, from the community's point of view, a crisis has been resolved because the heroine has been disciplined. However, whether she really acquiesces is an open question. Her life circumstances are by no means resolved. In the beginning she was a spinster, now she is a woman with a failed marriage and her parents have experienced an economic loss. On top of this, she has had to agree to marrying a one-eyed cross-cousin!

The prescriptive advice contained in both stories is implicit. In the discussions that followed the story-telling sessions, when I asked about the moral of the stories, the gathering emphatically stated that one should not go against the advice of the elders. 'Respect your elders and marry your cross-cousin!' What is interesting is that this prescribed behaviour is presented as an imperative fact of life, rather than an ideal 'happily-ever-after' solution for the woman concerned.

The Lost Woman

When reflecting on the relationship between a story and its social context, both of the above stories could be seen as solidly rooted in matrilineal social organization, which they describe and whose conventions they reflect. In matrilineal societies, marriage is often arranged by elder kin. Mothers or grandmothers may initiate the choice of a spouse, while the council of male elders have the final say. The girls are said to have the freedom to agree or not to agree, but the community has its ways of persuading them. Obviously, horror stories such as these can be counted among them. If story-telling is a discourse, it is one of persuasion whereby authority is constructed and reproduced for each new generation. Stories are used as ideological means to convince the girls to choose in the interests of the wider community. To impress the message upon the girls more effectively, it is couched in the form of a horror story which hints at dramatic losses not only to the girl but to her kin. Making the girl feel guilty is part of the strategy.

It is also with regard to matrilineal traditions that it becomes understandable that the stories warning about the choice of a wrong spouse are much more frequent than those of the type 'Hero gets a spouse' describing the efforts to gain a good partner and good fortune. When the ideal partner is prescribed by tradition, it is more vital to make youth agree to follow the tradition than to dream of faraway princes and princesses! It is not that such stories were not told to me, but they seemed to be less favoured.

Open-endedness of the story also accords well with the inner dynamics of a matrilineal culture. If the residence after marriage or throughout life has not necessarily been fixed, but has to be negotiated, stories provide one means of commenting on the issue. According to tradition, the newly-wed couple first resides with the wife's kin while the young man carries out bride-service, like the baboon in our first story. When the first child has been born and the husband has cultivated enough, the couple is free to move to the husband's kin, a status referred to in the beginning of the hyena story as 'after they had become man and wife'. But after that, the couple's residence can be negotiated again and is under the authority of the council of the male elders, while the ultimate authority lies with the maternal uncles. What has been coined the 'matrilineal puzzle' in anthropological literature describes the conflicting interests any man may have both as a father and as an uncle (Schneider and Gough 1961; Vuorela 1987). A man has the authority over his sister's children which culminates in his right to exercise authority over her marriage, while his own children will be under the authority of their maternal uncle and not their father. The authority of the uncle prompts a keen interest of men in their sisters' children, as was indicated in the story about the girl who married a hyena. This makes brothers more likely to be heroes than future husbands, as is the case in European stories.

A comparison with similar stories from a patrilineal society with strong fraternal interest groups will, however, demonstrate that the heroism of the brother is not a peculiarity of matrilineal societies. Stories of the monster as a husband have also been identified in patrilineal contexts of West Africa (Belvaude 1989). Calame-Griaule (1987) comments that such stories basically emphasize the 'illegality' of marriages based on sexual attraction, or which take place without the consent of the parents. In her analysis, the problem demonstrated in these stories is that no bridewealth is paid for the girl who runs away with a stranger without waiting for the proper transactions to take place.

If a brother in the matrilineal context has an interest in his sister's marriage, it can also be because he becomes the maternal uncle to her children and thus a brother's position of power and political authority is also built on the reproductive career of his sisters. In a patrilineal context, a young man's ability to marry may depend on the bridewealth paid for his sister. In both societies, brothers are constructed as 'heroes' in order to earn the respect from their sisters on whom they depend for their own reproduction. Respect is gained for the brothers as the protectors of their sisters, while in fact they are keenly guarding their sisters and their behaviour. Women are thus controlled both by their fathers as law givers and by brothers as their guardian/protectors who invigilate so that they are not 'lost' to the 'wrong' men, i.e. strangers who take them away.

The stories construct a dependence and respect between siblings, but this cooperation is not symmetrical. When age is more important than gender, then the younger brothers have to be constructed as elders to gain authority over their older sisters. A Limba story from Sierra Leone is a good illustration of how a hierarchy is constructed between a younger brother and a sister (Finnegan 1967). In a situation where a younger brother has rescued his sister, the brother speaks:

'My sister, now you understand that I am more than you. Well, let us go. I was able to free you. I was nearly killed for you. But it is all right. For you, I am the senior to you. My sense is the senior's. I am called the man, and I have more sense than you. Let us go!'

In the final passage, the story makes Kanu Masala, the god, speak:

'It was Sara [the brother] that had to say, "Here is the man you will marry", Kanu Masala saw this. That is what he told us in farewell, us Limba. Even if it is only a small boy, and you are the first born, you the woman, if he says to you, "Here is where you will be married", you the woman, agree with what he says. Even if you are known to be older, you the woman, you will not be able to stay in marriage by your own power. You will not be able to save your own life. Stand behind what the boy says. He is able to speak for you. Since Kanu told us that, all of us, Limba, now we follow that.'

In the patrilineal context, violation consists of a missing bridewealth payment, an essential payment creating enabling conditions for the brother's eventual marriage. In the matrilineal context, correct marital procedures are just as important. A number of social norms can be transgressed. The danger of losing a young woman to a stranger is particularly serious if the girl gets married to a man from a neighbouring, perhaps patrilineal culture. Her labour power and reproductive contribution will be lost, benefiting another community which does not acknowledge the matrilineal system of changing residence between husband's and wife's kin. This may also explain why the stories are more often concerned with the 'lost woman' rather than about the 'lost man'. There is, however, one example from Msoga which warns young men against obtaining a wife from afar.

The Boy who Married a Devil

Synopsis: 'There was once a king who had two sons. When they had grown up their father told them to marry. The elder son agreed but the younger one refused and asked the father to give him a horse instead. The elder brother got married and the younger brother got his horse. The younger brother set out on a journey with his horse. In a faraway seashore, he met two lovely young women and proposed to one of them. Then he went to inform his father and returned to collect his wife. While on the way back, the horse died and the wife asked her husband to carry her on his back. On arrival, the parents saw that their daughter-in-law was a devil. The husband asked his wife to get off his back so that they could sit down, but she refused and the husband had to sit down with his wife on his back. Whenever the husband asked his wife to come off his back, she refused. So the husband had to eat with his wife on his back. The husband had to take a bath with the wife on his back. The husband had to sleep with his wife on his back. The wife hung on the back of her husband until he died under her pressure. When his parents washed the body for burial the wife still hung on his back. When the parents dressed their son for burial, the wife still hung on. When the parents buried their son the wife finally got off his back and went back to where she came from.'[3]

Here, a male youth gets into peril because he rebels against the elders and violates the norms of preferential marriage. Again, marriage signifies a crisis because of the wrong choice of a spouse. But how does a story depicting a devilish woman as the villain fit into the matrilineal context?

Respect for the authority of the elders is expected from young girls and boys alike. But it is more dangerous if girls rebel, a fact signified by the greater frequency of feminine-centred tales of waywardness. But boys should not marry strangers either, which is to be expected if cross-cousin marriage is the norm.

A simple structural analysis of the story reveals elements which adjust this 'universal' into the cultural context of the story-telling community, be it a matrilineal or patrilineal community. In the above story, the devilish wife is immediately taken to her husband, whereas typical stories from Msoga carefully indicate that the custom of bride-service is followed, and the departure from the wife's relatives only takes place after the couple have had their first child. The horse, as an alien element in the local culture, indicates that the tale has either been adopted from outside the matrilineal domestic community, or has been told with reference to some neighbouring group of people.

The choice of a wrong spouse is not only something that concerns young women, but young men as well. The story of the devilish wife can be interpreted as part of the discursive tension between matri- and patrilineal social organization. The 'stranger' is now a woman from an alien tradition where women are strongly dependent on their husbands and can expect to be provided for by their husbands, i.e. 'sitting in purdah'. To the people of Msoga, observations of such norms can be made right in their midst due to the multiplicity of local cultures found in close proximity to one another.

The matrilineal domestic societies of the Tanzanian coast, such as the Kwere, have for centuries had strongly patriarchal cultures as its neighbours. In terms of oral traditions, the presence of Arab and Swahili cultures on the East African coast has also had an impact on the oral traditions of the area. Rich Arab cultures have flourished on the coast from the early years of Islamic penetration. Arab trading families have travelled and lived upcountry and their custom of female purdah has been observed by the local matrilineal people. Within the rich Arab trading class, women do not participate in any agricultural work, whereas Kwere women are important agricultural producers. To marry someone who depends on the man only is definitely uneconomical in the minds of Kwere elders. It is generally believed that if you marry a stranger from the coast, you will end up in peril because of a demanding wife!

The story of the devilish wife, a 'complete parasite', is not so much concerned with generational continuity through reproduction but with the daily maintenance of productivity. Here, a story from another context, or observations of a neighbouring culture have been adjusted to the political thinking of the matrilineal Kwere. As such, the story about the devilish wife does not belong to the theme of the 'lost woman', but depicts the economic losses of a young man and his community. Thus, swapping female and male roles in a seemingly similar story does not express symmetrical concerns. However, this story also contributes to setting the boundaries of the matrimonial alliances of the matrilineal society. As potential marriage partners, members of other domestic societies are depicted as strange, inhuman monsters and their kin are portrayed as dangerous cannibals.

Truth through the Voice of the Elders

Truth is a relative concept. Anything can sound true, given one's ideological persuasion and the spokesperson's convincing arguments.

In this light, all stories can be considered combinations of fact and fiction. The examples dealt with may be classified on the basis of formal criteria into magic tales, but they should perhaps be considered a sub-genre of their own. In essence, they are normative tales which express the ideology of the patriarchal mode of human reproduction (Vuorela 1987). If you marry against the will, i.e. interests, of your elders, you will get into peril. If you violate the norms, you will get lost, and you will lose your children. And to die childless is a fate worse than death in the ideology of the agricultural domestic community. But the adverse consequences extend beyond the individual. When the girl is lost, it is the community that loses her, her children and the labour contribution of the son-in-law.

Three commandments structure the aforementioned Msoga tales, namely: 1) respect your elders, which applies to both young women and men; 2) don't marry from afar, which also applies to both young women and men, but above all, to women; and 3) take care of your children. All of these dictums essentially express a concern for generational continuity and respect for the established hierarchy between old and young, men and women.

A different subjectivity is constructed for the male and female actors. Men, as fathers, are the speakers and enforcers of these norms, but they are not necessarily 'present' in the stories as speakers and actors. The patriarchal norms, aptly described by Tsala-Tsala (1982) as the 'Law of the Absent Fathers', is implicitly understood.

In the context of the agricultural domestic community, patriarchal law has to tame the woman's desire, so as not to lose her. A subjected identity is constructed for women who become victims if they show signs of individual wilfulness. Social reproduction has to be put ahead of individual desires. Desire of men is given more space because it does not necessarily conflict with generational continuity. Within the ideology of the patriarchal mode of human reproduction, desire is subjected to the concerns for generational reproduction.

Furthermore, respect for the elders is more essential in the patriarchal ideology of these stories than the respect that women must accord to men. In some stories, younger brothers are constructed as elders in order to give them authority over their elder sisters, while in other situations, older women join the ranks of the elders. Thus the social construction of age and gender is conditional on the concern for generational continuity and ideological consolidation of the elders as the managers of that continuity.

I had been puzzled by the fact that in Msoga, similar stories were told by women, men and children alike. As a feminist, I wondered why it did not make much of a difference whether the story was told by a man or a woman. The content was apparently the same. Did gender not matter at all in the construction of the fantastic realm? One comment gave me a clue to this question. In passing, one of the village elders told me about his second wife whom he 'inherited' from his brother, i.e. he had followed the leviratic practice of marrying the widow of a brother. 'She is not my wife,' he said, even though he had children with her and lived together with her. 'She is the wife of the voice of the elders.'

Likewise, a story is not the story of its teller only. In fact, it does not matter who tells the story, if it is the voice of the elders which speaks in them. I would argue that the voice of the elders is the voice of the patriarchal truth. The uppermost concern of the patriarchal truth is the generational continuity of the society which the patriarchs guard through marital strategies and land control. Over and over again, the stories construct the ideology of the patriarchal reproductive regime. The stories not only deal with male/female relations in marriage, but also with the generational relationship between the old and the young. This is cleverly achieved through a discourse of persuasion, which does not directly command but allows one to agree. Agreement is facilitated by the use of horror as a narrative element which makes the stories compulsive and powerful. The strange spouse is a threat to the community. Hence, he or she is depicted as a cannibalistic monster who not only devours the wife but devours children, or destroys the husband, as in the story about the boy who married a devil.

All of this expresses the concern for generational continuity of the agricultural domestic society, whereby patriarchs control the marital strategies for the common good of preserving women as reproducers in the community and not allowing men to import parasitic, dependent wives who do not wield the hoe. The voice of the elders demonstrates how women are valued both for their reproductive capability and for the contribution they make as producers.

To conclude, let us listen to the voice of the elders through the story of the bird as a baby-sitter. Perhaps it was told to me because I was somehow identified with efforts by UNICEF to bring a day-care centre to the village. A day-care centre never succeeded, despite the fact that the villagers seemed to be very cooperative and did their best in choosing girls to be sent for training. The following story may give a hint as to the kind of doubts people had in their minds about taking their children to a day-care centre. The dilemma of combining childcare responsibilities and agricultural production is salient even though the story is told by a male elder. But what is perhaps most noteworthy in the narrative is the voice of the elders endeavouring to ensure generational continuity, warning women about their role in raising the future generation.

The Bird as a Baby-sitter

'Quiet down Kidimu ...

Once upon the time there were a man and his wife. Together they cultivated a field. Unluckily, the man died. Luckily, the woman was left with a child.

This woman was a hard worker. She was very clever in hoeing. She hoed quickly and skilfully. Her field extended from here almost up to Dar es Salaam [approximately 75 km away].

Now if you have a big field and you have a child, you know that your problem is to get somebody to take care of the child while you work. And this woman had nobody to help her. She took care of the child on her own.

On the first day as she was hoeing alone, she put the child to sleep on a tree. On the second day, as she was hoeing, she did the same and put the child to sleep on a tree. On the third day as she was hoeing, she heard a big stream of very cold air descend from above, hrrrrRRRR!! Up to theeeeere! As she looked around, she could not see what kind of giant was moving around. But then, look! It was a very big bird which had lifted the child up on its wings. The mother's heart started beating with fear, because the child was small and the bird was huge. The mother cried: "HA! My child has been taken from me. What shall I do now?"

The bird alighted on top of the roof of a house that had been built near the edge of the field. The mother tried to prevent her tears from coming, because the bird had taken her child and she did not have the strength to catch the bird. While the bird perched high on the roof, the mother thought: "What shall I do when God puts me into a situation like this? First my husband died but luckily left me with a child. I am taking care of the child and then the bird comes and takes the child away!" The child was called Kidimu.

But the bird, you see, had come to be the baby-sitter! It descended on to the roof and put the child there. If the child cried, the bird sang a song to it and sang until the mother tired of hoeing. Then the bird brought the child down, putting it on a tree and flew off.

On the next day this happened again. On the fifth day, in the same way, the bird took care of the child. The mother hoed without worrying. When the mother came to the field with the child, as soon as they arrived, the bird appeared and looked after the child. The mother had no worries. The bird put the child on the roof and if the child cried the bird sang:

"Kidimu be quiet ..."

And the child did not cry since the bird kept the child happy. On the sixth day, the same happened and so on. The mother hoed. I can tell you, she hoed so that the dust flew all about. She mourned her husband's death. She mourned with her hoe. The hoe was her safety. The hoe was her wealth. She cried. She hoed and the bird looked after the child.

Well, on the seventh day, the danger started posing itself. A baboon came. You know these baboons? The mother feared that something bad was coming. Oh no! Where did that horrible creature come from? Perhaps it was forewarning of a lion, and so the mother rushed towards the child.

The baboon asked her, "Why do you rush to take the child?"

The mother replied, "Is this child mine or yours?"

The baboon said, "Listen! If it was your child, you would keep it on your back as you hoe!"

The mother tried to defend herself against the criticism, "Look at this field, how do you think I have got this field?"

But the baboon was even more accusing, "Aha, is that so? If that is your field, then this child cannot stay alive. You cannot deny that you are a human with five fingers on your hand and I am a human with five fingers on my hand. Am I not good enough to look after your child? If I am not good enough, then please go ahead and hoe with the child on your back! Then it can survive!"

The baboon set off. But before it left, a huge rain cloud appeared. It started raining heavily so that the mother got frightened and started thinking that the rain signified something. But luckily mother and child arrived home safely.

In the morning, the woman went to the field as usual. She put the child on to the tree to sleep, the very same old tree. Then she started hoeing. You know, when a woman hoes, she bends forward. She does not look around. She does not see very far in front of her, nor does she look back. She just hoes and does not know anything about the rest of the world.

Then the baboon arrived, the one who said that the child did not belong to her! The baboon came and snatched the child. The mother did not realize what happened. She did not know whether the child was there or not. As you hoe, all your thoughts get absorbed into it and so it was with this mother. It was a big job. She was so concentrated that the baboon took her child without her knowing it!

At about nine or ten o'clock the bird came PU! to the same place it always came and looked around but did not see the child. The mother noticed the bird.

The bird asked, "Mama, where is your child?"

"My child? Well, I placed it on the tree, as before."

The bird replied, "Mama, come and see where the child is!"

The mother went and saw that the child was gone. She started crying. She cried and cried. The woman started looking for the child, but the child was nowhere to be seen. No, however hard she looked for it, it was nowhere to be seen! Not where she always put it, not where the bird usually took it. So too, the bird looked everywhere for the child until it could do no more. The child had disappeared.

This is how our world is!

This calamity took place in days gone by. Did the baboon take the child? Did it eat the child? It was a mystery for the people of that time. The baby-sitter was quite incompetent and let the child disappear. They thought it was the baboon who robbed the mother of her child, but they did not know for certain. This could not be known.

This is where the story ended.'[4]

Clearly, this is another horror story. It pays tribute to the hoe, to the child and to the mother, yet at the same time, it pins the woman down to the field with a hoe in her hand and a baby on her back. The hoe is her wealth, and what the story-telling male elder does not say is that it is his wealth too.

Notes

* Parts of this paper have previously appeared in my article titled, 'From Oral to Written: The Theme of the "Lost Woman" in Some Tanzanian Narratives', in J. Gould (ed.), *A Different Kind of Journey: Essays in Honour of Marja-Liisa Swantz*, Helsinki, Finnish Anthropological Society, 1991, pp. 65–91.

1. Story told by Zena Shabani recorded by Ulla Vuorela, Msoga, 19 September 1985. Original in Kikwere.

2. Story told by Fatuma Halfani recorded by Ulla Vuorela, Msoga, 21

November 1985. Original in Kikwere.
3. Story told by Amina Salum recorded by Ulla Vuorela, Msoga, 22 November 1984. Original in Kikwere.
4. Story told by Nambari Kivunja recorded by Ulla Vuorela, Msoga, 5 January 1986. Original in Kiswahili.

References

Bascom, W., 'African Dilemma Tales', in R.M. Dorson (ed.), *African Folklore*, New York, Doubleday, 1972

Belvaude, C.E., *Amos Tutuola et l'Univers du Conte Africain*, Paris, Editions l'Harmattan, 1989

Calame-Griaule, G., *Des Cauris au Marché: Memoires de la Société des Africanistes*, Paris, 1987

Finnegan, R., *Limba Stories and Story-telling*, Oxford, Clarendon Press, 1967

Schneider, D.M. and K. Gough (eds), *Matrilineal Kinship*, Berkeley, University of California Press, 1961

Tsala-Tsala, J-P., 'La Loi des Pères Absents: Etude Psycho-Linguistique du Discourse Didactique Beti à Partir de Cinq Contes Didactiques', Ph.D., Centre des Etudes Africains, EHESS, Paris, 1982

Vuorela, U., *The Women's Question and the Modes of Human Reproduction: An Analysis of a Tanzanian Village*, Uppsala, Scandinavian Institute of African Studies, 1987

VI

CONCLUSION

14

Burying the Hoe?

Deborah Fahy Bryceson

The focus of this book has been on women agriculturalists in hoe-cultivating societies. Significantly, the largest concentration of hoe agriculturalists in the world resides in a band between the Sahara and Kalahari deserts of North and southern Africa respectively. This form of agriculture has been adapted to a wide range of ecological niches from lush forests to grass savannas. Within this vast terrain, hoe agriculture has been practised alongside or mixed with other modes of livelihood including hunting and gathering, pastoralism, ox ploughing and mechanized agriculture. The picture that emerges of rural societies in this zone is thus highly variegated. Nonetheless, the centrality of women's role in hoe agriculture tends to emerge as a notable feature throughout most of the territory.

This conclusion summarizes some of the lessons to be learned from prolonged study of women hoe cultivators in various parts of Sub-Saharan Africa. Areas of consensus and contention amongst the contributing authors regarding social relations of production and reproduction found in hoe societies are highlighted. The chapter concludes with a brief consideration of current evidence and possible future directions of women's role in African agriculture.

Discerning Patterns and Dynamics of Women Cultivators in Hoe Economies

Innumerable questions and interpretations regarding women hoe cultivators' working lives spring forth from the abundance of evidence that has been collected in rural Africa. The authors contributing to this volume have written on the basis of direct field experience in Tchad, Cameroon, Nigeria, Congo, Uganda, Kenya, Tanzania, Malawi, Zambia,

Botswana, and Mozambique. A majority of them are professional anthropologists, but several, by their own account, rejected their structural/functionalist training in the process of absorbing the information that local people communicated to them. Their sources of theoretical inspiration span participatory research, historical materialism, systems analysis, post-modernism, folkloristics, amongst others. But it would be a mistake to label individual analyses on the basis of any particular theory. Researchers with long experience of the field tend to abhor attempts to stuff the societies they study into theoretical pigeonholes. They have seen too many exceptions to the theory to be a willing party to such expedients.

Conventional Categories

Nonetheless, experienced researchers go into the field with the baggage of conventional terminology and they return to write up findings knowing that such terminology must be reckoned with if they are to succeed in imparting what they have observed to others. Ekejiuba focusses on the misconceptions perpetrated by the use of the term 'household'. She advocates adoption of another category, the 'hearth-hold', to denote the strong material bonds between a mother and her children which can be nested within the broader social unit of the household. She argues that recognition of hearth-holds can facilitate intra- and inter-household analyses and are vital to the study of reproductive strategies. Caplan's and Obbo's articles illustrate the latter point, showing how cooperation between hearth-holds goes some way to solving childcare and domestic labour constraints in situations of duress.

In a similar vein, Bryceson identifies misleading notions that arise from using the term 'household' with reference to women's work domain. She prefers the more all-encompassing term 'homestead', defined as a residential location as well as agricultural fields and the area in and around the village from which women derive the raw materials for basic needs provisioning. She argues that African rural women are not confined to work 'within the household' in a situation analogous to that of western women. Nonetheless, cross-cultural similarities have been generally assumed. The knock-on effect of western feminists' preoccupation with crushing female sterotypes of domesticity and challenging home economics as a field of study may have been the inadvertent diversion of attention away from the need for national government and donor agency efforts to seriously assist in finding a more *comprehensive* array of practical solutions to the rigours of African rural women's working day.

'Female heads of households' is a category of analysis which has gained currency over the past two decades, as Peters recounts. The incidence of female heads of households comes up in all the chapters dealing with the southern African labour reserve countries of Malawi, Zambia, Mozambique, and Botswana. Peters notes a disturbing tendency for aid project components taking account of, or focussing specifically on, female heads of households to be considered fulfilment of donor obligations to 'do something for women'. By dichotomizing male and female households, donors obscure differences among female-headed households and, more seriously, obscure the ways in which gender relations mediate production and consumption in *all* types of households.

'Good targeting', i.e. a precise identification of worthy project recipients and effectiveness of channelling funds or material support directly to them, has become a prime criterion for evaluating the success of donor assistance. Pursuit of this objective, however, often results in ready-made formulas that are too iron-cast to adapt to local circumstances. Broad categories of people are quickly labelled 'victims' or 'oppressors'. Female heads of households as victims are a case in point. Furthermore, single category targeting can be self-defeating. Bryceson maintains that donors' strong preference for small-scale, local-level women's projects beamed at married, childbearing women has, in most cases, failed to make a large or lasting impact. National programmes directed at unmarried teenage girls might have greater potential.

Cumbersome Concepts

Just as western units of analysis do not travel well, the superimposition of western concepts can severely distort perceptions of rural Africa. Several of the authors have argued that western researchers' over-concentration on 'male domination in gender relations' has caused a blinkered vision of reality. Dupré sees this as a mask for the more pernicious domination of the west over the non-industrialized population of rural Africa. Both Peters and O'Laughlin, from a more policy-oriented perspective, argue that the assumption that 'men don't matter' and that conjugality is not important leads to the application of lop-sided policies that have limited viability.

Some of the authors have taken issue with the notion of African rural women's 'relative autonomy' from men. O'Laughlin suggests that a false dichotomy between autonomy and dependence has arisen which eliminates the possibility of examining male/female interdependence and conjugal relations. Obbo, Ekejiuba, and Dupré take a related stance, emphasizing female agency, rather than female autonomy. This leaves room for a wide range of power relations between the sexes. Caplan, on the other hand, distinguishes agency from well-being, inferring that women may make decisions in such disadvantaged circumstances, that the 'freedom' to decide is virtually nullified by the culturally and materially restricted range of choice.

Conjugality is clearly operative in rural Africa. Obbo refers to her discussions with Ugandan rural women in which they unanimously held the view that it was better to have a husband during the hard times that prevailed. Skjønsberg cites the case of a middle-aged, once-divorced women who admits her current husband is useless, but for the sake of the children she tolerates him. It is revealing to contrast the views of African rural men. When asked, they tend to project themselves as 'pulling their weight' in the conjugal relationship. Caplan reports with some degree of irony a conversation she had with the husband of her main informant who asserted that 'men work as hard as women'. Similarly, Obbo records that men discount women's nursing activities and take the view that they are their families' chief 'health carers' because they pay for the medicines.

Western feminists have long admired African rural women for their 'female solidarity' networking. Both Caplan and Obbo vividly depict how female solidarity can be especially strong in times of physical duress, such as illness or pregnancy. Davison, however, cautions that cooperative behaviour amongst African women is not universal. Interestingly, she cites a case involving women from matrilineal groups where the women are highly competitive with regard to land access and earning cash. Under such circumstances women's projects based on assumptions of female solidarity are unlikely to succeed.

Obbo identifies another concept of duality which was most prevalent during the colonial period but has now reappeared in the context of AIDS, namely the distinction made between 'women of moral virtue versus vice'. By stressing the role of female prostitutes in the spread of AIDS, various western journalists, as well as some medical experts, have deflected attention away from the role of men who are infecting faithful wives. In so doing, they risk invoking a witch hunt against a small segment of the female population who are prostitutes, while ignoring the much larger numbers of women who as wives, mothers and sisters are nursing AIDS victims.

Vantage Point of the Researcher

Attempting to understand the position of African women hoe cultivators cannot be done on the basis of snapshots of particular moments in time. Guyer considers the value of different time-frames to reveal dynamic change. Her experimentation with various time-frames reveals shortcomings of neat evolutionary theories regarding African female farming. Likewise, Peters stresses the need for research which traces processes of change over time using units of analysis that are capable of accommodating the dynamics of gender.

Researchers' conscious decision-making regarding their subject matter are accompanied by several default choices which arise either through not fully anticipating what they will find in the field or being held in the grip of prevailing theories about what is significant and what is inconsequential. Both Skjønsberg and Vuorela refer to 'different forms of knowledge and consciousness' that distinguish them as 'researchers' from the 'researched'. Thus, Skjønsberg prefers a participatory research approach, where the researched and researchers merge into one and the research process becomes one of self-discovery.

Any consideration of the vantage point of the researcher must ultimately confront the inter-subjectivity between the researcher and the researched. This book concentrates on western perceptions of African women cultivators, but surely the tables should be turned. What do the women cultivators think of the researchers? Their views would probably provide a lively antidote to the volumes of sometimes turgid prose written by western observers about them.

Caplan's article, written in dialogue form from her research notes, provides some revealingly candid comments. During the course of a discussion about optimal family size and sex preference of children, Hadija 'turns the table' on Pat Caplan with her observations relating to Pat's relatively small family: '... men want boys and women want girls. It is best to have some of each. For there is the work of the bill-hook (*nyundu*, used by men) and that of the hoe (*jembe*, used more by women than men), so you need both, don't you? But in your country, since the work is that of the pencil, I suppose it doesn't matter which you get.'

Whether or not her remark was intended tongue-in-cheek, Hadija surmised what was relevant in a material context very different from

her own, unfettered by theories of western stages of development and
the role of women in western society. By contrast, western perceptions
too often fail to recognize, ignore or jettison local perspectives and
rationales in favour of what *should* matter in terms of prevailing theories.
Western theorists tend to project their own anxieties and social constructs
on African women. Perhaps this is why African female hoe cultivators'
lives have proved enigmatic to westerners. The role of women in lineage-
based African societies is a case in point.

'Mother Africa': Imaging Women's Place in Lineage Descent

Western scholars have long been occupied with the enterprise of
constructing theories centred on the significance of lineage organization
for social, economic and political change in rural Africa, as O'Laughlin
observes in her chapter. For decades, anthropological thought was
weighted towards the notion of the incompatibility of matrilineal
organization and wealth accumulation. Matrilineal societies were almost
exclusively associated with subsistence-based agriculture. Mary Douglas
challenged Goody (1962) and others in a seminal article entitled 'Is
Matriliny Doomed in Africa?' She argues that it is the appearance of
economic restrictions, not wealth *per se*, which causes matriliny to give
way to patriliny. Douglas (1971) lists the characteristics of matrilineal
social organization as:

> open recruitment of talent and manpower, strong inter-group alliance, [and]
> scope for achievement ... [M]atriliny provides the framework of a corporate
> descent group without making exclusive demands on the loyalties of males
> ... If there is any advantage in a descent system which overrides exclusive,
> local loyalties, matriliny has it.

According to Douglas, the need for cross-cutting social ties arises from
the nature of production in hoe economies. Harvests from rainfed
agriculture are erratic. The unit of production, the homestead, is smaller
than the ideal unit of distribution. There is a need to effect cooperation
and reciprocity between homesteads and between ecological zones. In
other words, matriliny operates as a social lubricant. Douglas hastens
to add that such attributes can be of value in societies where production
shortfalls are not prevalent and cites examples of business investments
facilitated by matrilineal organization.

Historical evidence provided by Davison supports the general view that external influences have facilitated the spread of patrilineality. Both Islam and Christianity have lent ideological support to patrilineality. Colonial governments, in their efforts to establish and maintain civil order, relied heavily on lineage structures and male elder control be it in a matrilineal or patrilineal form. But it is necessary to note a recent reversal in western orientation. As O'Laughlin observes, lineages are no longer seen as guarantors of political control but rather as perpetrators of a demographic deluge that thwarts economic development efforts. Current development thinking in international agencies is generally in line with western feminists in seeking to support African women's autonomy by affording them more educational and economic opportunity as a means of escaping the dictates of lineage authority and pressures to bear many children.

In any overview of African rural societies, it would be difficult to overlook the importance of lineage structures and ideology with respect to sanctioning women's rights and duties. For example, Caplan notes that her female informant rationalizes having another son on the basis of wanting to secure her marriage, since she has hitherto only succeeded in having daughters with her current husband. Vuorela's 'voice of the elders' invokes heavy penalties in the form of wild animals for marriage partners, kidnappings and cannibalistic feasts of one's children for those who do not adhere to the wisdom of their elders with regard to marriage partner selection. The 'lost woman' is a matrilineal dilemma which contrasts with the 'dutiful sister' who stays in her natal locality and works hard in the fields. Brothers rather than husbands, are cast as heroes.

But Kuper (1982) argues that lineage organization is largely the creation of western social anthropologists. Kuper's perspective highlights the fact that too much has been read into African lineages by anthropologists and non-anthropologists alike. Lineage is not necessarily the dominant form of association in African rural communities (Fardon 1984). Indeed it is usually very difficult for any particular society to be classified as 'matrilineal' or 'patrilineal' since combined elements of both are the norm. Thus, dualistic terminology has to be scrapped yet again. Even typologies are difficult. Each society seems to have a unique blend of matrilineal and patrilineal features. Furthermore, lineality/inheritance, locality/residence, production systems and control over resources can all evolve separately and be combined in any number of ways.

Perhaps it is most useful to get beyond the realm of lineage ideology and come down to one basic question. Do married women reside in the territory of their kin or their husband's kin? Their locality, not so much in the physical sense, but rather in terms of proximity to kin, is critical to their leverage both socially and materially. Different social strategies to secure resources must be exercised when living amongst one's husband's kin, as opposed to living with one's own kin.

But a woman's residence is not always a fixed 'here or there' situation. As Ekejiuba points out, women may move to their husband's home territory and then back to their own during their adult life. Often, not all women in a society follow the same pattern of residential location. A combination of matrilineal and patrilineal features gives individuals the means to rationalize their choice of residence on the basis of either. In such circumstances, material rather than ideological selection criteria prevail. As Davison notes, usually the most important consideration is whether good land is available amongst the husband's or the wife's kin. Once selection of a household location is decided on these grounds, the lineage-based rationale can follow *ex post facto*.

What all this suggests is that lineage structure and ideology do exist and are a real force in the construction of men's and women's identities in most of rural Sub-Saharan Africa. But this must be prefaced with the remark that lineage ideology is subject to endless re-interpretation and manipulation by its adherents. In effect, the 'voice of the elders' constitutes the parameters of an ongoing debate and a terrain for incessant negotiation regarding the roles and duties of individual men and women.

No doubt, this openness is what gives lineage structures their versatility and constancy. The versatility is not just in terms of the individual vis-à-vis his/her society, but also at an inter-society level. Intermarriage can be facilitated between social groups through a process of lineage interpretation or even lineage reconstruction. As for constancy, one need only look at the past three thousand years and the expansion of African agriculturalists into numerous ecological niches, their adaptation to a wide variety of historical circumstances against the odds of climatic hazards, infertile soils and political depradations. Lineages and women's roles within them have been shaped to contend with material adversity. Exhorted by lineage elders, African women hoe cultivators' food production and fertility have ensured human survival. Until such material adversity is removed, it is unlikely that lineage structures will be rejected by rural women *en masse*, regardless of western prescriptions in one direction or another.

Present and Future Agricultural Horizons

Is 'female farming' an illusion? How is 'femaleness' in farming measured? In terms of male/female ratios of labour time input or in terms of relative portions of male and female contributed output? While one can fairly safely say that women in rural Africa put more time into agricultural fieldwork than in Latin America and South Asia, it does not necessarily follow that women hoe cultivators put more labour time into agriculture than men do everywhere in rural Africa. As Skjønsberg demonstrates for rural Zambia, women were occupied in food processing two times longer than in agricultural fieldwork. O'Laughlin notes that women's agricultural efforts in Tchad achieved lower yields than that of men due to time constraints. In other words, domestic drudgery, renamed 'basic needs provisioning' by donor agencies, takes up an inordinate amount of women cultivators' time.

Despite the constraints on the amount and intensity of labour that women are able to devote to farming, even casual observation of women's work patterns reveal their unswerving commitment to agriculture. This was illustrated by Caplan's female informant who was thrown into a dilemma of having to choose whether to give immediate assistance to her pregnant daughter during an illness or bring in the harvest. She took the risk of temporarily neglecting her daughter's needs to carry on with harvest work. Obbo relates how women in rural Uganda under time pressure from the numerous funeral rituals of AIDS victims took the initiative in streamlining the ceremonies: '[f]unerals are stopping us from planting, weeding and harvesting. Surely we do not want to starve as well as die of AIDS.' The intensity of women's absorption in farming is related by the male raconteur in Vuorela's recording of the 'The Bird as a Baby-sitter':

You know, when a woman hoes, she bends forward. She does not look around. She does not see very far in front of her nor does she look back. She just hoes and does not know anything about the rest of the world.

But the 'rest of the world' is changing and women's labour input into African agriculture is changing with it. The 1960s and 1970s were years of African governments' optimism in 'modern' farming. State intervention in the form of settlement schemes for cash crops and promotion of fertilizers and improved seed packages in food crops were widespread. As attempts to capitalize peasant agriculture, these measures affected local combinations of land and labour. Injections of external money into the rural economy made agriculture more attractive for men. Women experienced increasing incursions on their usufructuary rights over land, as well as menfolks' heavier claims on their labour, as they were co-opted into new crop production whose yield was considered to 'belong' to men (e.g. Conti 1979; Dey 1981; Palmer 1985; Carney 1988). On the other hand, some field evidence suggests that men's labour input in more capitalized agriculture does increase. For example, Moore and Vaughan (1994) cite male/female agricultural labour time ratios ranging from .38 for those households with no commercial maize sales to .69 for those selling substantial surpluses consistently over time. Nonetheless, women's average working hours in surplus-producing households was greater than that of women in subsistence-based households. In other words, their working day superseded everyone else's, be it other women in the village or men within their own households.

Extension of women's working day is not solely due to increased agricultural labour. There is a spatial dimension to capitalized peasant agriculture which manifests itself in gender-differentiated patterns of land and labour allocation. Farmers choose to practise 'improved' farming on the fields closest to their villages, if they are at all agronomically suitable, to reduce the load-carrying requirements of transporting crop inputs to the field and transporting larger harvests from the field. One recent Zambian field study shows that it was primarily male, commercially-minded farmers who cultivated larger than average fields proximate to the village using improved inputs and modern agricultural techniques (Airey and Barwell 1991). The farmers who cultivated distant, scattered fields on the basis of traditional hoe agricultural techniques were predominantly women, even though their cooking and childcare duties required that they travelled more often between their fields and residence than men. Thus, women's travel time to fields was greater than men's. Similarly in Congo, men have been observed mechanically cultivating large areas of land close to villages while women are obliged to go further afield to cultivate (Zegers 1992). The same spatial dichotomy is documented by Chilver (1992) in Cameroon vis-à-vis men's coffee plots and women's food plots.

Structural adjustment has thrown the drive to capitalize African peasant agriculture into disarray. Before the imposition of structural adjustment programmes, most of the newly introduced agricultural inputs were sold at generously subsidized prices, while the prices of harvested crops were controlled at artificially high prices. The scrapping of government producer subsidies and market controls dealt a serious blow to farmers producing under these schemes. Now, labour must replace the recently introduced capital inputs which are no longer affordable. Female agricultural labour, be it own-account or at the behest of male household members, is under renewed pressure to produce more.

However, the demand on women's labour is influenced by land availability. Given that the population of rural Africa is anticipated to continue growing, one could argue that agrarian patterns of the densely populated parts of Sub-Saharan Africa could be suggestive of trends appearing elsewhere in the future. One can take the fertile, highland areas of East Africa as an example. The plough is not commonly used in these areas due largely to extreme land fragmentation and small farm plot size. Thus, hoe agriculture continues to be the norm. Two distinctive patterns seem to be emerging in severely land constrained areas of the East African highlands: that of exclusively female 'vestige farming' or alternatively, the dominance of male commercial farming.

In many rural areas experiencing extreme population pressure, one tends to find a 'women left on the land' phenomenon. A 1986 survey of Rwandese households showed that smallholdings had intensified their on-holding labour input using female labour while men were engaged in a higher than average incidence of off-farm activities (von Braun, de Haen and Blanken 1991). Raikes (1992) documents a similar phenomena in a mountainous area of western Kenya. In the Uluguru mountains of Tanzania, van Donge (1992) observes men of economically active ages migrating to Dar es Salaam, leaving women to farm sub-optimally sized plots which are often incapable of producing subsistence food needs of the household. He notes that the land is at a premium and 'may be a major reason why there is continued support for those women who are left behind. It is striking that it is said of such women that they guard the land *(wanatunza ardhi)* and not that they farm the land *(wanalima)*. The connotation of farming generating income from land has been lost.'

In other densely populated societies that have evolved specialized market niches for their agricultural products, men commonly have an entrenched position in agriculture and may encroach on women's land rights to the point of undermining their ability to produce household food supplies. Mersmann (1994) traces how over the years women's food crop fields were pushed further and further up the slope of the Usambara mountains in Tanzania, until their production became untenable. Women were forced into wage-labour, either as casual labour on neighbour's fields or as workers in nearby tea plantations (Sender and Smith 1990). This pattern is not restricted to East Africa. Chilver relates similar circumstances in the northwest Province of Cameroon where pressure on available land was 'driving women from the more sheltered valleys to farm on higher slopes' in competition with men's cash cropping.

While the marginalization of women hoe cultivators from agriculture sounds extreme, a steady accumulation of case study evidence does hint that women hoe agriculturalists, as household food producers, may be the first to become 'redundant' in the new market-driven agrarian landscape of the continent. O'Laughlin has noted the dilemma of asset-deprived women-headed households whose semi-proletarianized status does not make it possible for them to benefit from development projects focussed on women's own-account farming. In these situations, female smallholder farming is a lost option. Even where it is not, the current climate of market supremacy in donor thinking does not give much scope to women hoe cultivators. Their inferior command over rural resources puts them at a disadvantage vis-à-vis men in commodity production. A recent pan-African study of women farmers sponsored by the World Bank found: '30 per cent higher labour input per hectare on women's plots compared with men's in Kenya and Nigeria due to the use of low productivity technology' (Saito et al. 1992). The conclusion was yet another call for more extension advice and credit to women (World Bank 1992). But these calls take place amidst crumbling national and regional government structures which, under ordinary circumstances, would be expected to provide such services.

There are, however, notable exceptions to the general pattern of men's superior market advantage. Seur's (1992) in-depth study of Serenje district, Zambia, documents women reaching a position of competitiveness with men in the production of cash crops such as hybrid maize using ox ploughs, over the course of two generations. A small group of divorced women migrants, recently returned from town, were the first to see cash crops as a means of securing a good livelihood. Against male censure and interference, they used their rights of access to land of deceased matrikin. As role models, they paved the way for a broader based subsequent generation of women who took up commercial maize and bean production and became responsible for more than one-third of total hybrid maize output in the area. The combination of maize and beans was especially suitable for women because it provided a means of producing cash crops without necessarily sacrificing time and effort on household food crop production. The division between household and market-destined produce could be determined after the harvest. Furthermore, and significantly, this successful female venture into plough agriculture and cash cropping was in the context of a society which had been exposed to the Jehovah Witness religious ideology, propagating attitudes towards work and gender that contrasted with the dictates of the society's male elders. In this example, African women farmers had clearly sidestepped the Boserup model, and were actively engaged in ploughing, very far removed from agricultural retirement.

Plough agriculture is found quite widely in southern Africa yet women maintain a strong presence in farming. In southern Africa, plough technology was already being adopted in the late nineteenth century by African men who had worked on European farms or had come under the influence of Christian missionaries (Bundy 1988). This is illustrative of the fact that it is myopic to think of African agriculture in isolation from agrarian influences in the world at large over the past century. Furthermore, it infers the impossibility of proving Boserup's theory one way or the other on the basis of African case material. Evolutionary theories, such as the transition from female hoe to male plough agriculture argued by Boserup, are only testable in a closed system.

But stages of agricultural transformation *per se* are not at issue in this book. Rather the aim has been to explore the productive and reproductive patterns of African women cultivators. In this regard, it is sufficient to observe that the ox plough and the tractor have not displaced 'women wielding the hoe'. Women's hoe agriculture endures over vast expanses of the continent as well as appearing in innumerable interstitial places where hoes are uncommon but expedient for individual use. Because of its low capital requirements, the hoe is accessible to most rural women and is easily combined with non-agricultural activities or other agricultural techniques of production. Thus, hoe agriculture continues to be feasible as a mainstay, a last resort, or even as a basis for accumulation. It is extremely versatile, just as the social systems in which it is embedded are remarkably malleable under changing circumstances. This is borne out as much by women cultivators' staying power during this century under the widening influence of the state and most recently the market, as by the far-flung imprint of agriculture throughout the continent and women's largely unacknowledged role in its spread in earlier millennia.

There is no denying that hoeing the tropical soils of Africa is hard work, but given the individualized nature of hoeing as a physical activity, the hoe has, over time, offered women a means of supporting themselves and their dependents with or without male involvement. The depressed economic situation of rural Africa at present increases the probability of hoe technology's continued dominance. The agricultural technology capable of liberating African women cultivators from hard toil and affording them a reasonable livelihood within their control has not appeared on the horizon nor is such a neat technical fix likely. It is for all these reasons and more that the broad masses of African rural women retain a strong grip on the hoe.

References

Airey, T. and I. Barwell, 'Village-Level Transport and Travel Surveys and Related Case Studies: Report on Interim Analysis of First Village-Level Survey in Zambia', IT Transport Consultancy commissioned for the Sub-Saharan Transport Programme by the ILO/World Bank, October 1991

Braun, J. von, H. de Haen and J. Blanken, *Commercialization of Agriculture under Population Pressure: Effects on Production, Consumption and Nutrition in Rwanda*, International Food Policy Research Institute Research Report 85, 1991

Bundy, C., *The Rise and Fall of the South African Peasantry*, London, James Currey, 1988, 2nd edition

Carney, J.A., 'Struggles over Crop Rights and Labour within Contract Farming Households in a Gambian Irrigated Rice Project', *Journal of Peasant Studies*, vol. 15, no. 3, 1988

Chilver, E.M., 'Women Cultivators, Cows and Cash Crops in Cameroon', in S. Ardener (ed.), *Persons and Powers of Women in Diverse Cultures*, Oxford, Berg, 1992

Conti, A., 'Capitalist Organisation of Production through Non-Capitalist Relations: Women's Role in a Pilot Scheme in Upper Volta', *Review of African Political Economy*, vol. 15/16, 1979

Dey, J., 'Gambian Women: Unequal Partners in Rice Development Projects?', in N. Nelson (ed.), *African Women in the Development Process*, London, Frank Cass, 1981, pp. 109–22

Donge, J.K. van, 'Agricultural Decline in Tanzania: The Case of the Uluguru Mountains', *African Affairs*, No. 91, 1992, pp. 73–94

Douglas, M., 'Is Matriliny Doomed in Africa?', in M. Douglas and M. Kaberry (eds), *Man in Africa*, New York, Doubleday, 1971

Fardon, R., 'Sisters, Wives, Wards and Daughters: A Transformational Analysis of the Political Organization of the Tiv and their Neighbours', *Africa* vol. 54, no. 4, 1984

Goody, J., *Death, Property and the Ancestors*, London, Tavistock, 1962

Kuper, A., *The Invention of Primitive Society: Transformations of an Illusion*, London, Routledge, 1988

Mersmann, C., 'The Impact of Indigenous Knowledge Systems on Changing Patterns in Land Endowment: The Case of Mbaramo Village in the Usambara Mountains, Tanzania', Paper presented at the 'Changing Rural Structures in Tanzania', Symposium at the University of Bayreuth, Germany, June 1994

Moore, H. and M. Vaughan, *Cutting Down Trees: Gender, Nutrition, and Agricultural Change in the Northern Province of Zambia, 1890-1990*, London, James Currey, 1994

Palmer, I., *The Impact of Agrarian Reform on Women*, West Hartford, USA, Kumarian Press, 1985

Raikes, P., 'Crop Marketing and Food Security in Kisii District, Kenya', Paper presented at the Institute of Social Studies, The Hague, February 1993

Saito, K., et al., *Raising Productivity of Women Farmers in Sub-Saharan Africa*, Washington, D.C., World Bank, Women in Development Division, 1992

Sender, J. and S. Smith, *Poverty, Class and Gender in Rural Africa*, London, Routledge, 1990

Seur, H., 'Sowing the Good Seed: The Interweaving of Agricultural Change, Gender Relations and Religion in Serenje District, Zambia', Ph.D. Thesis, Wageningen University, The Netherlands, 1992

World Bank, *WIDLINE: Population and Human Resources Department*, no. 6, Washington, D.C., November 1992

Zegers, M., 'Strategies for Women and Development in the Republic of Congo', Geneva, International Labour Office, Labour and Population Series for Sub-Saharan Africa, Working Paper, 1992

Notes on Contributors

Han Bantje studied social anthropology at Leiden University and has worked in development programmes in Zambia, Jamaica and Tanzania for over twenty years. He was associate professor at the University of Dar es Salaam from 1981 to 1987. His main research interest is in systemic linkages between nutrition, health and agriculture. He has researched farming systems in several areas of Tanzania and has published a series of articles on variations in birthweight distributions. He is presently employed as a researcher at the Institute of Infrastructure, Hydraulics and Environmental Engineering, Delft, The Netherlands.

Deborah Fahy Bryceson, an economic geographer by training, is currently a Research Fellow at the Afrika Studiecentrum, Leiden. In addition to her academic and consultancy work on rural women in East Africa, her research activities have concentrated on issues of food marketing, urbanization, rural transport and mobility patterns and the impact of public investment on rural welfare. Her recent publications include the books, *Food Insecurity and the Social Division of Labour in Tanzania, 1919-1985* (1990), and *Liberalizing Tanzania's Food Trade* (1993). She is presently involved in organizing a research programme on rural employment and land accessibility in Sub-Saharan Africa.

Pat Caplan is Professor of Anthropology at Goldsmiths College, University of London. She has been carrying out research in Tanzania since 1965, and has also done field research in Nepal and South India. Her recent books include *The Cultural Construction of Sexuality* (1987), *Les Swahili entre Afrique et Arabie*, edited with F. Le Guennec-Coppens, (1991), and *Gendered Fields: Women, Men and Ethnography*, edited with D. Bell and W. Jahan-Karim (1993). She is currently directing a study of food in Britain.

Jean Davison's major research interests are in gender relations of production and land tenure issues as they affect women's food production. She was a Senior Lecturer in Sociology and Coordinator of the MA Programme in the Sociology of Women in Development at the University of Malawi from 1989 to 1992. She is currently a Visiting Scholar at the Institute for Research on Women and Gender, Stanford University. Dr Davison is the author of two books, *Agriculture, Women and Land: The African Experience* (1988), and *Voices from Mutira: Lives of Rural Gikuyu Women* (1989). She is now completing the manuscript for a third book, *Labours Lost: Gender and Ethnicity in Southern Africa's Clan-based Societies*, as well as a chapter for a book on Kenyan women's roles in the Mau Mau liberation movement. She has published articles on women and girls' education constraints in Kenya and Malawi, and on gender relations of production in Kenya, Malawi and Mozambique.

Marie-Claude Dupré, a member of the Centre Nationale de la Reserche Scientifique (CNRS), did her main fieldwork with the Tsayi, Lali Teke and the Bembe between 1966 and 1973. Her research has centred on healing rites, iron smelting, political history, deciphering the Kidumu masks, relations between structure and local systems, and cognitive science. She is presently completing a book on the history of Teke metallurgy with the archaeologist Bruno Pinçon. Her interests have embraced recent scientific trends including systems and cognitive science as well as ecology. She collaborates with the Swiss Institut de la Méthode in Bienne.

Felicia I. Ekejiuba is a Professor of Anthropology and currently a Regional Programme Adviser for the United Nations Development Fund for Women (UNIFEM). Since graduating from Harvard University in 1976, she has taught at the University of Nigeria, Nsukka, and at several American universities including Colgate University, Hamilton, New York. Her fieldwork has been in rural eastern Nigeria where she has focussed on processes of socio-economic formation and transformation of African society, gender relations and the changing roles and status of women in Nigeria. Her publications include a book entitled *The Aro of South Eastern Nigeria: A Study of Socio-Economic Formation and Transformation* and diverse journal articles, namely: 'Social Capital and the Changing Social Status of Igbo Women', 'Participatory and Sustainable Development with Rural Women: Field Experiences from Eastern Nigeria' and 'Currency Instability and Social Payment in Eastern Nigeria'.

Jane I. Guyer is Associate Professor of Anthropology, Boston University. Besides the work summarized here on the division of labour and agricultural practice she has published on African urban food supply, the history of currencies and value in West and Equatorial Africa, and change in kinship. The current Nigerian restudy is being composed as a book, comprising all the major changes in this rural economy in the Ibadan food supply hinterland.

Christine Obbo is a Ugandan social cultural anthropologist currently working as an independent research consultant on HIV/AIDS and gender issues in Africa. She is carrying out research on changes in family obligations and entitlements and writing a book on women, HIV/AIDS, and the cultural construction of disease and death in Buganda. Currently she is an associate of the Centre of African Studies at the School of Oriental and African Studies at the University of London.

Bridget O'Laughlin is a Senior Lecturer in Social Anthropology in the Population and Development Programme at the Institute of Social Studies in The Hague. She has done rural field research in southern Tchad, and in many different areas of Mozambique. Most of her research was published in reports of the Centre of African Studies (CEA), Eduardo Mondlane University in Maputo, where she first went to work on questions of socialist transition in agriculture under Ruth First, then research director of the CEA.

Pauline E. Peters is a Research Associate at the Harvard Institute for International Development and Lecturer in the Department of Anthropology, Harvard University. She is a social anthropologist with a Ph.D. (1983) from Boston University and earlier degrees from the University of Wales and the London School of Economics. She has conducted field research in Botswana and Malawi. Her recent publications include 'Manoeuvers and Debates in the Interpretation of Land Rights in Botswana', *Africa* (1992), 'Is "Rational Choice" the Best Choice for Robert Bates? An Anthropologist's Reading of Bates' Work', *World Development* (1993), and a book entitled *Dividing the Commons: Politics, Policy and Culture in Botswana* in press.

Else Skjønsberg is a sociologist with more than twenty years of experience in the field of development research. She has worked as a consultant to the UN, and as a programme officer with the Norwegian Agency for International Development (NORAD). Since 1985 she has run Women in Development Consulting – Norway which specializes in rural development and women's issues. Among her publications are *A Special Caste? Tamil Women of Sri Lanka* (1982), the prize-winning *Change in an African Village – Kefa Speaks* (1989), and a recent book on women in the European Community (1993).

Ulla Vuorela, Ph.D., is an Associate Professor of Social Anthropology at the University of Tampere, Finland. She did research in Tanzania from 1976 to 1986, associated with the Ministry of Culture and Youth. She was also a member of the Women's Research and Documentation Project at the University of Dar es Salaam. She is now head of the Women's Studies Unit at the University of Tampere and is particularly interested in feminist theory in anthropology.

Index

277